Coming to Voice

Writing Personal, Civic, and Academic Arguments

SECOND EDITION

Edited by

Kelly Kinney and Sean Fenty

HAYDEN
HM
McNEIL

Hayden-McNeil Publishing
14903 Pilot Drive
Plymouth, MI 48170
www.hmpublishing.com

Kinney 6652-3 F14-S

Table of Contents

1. **Front Cover:** Rally on October 18, 1996, to protest the use of pepper spray by public safety officers during a Student Assembly Meeting the week prior. Photo by Evangelos Dousmanis.

2. **Back Cover:** Students protesting investments in South Africa in front of the Administration Building in 1985.

Chapter Three: The Op-Ed Essay Assignment   167

Chapter Four: The Researched Argument Assignment   207

Preface

Acknowledgements

This text is the product of contributions made from many members of the Binghamton University Writing Initiative, not just the two faculty members who serve as its editors. We would like to begin by thanking those who have contributed most to this collective pedagogical effort.

First and foremost, we need to acknowledge the expert work of Robert Danberg, Wendy Stewart, and Paul Shovlin, who have been responsible for fine-tuning the respective materials for the Personal Essay, Op-Ed, and Researched Argument. Danberg, Stewart, and Shovlin also help us support the graduate student teaching assistants who make up the backbone of our First-Year Writing program, and without their contributions this textbook would not be possible.

We also owe a special note of thanks to those graduate student teaching assistants who serve as classroom instructors of Writing 111, Coming to Voice, and who have given us countless insights on how to improve assignments and classroom materials. Their feedback on the course and expert instruction are what make this program strong, and their commitment to excellent teaching is in large part responsible for our program being honored with the Conference on College Composition and Communication's Certificate of Writing Program Excellence, an award given to top writing programs across the globe.

Some of our former colleagues and mentors also deserve mention here. They include our former co-editor, Kristi Murray Costello, now an Assistant Professor at Arkansas State University, and Mark Brantner, now of the National University of Singapore, who helped to spearhead earlier iterations of the Rhetorical Analysis assignment; Connie Mick, Kim Orlijan, Nicole McLaughlin, and Ed Kelly, all of the University of Notre Dame, who contributed to earlier iterations of some reflective activities in this text; Roger Gilles and Dan Royer, of Grand Valley State University, who were the original architects of the portfolio grading system we have adapted here; Sherrie Gradin, of Ohio University, whose mentorship influences the entire Writing 111 curriculum; and former graduate student assistant directors of First-Year Writing Thomas Girshin (Ithaca College), Barrett Bowlin (Binghamton University), and Virginia Shank (Irvine Valley), who also helped fine-tune many of the assignments and materials students engage in in this text.

Finally, a special word of thanks to Lisa Wess and the entire production team at Hayden-McNeil Publishing, whose professionalism is matched only by their good humor.

Kelly Kinney
Director, Writing Initiative and First-Year Writing

Sean Fenty
Associate Director, First-Year Writing

How to Use This Guide: A Letter from the Editors

Dear Writers:

On behalf of the Writing Initiative, we welcome you to Binghamton University and to First-Year Writing. In this course guide, *Coming to Voice: Writing Personal, Civic, and Academic Arguments*, you will find policies and evaluation criteria for Writing 111, as well as many of the assignments, readings, and in-class activities you will complete throughout the semester.

We have designed this book in order to help you become acclimated to the policies, assignments, and evaluation criteria we use in this course, and to ensure that students have common experiences across sections. As you can see from the Table of Contents, there are six components to this text: a Preface, four Unit Chapters, and an Appendix. The Preface contains information about Writing 111, including our course policies and grading procedures. The Unit Chapters each begin with the assignment overview, followed by invention, revision, and reflection activities that will help you develop ideas and refine your writing. The Unit Chapters also contain a selection of related readings to help further guide your efforts. In the Appendix, you will find guidelines and advice for making final revisions to your three portfolio essays. You will also find instructions for the option of submitting your work to *Binghamton Writes*, a journal we publish each semester that highlights some of our best student writers.

As you may be aware, Writing 111 at Binghamton University uses a portfolio evaluation system. This means that in addition to commenting on your writing throughout the semester, your instructor will give you the chance to revise your formal assignments up until the very last day of class. By using a portfolio system, we hope to ensure that your writing will improve throughout the semester, and thus, that your assignments will be in their best shape when you turn them in for a grade. Because we use such a system, you can work hard to both improve your writing and reach the grade goal you hope to achieve. While satisfying the criteria to earn high marks in the course is no simple feat, we have designed the portfolio system to help you reach your maximum potential as a writer. Please keep this in mind as you work through each of the chapters in this text, as every activity may contribute to your ability to improve your portfolio, and more importantly, help you improve your writing skills.

As this is the inaugural edition of this guide, we are excited to get your reaction about its organization and how we can make it better in the future. If you have any questions about these materials or would like to give us feedback, please email your suggestions to Kelly Kinney <kkinney@binghamton.edu> or Sean Fenty <sfenty@binghamton.edu>. As the editors of this guide, we would appreciate your input.

We wish you a productive and successful semester!

Sincerely,

Kelly Kinney
Director, Writing Initiative and First-Year Writing

Sean Fenty
Associate Director, First-Year Writing

First-Year Writing: Mission and Philosophy Statement

Committed to providing highly motivated students an outstanding education grounded in the liberal arts, the First-Year Writing Program is a central component of the Binghamton University Writing Initiative. Our mission is to foster the academic and civic literacies essential for success at the university and beyond. To this end, we offer students rigorous courses that meet a range of educational goals, and faculty and graduate assistants an intensive mentoring program that supports state-of-the-art instruction.

The course central to this commitment is Writing 111: Coming to Voice: Writing Personal, Civic, and Academic Arguments, for which this textbook was created. Writing 111 asks students to communicate in different genres for a range of audiences, engage in intensive revision, and practice critical thinking through researched argumentation. Laying a general foundation for writing, the course maintains a significant emphasis on scholarly research, including how to formulate appropriate research questions; how to find, evaluate, and integrate a range of credible sources; and how to add one's perspectives to an ongoing civic or scholarly conversation.

By focusing on salient social issues important in the civic and academic spheres, Writing 111 is also in keeping with one of Binghamton University's most time-honored traditions: that is, to nurture in students an active engagement in the most pressing matters of our time.

Writing 111 Learning Outcomes and Course Description

Writing 111 is designed to help first-year students become stronger writers, speakers, and critical thinkers, and it features assignments that allow students to explore their personal, civic, and academic interests. The course requires you to engage in different genres for a range of audiences, emphasizes revision, and gives you practice in critical thinking and researched writing, reinforcing the notion that writing conventions differ according to their rhetorical situations. The course's emphasis on civic discourse is in keeping with one of Binghamton University's central missions: to help reinforce in students a sense of responsibility for adding their voices to important public conversations.

Writing 111 satisfies Joint (J) general education designation for Composition (C) and Oral Communication (O). By the end of the term, students who successfully complete the course will demonstrate the following:

- The ability to write coherently for a general, university-level audience.

- The ability to revise and improve writing in both content and form.

- The ability to write in different genres and in a variety of rhetorical contexts.

- The ability to build arguments based on observation, critical analysis, and the integration of academic sources.

- The ability to cite sources according to general academic conventions, which includes knowing when and how to integrate summary, paraphrase, and direct quotation.

- The ability to confidently participate in important civic conversations—that is, to add one's own perspectives to conversations about salient community, national, and global issues.

- Proficiency in oral presentations.

- The ability to improve oral presentation skills in response to peer and instructor feedback.

- Skill in listening to and offering critical feedback on oral presentations.

Course Structure

On many days, the class will be conducted in seminar format, which means you will engage in discussions about reading, writing, and speaking assignments and examine the rhetorical strategies used to persuade audiences. As a class, we will raise questions, pose problems, interpret readings, challenge one another's ideas, and develop strategies for successfully completing assignments. There will also be many class sessions in which we perform small group activities, including peer review, drafting, and editing, and there will be mandatory one-on-one conferencing sessions, outside of class, to help you develop your ideas and revise your work. Although there will be mini-lectures on a variety of writing-related topics, we will spend the majority of class time engaging in collaborative discussions and activities.

Writing Assignments and Portfolio

Personal Essay: This assignment asks you to write an essay that considers the relationship between a memorable aspect of your personal experience and its broader political, social, cultural, educational, or humanitarian significance. The experience can be common, intense, tragic, or even humorous, but it must also reveal its relationship to the way we negotiate our lives, our political beliefs, or our roles in society. In short, this Personal Essay should do more than tell a story; it must also reflect on a significant political, social, or cultural issue.

Opposite Editorial (Op-Ed): This assignment asks you to respond to a public issue in the form of an Opposite Editorial. Unlike an editorial, which represents the collective views of a newspaper's staff, an Op-Ed represents the views of the writer alone. Engaged citizens write Op-Eds to give their viewpoints public expression. You will have the option of writing your Op-Ed in response to texts we read in class, or to texts you find on your own.

Researched Argument: Building on earlier assignments, the Researched Argument asks you to collect different kinds of research on a social, cultural, or disciplinary issue that interests you. In preparation, you will collect a range of perspectives on the issue by performing library research. You will use this research to create an academic argument, establishing what has already been written and said, and adding your perspectives to the conversation. Your teacher will help you identify appropriate issues and develop an academic research question, but in the end the focus will be up to you. What is important is that you invest in the issue you research, and you allow your writing to be a genuine form of scholarly inquiry.

Course Portfolio: This course uses a portfolio system, which means that throughout the semester you will turn in polished drafts of writing assignments for both peer review and instructor commentary, but will not receive formal grades until the end of the semester, when you submit a course portfolio showcasing your very best work. The portfolio system ensures that you have plenty of time to get feedback on, re-imagine, revise, and polish your writing. Instructor comments on early drafts may include a good-faith estimate of the potential grade of a draft in progress, but such comments have absolutely no bearing on the grade you receive on your course portfolio. Instead, teachers assign your portfolio a holistic grade based on the quality of the work you submit at the end of the semester.

In your course portfolio, you will resubmit the three essays you have written in this course. Because your course portfolio constitutes 80% of your grade, it is paramount that you revise your writing rigorously, taking into account feedback from peers and your instructor as well as your understanding of the Writing 111 grading criteria. Note: Teachers will not accept course portfolios that contain papers on topics they have not previously commented upon or approved. If your portfolio contains work that has not been previously commented upon or approved, you will receive an "F" for the course.

Oral Presentations

Rhetorical Analysis Presentation: A Rhetorical Analysis asks you to examine the strategies of persuasion within a text, analyzing and assessing the techniques used, reading the text closely, making strong claims about it, and mining the text for evidence of support. You and a small group of peers will engage in rhetorical analysis of an essay from *They Say, I Say* (or a different essay assigned by your instructor) and present it to the class.

Research Presentation: For this assignment, you will create an individual oral presentation to introduce your peers and instructor to your Researched Argument, establishing what has already been written and said on the issue you explore, and adding your interpretations and perspectives to the conversation.

Writing 111 Course Policies

Attendance Requirements

It matters that you come to class on time, every day. If you are repeatedly late, it will negatively influence your grade. Excessive tardiness, early departure, or lack of preparation will result in an absence. Your participation grade will be lowered if you miss more than two classes on a Tues/Thurs schedule or three classes on a Mon/Wed/Fri schedule. **Your final grade will be reduced a full letter grade if you miss four classes on a Tues/Thurs schedule or six classes on a Mon/Wed/Fri schedule. You fail the course if you miss six Tues/Thurs classes or nine Mon/Wed/Fri classes.** If you know you will be absent, turn in work in advance. If you experience a crisis that prevents you from completing your work, speak to your instructor or ask an appropriate campus official to document your situation. Instructors may not accept doctors' notes to excuse absences, as only an appropriate campus official can document extenuating health circumstances. Reserve all absences for illness or other unpredictable events such as transportation problems, unforeseen family obligations, and the like. Regardless of when you add the course, all classes missed after the first week count toward absences.

Drafting Requirements, Due Dates, and Deadline Extensions

You must turn in drafts of assignments and perform your oral presentations on the days they are due: *failure to do so can result in failure of the course.* If you anticipate needing a deadline extension for a draft, you may request one a week in advance of the due date. Teachers have the right to deny deadline extensions and/or implement appropriate penalties when you turn in late work. Important note: *Teachers will not give deadline extensions for course portfolios.*

Classroom Participation and Oral Presentations

You are expected to be in every class, on time, fully prepared. You are expected to fulfill all homework, presentation, and reading requirements. Invest yourself in presentations, readings, and discussions—doing so will pay off in your writing. Because one of the objectives of Writing 111 is to make you comfortable engaging in different forms of public discourse—both written and oral—you should make an effort to add your voice to discussions during every class: failing to do so will negatively impact your course grade.

Technology Requirements

You need consistent access to a working computer and printer for this course. BU students have limited computer and printing privileges in campus labs, called "PODs": you may use campus computers during regular PODs hours and print up to seventy-five pages per week at no cost, but if you go over quota, you must use a BUC$ account to pay for material printed on campus. Whether you use your private computer and printer or public ones, however, you alone are responsible for saving and backing up all of your written work: if you fail to do so, you risk missing course deadlines, which can lead to a lowered grade.

Plagiarism and Binghamton's Academic Honesty Code

A primary goal of this class is to teach you how to use and document sources appropriately. If you have questions or are confused, please do not hesitate to ask. Any violation of the Academic Honesty Code, however, constitutes plagiarism, which can result in failure of the course or suspension from the University. The Academic Honesty Code defines *plagiarism* as:

> Presenting the work of another person as one's own work (including papers, words, ideas, information, computer code, data, evidence-organizing principles, or style of presentation of someone else taken from the Internet, books, periodicals or other sources). This includes:
>
> - quoting, paraphrasing, or summarizing without acknowledgement, even a few phrases;
> - failing to acknowledge the source of a major idea or ordering principle central to one's work;
> - relying on another person's data, evidence or critical method without credit or permission;
> - submitting another person's work as one's own or using unacknowledged research sources gathered by someone else. (http://buweb.binghamton.edu/bulletin/program.asp?program_id=703)

Please note that the Academic Honesty Code also prohibits *multiple submissions*, which it defines as:

> Submitting substantial portions of the same work for credit more than once, unless there is prior explicit consent of the instructor(s) to whom the material is being or has been submitted. (http://buweb. binghamton.edu/bulletin/program.asp?program_id=703)

Writing 111 Feedback and Grading

How Instructors Give Feedback in Writing 111

Writing 111 uses a portfolio approach to grade student writing: this means that your teacher not only responds to your writing in various stages of progress, but that you may revise your work until the very last day of class. You will also have multiple opportunities to get feedback from your classmates, and are encouraged to seek feedback from Writing Center tutors, fellow students, and campus support services.

At the end of each assignment, you will turn in a polished draft, and your instructor will carefully respond to it, noting what you have done well, possible strategies for improvement, and your draft's potential for success in the course portfolio. Any good faith grade estimate of a draft in progress, however, is not a recorded grade and has no bearing on your course portfolio; instead, your course portfolio is graded given the quality of work you turn in at the end of the term alone.

Workshop, Peer Critique, and Sharing Your Work

When you meet in groups to receive peer feedback, it is your responsibility to have a complete draft and to bring enough copies for everyone in your group. Students who arrive without multiple copies will be marked absent. Sharing your writing is perhaps the single most important activity of this course. Take it seriously and work hard to establish the kind of climate that will make it successful. Your teacher may request drafts to share with the entire class or with other instructors of Writing 111. Although you may decline such requests, you can trust that all work shared in public settings will be treated with respect.

Classroom Participation and Oral Presentations

Your classroom participation and oral presentations make up 20% of your course grade and will be holistically evaluated by your teacher based on grading guidelines, which include: the quality and consistency of your contributions to class discussions and activities, timely and satisfactory engagement in and completion of assignments and readings, and the quality of your oral presentations. Your classroom participation and oral presentations grade is also influenced by factors such as consistent attendance—you can't do well if you don't show up regularly.

Portfolio Team Grading

Your course portfolio will be evaluated by your classroom instructor and at least one additional Writing 111 instructor. If these two instructors do not agree on the same letter grade, then a third instructor evaluates the portfolio and helps the team come to consensus on a grade. The team grading system brings instructors together for productive small-group discussions of teaching and grading throughout the term, allows instructors to coach students as they draft and revise their writing, and ensures that the grades students receive are representative of the common grading standards endorsed by the First-Year Writing program as a whole. Instructors meet weekly to discuss teaching and grading and report these discussions back to their students. In turn, students are better prepared to revise their work for the course portfolio.

At the end of the semester, you will submit a course portfolio, which includes revised versions of your writing. Course portfolios are graded with a simple letter grade: A, B, C, or D (Fs are reserved for students who miss too many classes, do not fulfill assignment guidelines, do not submit all drafts, do not submit course portfolios on time, or engage in plagiarism). Your classroom instructor will adjust your portfolio letter grade with a plus, minus, or no adjustment to reflect your engagement in the course. The course portfolio grade—the grade agreed upon by at least two instructors—constitutes 80% of your course grade.

Class Participation and Oral Presentations
20% of course grade ~ 200 points

Includes two oral presentations, timely and satisfactory completion of class readings and homework, and your overall participation in the course.

A	186–200 points		C+	154–159 points
A–	180–185 points		C	146–153 points
B+	174–179 points		C–	140–145 points
B	166–173 points		D	120–139 points
B–	160–165 points		F	0–119 points

Although instructors have some flexibility when assigning a point value for a letter grade, they are encouraged to use a generous median within the ranges provided previously. The suggested point values for class participation and oral presentations are as follows: A: 193; A–: 183; B+: 177; B: 170; B–: 163; C+: 157; C: 150; C–: 143; D: 130.

Course Portfolio

80% of course grade ~ 800 points

Includes your final revised drafts of all three Major Writing Assignments.

A	745–800 points	C+	616–639 points
A–	720–744 points	C	584–615 points
B+	696–719 points	C–	560–583 points
B	664–695 points	D	480–559 points
B–	640–663 points	F	0–479 points

Although instructors have some flexibility when assigning a point value for a letter grade, they are encouraged to use a generous median within the ranges provided above. The suggested point values for portfolio grades are as follows: A: 773; A–: 732; B+: 708; B: 680; B–: 652; C+: 628; C: 600; C–: 572; D: 520.

Course Grading Scale

1000 points total

A	930–1000 points	C+	770–799 points
A–	900–929 points	C	730–769 points
B+	870–899 points	C–	700–729 points
B	830–869 points	D	600–699 points
B–	800–829 points	F	0–599 points

Course Portfolios Due During Your Last Class Meeting

Course portfolios *must be submitted in paper copy and are due at the beginning of your last class meeting.* Late portfolios result in an "F" for the course. There is no final examination in Writing 111.

Frequently Asked Questions (and Answers) about Grading in Writing 111

1. When I hand in drafts of my work, my teacher's comments suggest that my writing is much weaker now than it was in high school. For example, I took AP English and earned an A, but my Writing 111 instructor thinks my draft is closer to a C. Was my teacher in high school wrong? Is my college teacher?

   Answer: No, not at all. The writing conventions high school teachers teach, the goals they set for students, and the standards they use to grade student work are different than the conventions, goals, and standards of university instructors. That's appropriate, because the goal of a high school education is to ensure adolescents are prepared to function as adults, while the goal of a college education is to ensure adults have mastery of academic subject matter and conventions. One of the primary goals of Writing 111 is to make you aware of new expectations for your writing, to prepare you to succeed *on the university level*. Use your teacher's comments to set goals for your next draft and for future writing assignments. While comments on early drafts may sting, it's your teacher's job to point out where you can improve, to coach and motivate you to produce writing that satisfies academic conventions. Remember, too, that you have time to rewrite your essays before you submit them for a final grade in your portfolio. Don't be hard on yourself (or your teachers!) and don't let an unexpected comment about the quality of your work discourage you. Visit your teacher during office hours, visit the Writing Center, and start revising.

2. Why is a group of Writing 111 teachers evaluating my portfolio rather than just my own teacher?

   Answer: A group of four or more teachers (including your own teacher) has been reading samples of your class's writing throughout the semester to discuss and agree about what constitutes A, B, C, D, and F writing. The goal of the group is to create clear and fair grading standards that teachers communicate and reinforce in their classrooms. One advantage of our team grading system is that it protects Writing 111 students from being misled by "easy" graders or penalized by "hard" graders. When you leave this course, you should have an accurate sense of what you do well, areas for improvement, and how your writing measures up to the university community's standards.

3. **Does my teacher have any say on my grade in Writing 111 and my portfolio?**

   Answer: Yes. Your teacher will always be one of at least two readers of your portfolio. If the second reader in the group agrees with your teacher, then the grade your teacher gave your portfolio is the grade you will receive. (First and second readers agree about 70–80% of the time.) If the second reader does not agree with your teacher, then a third reader will join the conversation and help the other readers come to consensus on a fair grade. Rather than grading in isolation and without the guidance and support of other members of the university community, Writing 111 teachers work together to ensure that the grade you receive is in keeping with standards agreed upon by our academic community.

4. **What happens if one person in the portfolio group grades much harder than the others? Doesn't this mean I'll get a lower grade?**

   Answer: No, not in our system. If the first two readers of your portfolio don't agree on a grade, a third reader is asked to read your portfolio and decide what grade is most in line with the standards agreed upon by the team of graders. So if one reader does have unreasonable standards, the other two readers will help determine an appropriate grade.

5. **I think each teacher should grade his or her own students' work.**

   Answer: Each teacher does have a hand in grading student work: all teachers serve as the first reader in a multi-reader grading system. What's more, your teacher alone evaluates your performance on oral presentations and classroom participation, which constitute 20% of your course grade.

6. **My teachers said that I have to meet specific guidelines that are particular to my section of Writing 111. If other teachers in the grading group have different guidelines, are they going to penalize me?**

   Answer: No. Teachers often have minimum requirements they want every paper to meet. For example, some teachers require students to use particular kinds of research sources, while others may ask students to approach one of the major assignments in an innovative way. When teachers have different requirements, they enforce them by making sure that students meet them. If you don't meet your teacher's minimum requirements, then your teacher doesn't allow your portfolio to move on to group grading—and, by extension, you will fail the course.

7. **Could two people in the team grading group agree that I deserve a B and then my teacher give me a C or lower because of absences or class participation?**

   Answer: It depends, so take careful note of the following. Your portfolio grade is 80% of your grade for the semester. 20% of your grade is devoted to oral presentations and your overall classroom participation. While teachers cannot lower your *portfolio grade* because of poor attendance or participation, they can and will lower your *course grade* because of excessive absences or poor performance and participation. For instance, the syllabus makes clear that students who violate the attendance policy or who do not turn in drafts of all assignments may not submit a final portfolio and thus fail the course. (Please forgive our emphasis here and above on different ways to fail—few students do—but it is our job to be clear about how grading in Writing 111 works.)

8. **Just looking at my portfolio at the end of the term doesn't show how much I've improved. Shouldn't my grade be based, at least in part, on my improvement?**

   Answer: Yes, we agree that it should. That's why teachers adjust the portfolio grade with a plus or minus (or make no adjustment) given your hard work and improvement. Improvement in your writing over time can and does positively influence your grade in the course.

9. **I like to have grades during the semester so that I know how well I am doing. I don't want my grade at the end of the term to come as a big surprise.**

   Answer: We don't either. Your teacher should be reading your writing throughout the semester and responding to it with marginal comments, in personal conferences, and with endnotes and suggestions for revision. In his feedback, your teacher should indicate what members of his grading group have been saying about writing like yours, and discuss what grade characteristics your drafts-in-progress embody.

Still, if you're concerned about the status of your grade or have questions about the quality of your work, don't hesitate to schedule additional conferences with your teacher. That's what he's here for. If you feel you aren't getting satisfactory feedback, please discuss your concerns with your teacher, or contact the Writing Initiative (777-6725).

10. **The team grading group read my portfolio but didn't give me feedback. Why not?**

    Answer: Your teacher has given you written feedback on drafts as well as opportunities to discuss your work in a variety of classroom, office hour, and Writing Center settings. At the end of the semester, because there are no longer opportunities for revision, grading groups are focused on determining your grade, not on giving you feedback. Your teacher is helping to set standards in the grading group throughout the semester, so take her feedback seriously and work hard to implement it in your writing.

11. **What is supposed to be in my portfolio?**

    Answer: You must submit the three major writing assignments, plus any forms or additional materials requested by your instructor. Ask your teacher if you have questions.

12. **Can I include a paper in my portfolio from another class or from high school?**

    Answer: No. All papers in your portfolio must have been assigned and seen by your Writing 111 teacher. Students who submit work from another class or submit work not previously reviewed by the teacher not only risk facing academic dishonesty charges, they will receive an F for the course.

13. **What do I do if I have questions about my final grade? Can I get a report on how my course grade was calculated?**

    Answer: If you have questions about how your teacher arrived at your final grade, contact your instructor via email and request to see your percentage breakdown for your final portfolio grade and your oral presentations and classroom participation grade. After you receive a response, if you still have questions, concerns, or believe there may have been an error in calculating your grade, please contact the Writing Initiative (777-6725). We will be happy to follow up on your situation.

14. **It seems to me that the portfolio grading system is all about judging final products. I thought we were supposed to be interested in the writing process.**

Answer: We use portfolio team grading to respond to the university community's desire to ensure that entry-level students understand and have the opportunity to study and practice college writing conventions before moving on to upper-division courses. We want you to be prepared for the challenging writing assignments you'll face throughout your four years at Binghamton. So yes, Writing 111 focuses primarily on writing process strategies that will help you succeed as a college writer. But that doesn't mean we don't have high expectations for your writing. After all, not only do you have an entire semester to revise your work for the final portfolio, but Binghamton University attracts some of the most talented students in the region and across the globe. We know you're up to the challenge, so stay focused and keep revising!

Grading Criteria for Written Work: Characteristics of ABCD Writing

Characteristics of "A" Writing

Content

- The material challenges the intelligence and sophistication of a college audience, and is clear to readers beyond the writer's classroom.
- A single focus is emphasized through the entire paper.
- The focus is developed with significant and interesting details, examples, and discussion.
- Relevant outside sources are clearly introduced and integrated into the discussion.
- The writing artfully fulfills the assignment criteria.

Organization

- The argument or focus of the paper is clearly emphasized.
- The overall pattern is artfully conceived.
- The focus is developed through a sequence of related paragraphs.
- Paragraphs are purposefully organized and substantially developed with supporting evidence or detailed examples.
- The opening and closing are inviting, challenging, and appropriate.
- Transitions between and within paragraphs are explicit, clear, and purposeful.

Style and Mechanics

- Sentence structure varies according to the content and purpose of the assignment.
- Sentences are clear, logical, and enjoyable to read.
- Word choice is precise, interesting, and appropriate to the writing task.
- The language is mature and idiomatic.
- The tone complements the writer's purpose and suits the audience.
- References to sources are cited and documented using MLA style.
- Problems in grammar, spelling, punctuation, or usage do not interfere with communication.

Characteristics of "B" Writing

Content

- The material is thoughtful and engaging to a college audience, and is clear to readers beyond the writer's classroom.
- A single focus runs through the entire paper.
- The focus is developed with appropriate details, examples, and discussion.
- Outside sources are used clearly and purposefully.
- The writing clearly fulfills the assignment criteria.

Organization

- The argument or focus is clearly identifiable.
- The overall pattern is clear and sensible.
- The focus is developed through a sequence of related paragraphs.
- Paragraphs are clearly organized, but some may lack richness of detail or evidence.
- The opening and closing are appropriate to the focus.
- Transitions between and within paragraphs advance the writer's ideas.

Style and Mechanics

- Sentences are varied in structure, only occasionally choppy or repetitive.
- Sentences are generally clear, logical, and readable.
- Word choice and vocabulary are appropriate to the writing task.
- The language is idiomatic.
- The tone is appropriate to the writer's purpose and audience.
- References to sources are generally cited and documented using MLA style.
- Problems in grammar, spelling, punctuation, or usage rarely interfere with communication.

Characteristics of "C" Writing

Content

- The material is reasonable, but may not fully engage a college audience; sections may be unclear to readers outside the writer's classroom.
- A single focus runs through the paper, although parts may wander from the central idea.
- The focus is generally developed with details, examples, and discussions.
- Outside sources are generally relevant, although not always clearly introduced or integrated into the discussion.
- The writing reasonably fulfills most assignment criteria.

Organization

- The argument or focus is identifiable.
- The writer establishes an overall pattern for the paper to follow.
- The focus is generally developed throughout the paper, although some paragraphs may appear out of sequence or slightly off-track.
- Paragraphs tend to lack richness of evidence or detailed examples.
- The opening and closing generally support the topic and focus.
- Transitions are evident, but may be abrupt or mechanical.

Style and Mechanics

- Sentences tend to be basic, choppy, or structurally repetitive.
- Sentences are generally readable, but ideas may be hard to follow from one part of the paper to the next.
- Although most words appear to be well-chosen, some may not be as precise or apt as they could be.
- Occasional lapses from standard idiom occur.
- The tone, though generally consistent, at times appears inappropriate to the writer's purpose and audience.
- References to sources are generally cited and documented, but not always according to MLA style.
- Problems in grammar, spelling, punctuation, or usage occasionally interfere with communication and impair the writer's credibility.

Characteristics of "D" Writing

Content

- The material does not fully engage the abilities of a college audience, or is unclear to those outside the writer's classroom.
- No single focus runs through the entire paper.
- Ideas are stated, but not developed with details, examples, and discussions.
- Outside sources, if used at all, are not clearly introduced or integrated.
- The writing fails to fulfill several assignment criteria.

Organization

- The argument or focus is overly general, missing, or unclear.
- The writer hasn't established a clear pattern for the paper to follow.
- Attempt at focus development is evident but unsuccessful; paragraphs frequently seem unrelated or repetitive.
- Paragraphs are poorly constructed and contain little supporting detail.
- The opening and closing are overly general, missing, or misleading.
- Transitions are weak, ineffective, or missing.

Style and Mechanics

- Sentences are frequently basic, choppy, or repetitive.
- Sentence problems impede effective communication.
- The reader must reread many sentences in order to comprehend them.
- The writer displays inadequate control of diction; word-choice problems are frequent.
- There are many problems with standard idiom.
- The tone frequently appears inappropriate to the writer's purpose and audience.
- References to sources are not clearly cited; documentation consistently ignores MLA style.
- Many errors in spelling, grammar, punctuation, and usage impede communication and damage the writer's credibility.

Characteristics of "F" Writing

In addition to reflecting many "D" characteristics, the writer does not fulfill basic assignment criteria, including submission of early drafts, page count expectations, source integration requirements, and the like.

Grading Criteria for Classroom Participation and Oral Presentations

Characteristics of "A" Class Participation and Oral Presentations

Classroom Participation

- The student attends every class period, prepared and on time.
- The student contributes fruitfully, appropriately, and frequently to class discussions.
- The student completes all assignments and readings superbly and on time.
- The student actively and enthusiastically participates in all class activities.
- The student always provides thoughtful and substantial feedback to peers during presentations, workshops, and related activities.
- The student always actively listens and responds to peers and the instructor.
- The student always engages in the practices of good classroom citizens.

Oral Presentations

- The material challenges the intelligence and sophistication of a college audience, and would be clear to audiences beyond the student's classroom.
- The focus of each presentation is clearly emphasized.
- Presentations are purposefully organized and substantially developed with supporting evidence or detailed examples.
- The openings and closings are inviting, challenging, and appropriate.
- The student masters the basics of oral communication including eye contact, clarity, delivery speed, volume, meeting time requirements, and professionalism.
- The presentations artfully fulfill the assignment criteria.

Characteristics of "B" Class Participation and Oral Presentations

Classroom Participation

- The student attends nearly every class period, prepared and on time.
- The student contributes productively and consistently to class discussions.
- The student regularly completes assignments and readings well and on time.
- The student actively participates in class activities.
- The student consistently provides thoughtful feedback to peers during presentations, workshops, and related activities.
- The student actively listens and responds to peers and the instructor.
- The student frequently engages in the practices of good classroom citizens.

Oral Presentations

- The material is thoughtful and engaging to a college audience, and would be clear to audiences beyond the student's classroom.
- A single focus runs through each presentation.
- The focus of each presentation is developed through supporting evidence or detailed examples.
- The openings and closings are appropriate.
- The student successfully exhibits the basics of oral communication including eye contact, clarity, delivery speed, volume, meeting time requirements, and professionalism.
- The presentations clearly fulfill the assignment criteria.

Characteristics of "C" Class Participation and Oral Presentations

Classroom Participation

- The student attends most class periods, prepared and on time.
- The student sometimes contributes productively to class discussions.
- The student completes most assignments and readings satisfactorily and on time.
- The student participates in class activities.
- The student generally provides thoughtful feedback to peers during presentations, workshops, and related activities.
- The student pays attention in class and listens to peers and the instructors.
- The student generally engages in the practices of good classroom citizens.

Oral Presentations

- The material is reasonable but may not fully engage a college audience; portions of the presentations may be unclear to audiences beyond the student's classroom.
- A single focus runs through each presentation, although parts may wander from the central idea.
- The focus of each presentation is generally developed throughout the presentation, though some information may seem slightly off-track.
- The openings and closings generally support the topic and focus.
- The student satisfactorily exhibits most of the basics of oral communication including eye contact, clarity, delivery speed, volume, meeting time requirements, and professionalism.
- The presentations reasonably fulfill most of the assignment criteria.

Characteristics of "D" Class Participation and Oral Presentations

Classroom Participation

- The student routinely misses, is late, and/or arrives unprepared to class.
- The student rarely and/or inconsistently contributes to class discussions.
- The student completes some assignments and readings well and on time, but routinely demonstrates that he/she has not completed assigned tasks.
- The student participates in class activities though perhaps without full ambition, attention, and/or enthusiasm.
- The student seldom provides appropriately thoughtful and substantial feedback to peers during presentations, workshops, and related activities.
- The student routinely seems distracted during class and/or occasionally distracts others.
- The student typically engages in the practices of good classroom citizens.

Oral Presentations

- The material does not fully engage the abilities of a college audience, or is unclear to audiences beyond the student's classroom.
- The focus of each presentation is overly general, missing, or unclear.
- The student hasn't established a clear pattern for the presentation to follow.
- The openings and closings are overly general, missing, or misleading.
- The student does not exhibit many of the basics of oral communication including eye contact, clarity, delivery speed, volume, meeting time requirements, and professionalism.
- The presentations fail to fulfill several of the assignment criteria.

Characteristics of "F" Class Participation and Oral Presentations

In addition to reflecting many "D" characteristics, the student does not fulfill basic classroom expectations and/or assignment criteria.

About the Binghamton University Student Writing Center

We tutor all students, from all disciplines, on all assignments.

The Writing Center provides free tutoring in college writing for *all* students. Our excellent tutors are available Monday–Friday to assist you with any assignment from any class: essays, arguments, research papers, reports, analyses, editorials, proposals, abstracts, and lab reports, as well as critical reading and citing sources.

Our friendly, qualified tutors are here to help *every student from every department and school.* Whether English is your home language or not, whether you're an undergraduate or graduate student, we're here to help you become a better writer. We guide and advise you as you work on your writing. There are three ways to use our tutoring services:

1. You can drop in as needed.

2. You can make an appointment so that a tutor is available when you arrive.

3. You can establish a regular weekly appointment with the same tutor.

What Tutors Do: We provide insight to college-level writing as we work with you to

- understand the assignment
- plan your paper or project
- read critically
- select and narrow a topic
- focus your thesis
- choose credible source material
- integrate source material
- use citation styles such as APA, MLA, and Chicago
- avoid plagiarism
- write with audience and purpose in mind
- develop logical structures
- craft your tone, transitions, and language
- recognize and revise sentence-level problems related to style and mechanics

What Tutors Don't Do:

- fix the writing for you—we are tutors, not editors; we coach and advise
- comment on writing without the author present

Location:	Library North (LN) 2412
Hours:	Monday through Thursday 10–4 Friday 10–3:15
Information:	607-777-6725
Website:	http://www2.binghamton.edu/writing/
Appointments:	http://binghamton.mywconline.com/
Director:	Dr. Paul Shovlin pshovlin@binghamton.edu

About Writing Initiative Faculty Outreach

The Writing Initiative's Faculty Outreach program is committed to the development of writing as a central part of the intellectual life and learning goals of Binghamton University students and faculty. Writing Initiative Faculty Outreach works to strengthen the teaching of writing across campus in many ways, from providing one-on-one consulting services for faculty, to developing and making available writing pedagogy resources to faculty, to sponsoring workshops and programs that support writing instruction. These services are designed to attend to the needs of writers in different disciplines and give faculty members the support they need to help students achieve the goals set for writers in their classrooms. In addition to work with faculty, Writing Initiative Faculty Outreach supports graduate student teaching assistants who work with writers in the classes they teach, and the staff of programs that provide writing support to students.

Faculty Outreach Coordinator: Dr. Robert Danberg
rdanberg@binghamton.edu

Chapter One

The Rhetorical Analysis Oral Presentation

Assignment Overview

Rhetorical Analysis Oral Presentation

In this unit, you will think about the relationship between invention and arrangement by closely reading and discussing several kinds of texts to learn what rhetorical features make them work. John Ruszkiewicz describes the essence of rhetorical analysis in his textbook, *How to Write Anything*:

> Rhetoric is the art of using language and media to achieve particular goals. A rhetorical analysis is an argument that takes a close look at the strategies of persuasion within a text; it lists and describes specific techniques that a writer... has employed and then assesses their effectiveness. (222)

As you prepare your presentation, you must take words seriously, know your audience, and read closely so that you can offer strong claims about the text and support those claims with textual evidence.

Content and Audience

You will work with your peers to create a group presentation based on your analysis of an essay from *They Say, I Say*, or another essay of the instructor's choosing. Your presentation will include reporting your rhetorical analysis to the rest of the class, emphasizing how the essay could be used as a touchstone for each of the major assignments, and leading a sophisticated discussion of the text. Your instructor will offer you strategies for successfully tackling the assignment and point you to essays that are appropriate for analysis.

As you prepare your presentation, think of your audience as not just the members of our classroom, but also the wider Binghamton University campus community. Members of the Binghamton University community are bright, intellectually adventurous, and sophisticated—they know a lot about many things. But they don't know everything about everything. Thus, you will need to explain key concepts and define terms in your presentation. You will also have to persuade your audience that you have something valuable to contribute to their intellectual understanding of the text. As you plan your presentation, consider the following questions, as well as questions that you develop as a group:

* What ideas are important in the text? How and to what extent are ideas supported?

* What principles of organization govern the text, and how does structure influence its success?

* How does the author appeal to the reader's feelings, intellect, and sense of self, and what rhetorical strategies does the writer use to affect readers' understanding?

* Who is the intended audience for this piece, how did the author attempt to reach this audience, and how successful was the author in doing so?

* What challenges did you face as you analyzed this text and how did you overcome them?

* How could you use this piece as a touchstone for future assignments in Writing 111?

Organization and Format

Your Rhetorical Analysis Oral Presentation group should develop a claim based on your analysis and support this claim by referring specifically to the text in your analysis, using summary, paraphrase, and direct quotation. As a class, we will practice doing rhetorical analyses, examine sample rhetorical analyses, and generate grading criteria for this genre. Your presentation should be fifteen minutes long (no less than twelve, no more than sixteen). Time requirements will be strictly enforced.

Evaluation

Your group will be evaluated on the grading criteria developed by you and your classmates, the sophistication of your analysis, your thorough preparation for the presentation, your ability to generate understanding and enthusiasm about the text in your classmates, and your contribution to discussion when groups other than your own present.

INVENTION: **Rhetorical Analysis Group Charter**

Group Members/Personal Information

Name   Email

_____ _____

_____ _____

_____ _____

_____ _____

_____ _____

Team Member Skill Inventory

(Areas individual members can contribute/want to develop; include research skills, speaking skills, technology skills, and organization/project management skills.)

Team Presentation Goals

(May include RAOP assignment goals, group process goals, quality level goals, etc.)

What are potential barriers to the achievement of these goals?

Ground Rules

Meeting schedule, locations, attendance expectations, agenda, assignment completion, communication methods, etc.

Conflict Management

What are potential conflicts that might arise among or between team members during this course? How will team members deal with these and other conflicts?

INVENTION: **The Rhetorical Appeals, the Rhetorical Triangle, and Academic Argument**

The Three Rhetorical Appeals: Ethos, Logos, and Pathos

Effective arguments usually include all three of the following appeals, or types of arguments:

Ethos: An ethical appeal is an argument based on two different but related conceptions of the term "ethics."

1. The first sense of ethics is like "medical ethics:" doing what is good, or in the best interest of those people involved in the situation.

2. A writer's ethos is his or her credibility. Do you believe the author? Do you trust him or her? To demonstrate the use of ethos in an argument, a writer can establish one's credentials, cite authorities on a topic, establish common ground with an audience, and demonstrate open-mindedness.

Logos: A logical appeal is an argument based on reason. To demonstrate the use of logic in an argument, a writer can define his or her terms specifically and use those definitions as part of his or her argument, use sufficient, relevant, and timely evidence, draw conclusions from facts or data, etc.

Pathos: A pathetic appeal is an argument based on emotion. To demonstrate the use of pathos in an argument, a writer might use vivid description of an event, figurative language, appeal to an audience's emotions (pity, anger, love, patriotism...), use personal stories or anecdotes, etc.

The Rhetorical Triangle: Writer, Audience, Purpose

Effectively written arguments will show that the writer has carefully thought about all three of the following aspects of writing:

Writer: For the purposes of writing and crafting arguments, one needs a clear conception of the writer: the stances he or she takes, what preparation he or she has done for the argument, how qualified he or she is to write or speak about a topic. A writer also needs a clear conception of his or her audience and purpose for writing. This relates to the second definition of ethos above.

Audience: For an argument to be convincing, a writer must know to whom she or he is writing. Simply put, a letter to one's sibling is going to be different from a letter to an elected official, a potential employer, and so on. A writer needs to research his or her audience and then write an argument that is appropriate to that audience. The writer will use different appeals to different degrees depending on the expectations and attitudes of the intended audience.

Purpose: The purpose of writing an argument can vary—one's purpose can be to seek the truth, to persuade or convince an audience to think a certain way or to take a certain action. One can have many different purposes for writing: to convince, to explain, to interpret, to enlighten, to entertain, etc. Again, depending on your purpose, or what you hope to achieve, you will choose to use different appeals to different degrees.

What Is an Academic Argument?

An academic argument is not a fight or a quarrel. An academic argument is a claim with justifiable reasons to back it up. Another way to think of academic argument is like a thesis statement with supporting evidence. Most academic arguments will also explore counterarguments. More often than not, academic arguments attempt to find the best solution to a problem, attempt to find the truth, or attempt to persuade an audience. By and large, Writing 111 asks you to focus on persuasion.

For example, this is an example of a persuasive argument:

Binghamton University is the best university in the nation, because it attracts the best students, it provides a high-quality liberal arts education, and it offers excellent opportunities for student support.

Claim:	Binghamton University is the best university in the nation.
Reason #1:	Because BU attracts the best students from around the world.
Reason #2:	Because BU provides a high-quality liberal arts education.
Reason #3:	Because BU offers excellent opportunities for student support.

Could someone disagree with this argument? Yes—some may argue that Cornell University, for example, is a better university, and they would need to be able to come up with reasons for their argument.

Truth and Persuasion

Academic arguments are not only about finding "the truth" or what is correct; they are about persuasion—convincing someone else about your ideas or positions. Arguments are often not about finding the absolutely correct answer, but rather finding ground in a debate. Arguments are often about distinguishing between shades of gray, rather than distinguishing between black and white. Will our argument about Binghamton University lead to "the truth"? Probably not (especially to Cornell students), but it might persuade some people.

Are All Arguments Equally Valid?

No. Argument is not the same as opinion: we can have opinions on all sorts of things, but an argument is different because it is a claim that is backed up by justifiable reasons. The difference between right and wrong may not always be clear to us, but through argumentation, we seek to clarify our positions and take stands based on our claims and reasons. We cannot always claim to be correct simply because of "our opinions." Argumentation means that we can be persuaded to think something different if convinced; argumentation means that we can hold a position until we are persuaded otherwise.

Activity: Identifying Rhetorical Appeals and Argumentative Strategies

Consider a text we have read in this class or that you have been assigned. How is that text using rhetorical appeals? What other argumentative strategies does the writer employ and what claims does the writer make? What techniques and strategies are most effective to you?

● REFLECTION: Rhetorical Analysis Cover Letter

Guidelines: Approximately 200 Words

Please consider the following questions in the format of an informal letter to your instructor. You are not obligated to discuss all of these questions; instead, answer the three or four that will give your instructor the best insight into your work and your experience with this assignment. Instructors will use this statement to guide their feedback, so do your best to reflect on both the strengths and weaknesses of your project.

Before You Write Your Cover Letter

Prior to putting pen to paper, consider your recent Rhetorical Analysis Oral Presentation carefully.

Question 1: Getting Started

Explain how your group began the project. Did you all read the essay independently and then unite to share notes? Describe the process by which you all began your analysis. Did you reread the essay? Did you jump in and plan your presentation from top to bottom? Or did you start in some other way? How did this process work or not work? Explain your contributions to the presentation.

Question 2: Focusing

What was your purpose with the presentation? What re-vision of the text did you hope to communicate?

Question 3: Improving

Following your presentation, what advice did you seek from your classmates? What specific concerns and praise did they offer? Were their suggestions helpful? Why or why not?

Question 4: What's Working Well? What's Not?

What were you happiest with in this presentation? Did you try a particular technique that seemed to work for you? Did your classmates confirm that? What are you least satisfied with? Were there any approaches that you or your fellow group members tried that didn't seem to work?

Question 5: Goals for Future Presentations

When planning your individual Researched Argument Oral Presentation, what priorities will you set for revision in regards to the way you prepare and conduct oral presentations? What are your specific goals for improvement?

Question 6: Characteristics of ABCD Classroom Participation and Oral Presentations

Take a few minutes to reflect on the major criteria you and your classmates developed in accordance with the Rhetorical Analysis Oral Presentation as well as the Characteristics of ABCD Classroom Participation and Oral Communication. Which of the criteria do you feel most confident about? Which one are you the least confident about? Why?

Related Readings

"INVITING TRANSFORMATION"

On the next pages is a reading—"Inviting Transformation"—which is a chapter from a book by Sonja K. Foss and Karen A. Foss, *Inviting Transformation: Presentational Speaking for a Changing World.*

"Inviting Transformation" asks us to look at the aim and practice of public speaking in a different way than we are used to, not as "persuasion" so much as "inviting transformation." The difference is in the nature and quality of the relationship between the speaker and the audience. Persuasion, some feel, directs the speaker to try to change the audience through her use of words and occasion, whereas a speaker who invites transformation leaves the audience room to move, to make decisions, to play a role in the event of communication.

We have included "Inviting Transformation" at this point in the chapter because it gives you further ways to think about *preparing a talk*. A reading about the aim of speaking and the kind of relationship you strike up with your audience will be most useful as you begin to think about preparing to talk, as you plan how you will go about saying what you have to say.

Inviting Transformation

By Sonja K. Foss and Karen A. Foss

Presentational speaking is an invitation to transformation. Speakers initiate communications with others because they are seeking opportunities for growth and change and because they believe they can offer such opportunities to others. As a result of communication, an audience may accept a speaker's invitation and leave the interaction changed in some way. A speaker, too, may re-think ideas and gain new insights as a result of the interaction that occurs. This notion that presentational speaking is an invitation to transformation, which is crucial to understanding and applying the principles of speaking discussed in the rest of this book, can be clarified by exploring the primary concepts it entails—presentational speaking, transformation, and invitation.

Presentational Speaking

When you think about giving a speech or making a presentation, what probably comes to mind is a situation in which one person is standing in front of an audience composed of at least several people and probably more. The speaker does the talking, and any oral participation by the audience, more often than not, is limited to asking questions at the end of the speech. You probably associate this kind of speaking with public settings such as lecture halls, classrooms, senate chambers, courts of law, churches, and campaign rallies. If you suffer from stage fright at all, this is the kind of speaking situation that tends to make you nervous.

In contrast to public speaking is conversation or interpersonal communication, where two or three people talk informally, with everyone participating equally in the interaction. This type of interaction, which most people find comfortable and enjoyable, usually is associated with private places such as homes or offices or perhaps places where private spaces can be created within public spaces, such as restaurants or bars.

Some oral communication cannot easily be put only into one format or the other: it can occur in conversational formats as well as in more formal speech contexts. We have chosen to call this kind of communication presentational speaking, and it is distinguished by two features. The first is that one person has more responsibility for the communication than do the others involved in the interaction. Perhaps that person has been asked by others to share her perspective on a subject, she has an idea she thinks will be useful to her coworkers, or she might be leading a discussion to generate ideas to solve a problem. For whatever reason, she has been given a greater role in the interaction, and other participants will expect more from her than they will from the others involved. Her communication will be somewhat more important than theirs in creating the nature, tenor, and environment of the interaction.

A second feature of this kind of oral communication is that at least one of the individuals involved in the interaction has done some thinking about the message or the ideas to be conveyed prior to the interaction. This person will not always have had a lot of time to prepare, but he will have in mind a goal for speaking, the basic message he wants to convey, and some thoughts about how to present that message.

Presentational speaking is the kind of oral communication with which this book is concerned. It deals with communication in which you have had some prior preparation time. This communication may occur in the format of a public speech, a private conversation, or something in between. It simply involves some kind of presentation—even if it is only a few sentences long and is designed to get discussion started.

Presentational speaking, then, involves a variety of forms. The answers a candidate gives during a job interview constitute presentational speaking; the interviewer in this situation also is engaged in presentational speaking. A coach who gives a pep talk to a wrestling team is giving a presentation, as is the new manager who begins the first meeting of her staff by introducing herself. In all of these situations, one person has primary responsibility for communicating a message thought about ahead of time. When members of a group explore an issue together to figure out what they know and believe about it, they also are engaged in presentational speaking. Although this interaction produces presentations that may contain many of the hesitations, incomplete thoughts, and overlaps of spontaneous conversation, it counts as presentational speaking because the convener of the meeting has thought about the issue, asks others to participate, and assumes responsibility for starting the discussion.

Transformation

Transformation means growth or change. It may involve changing your opinion on an issue, gaining information about a subject you did not have before, or adopting a new behavior. Transformation also includes the more subtle kind of change that occurs when you incorporate new information into your systems of thought, allowing you to imagine and generate new ideas. A student at Ohio State University, Sherveen Lotfi, provides a good summary of this kind of transformation, which he hopes his presentations facilitate: "I'm hoping that after the speech is over, the kernels of information represented by the key words will expand in their minds as they did in mine and lead to other images.... I try to challenge them to take the next step on their own and to infer additional conclusions based on their own circumstances and understanding."

Transformation happens only through the process of interaction: it cannot occur in isolation. When, for example, you see your position as the only right or correct one and are not willing to consider or to try to understand other positions, transformation is not possible. Neither can it occur when one perspective is privileged over others. Transformation is generated when you share your perspective with others—when it is subject to comparison with other perspectives in a process of discovery, questioning, and rethinking. The transformation that may be engendered in presentational speaking, then, is not the result of the skill or expertise of one speaker. If it occurs, it results from the exchange and interaction to which the speaker's presentation contributes. Your role as speaker is to keep the conversation going—to sustain interaction—so that new ways of thinking and acting are able to emerge.

Invitation

Invitation is a critical concept in the notion that presentational speaking is an invitation to transformation. Any change that results from presentational speaking is not forced on the audience. Your efforts are directed at enabling transformation—making it possible for those who are interested—not imposing it on those who are not. The speaker's invitation is an offering, an opening, an availability—not an insistence. Some in the audience may choose to accept this invitation; others will not. Your communication may not appear to change thinking and behavior, but you do not and cannot change others. Such changes are the results of decisions by listeners who choose to hear others or to learn from others. Transformation occurs only through the process of self-change generated by interaction with other perspectives.

When you offer an invitation to transformation and do not impose it, you recognize that audience members have had experiences and hold perspectives that are as valuable and legitimate as your own. You view audience members as the authorities on their own lives who hold the beliefs they do and act as they do for reasons that make good sense to them. You respect, then, the integrity and authority of audience members by offering your ideas to them rather than imposing your ideas on them. Sherveen Lotfi uses a metaphor of baking cookies to convey this notion: "Giving a speech is like sharing cookies we've baked with the people around us. They may or may not like them. I hope that the cookies are so tasty that the people who ate them want to go and bake some of their own." Audience members may refuse the invitation—may not take any cookies from the plate that is passed—for any number of legitimate reasons.

Although you cannot force transformation on your audience, what you can do is create, through the communicative options you select, an environment in which others may change if they are inclined to do so. As Sally Miller Gearhart explains, "No one can change an egg into a chicken. If, however, there is the potential in the egg to be a chicken ... then there is the likelihood that in the right environment (moisture, temperature, the 'external conditions for change') the egg will hatch."

Four external conditions are particularly critical for the creation of an environment in which self-change may take place—safety, value, freedom, and openness. When these conditions are present, self-change is more likely to occur. As you prepare your presentation, you can select communicative options that either facilitate or impede the development of these conditions in your particular speaking situation.

Safety is the condition of feeling free from danger, of feeling secure. Your communication contributes to a feeling of safety when you let audience members know that the ideas and feelings they share with you will be received with respect and care. You also help create a safe environment when you do not hurt, degrade, or belittle your audience members or their beliefs. Providing a means for your audience members to order their world in some way so it seems coherent and makes sense to them is another way to contribute to their feeling of safety. When people feel their sense of order is threatened or challenged, they are more likely to cling to familiar ways of thinking and to be less open to possibilities for change. When you create safety in a speaking situation, audience members trust you, are not fearful of interacting with you, and feel you are working with and not against them.

Value is the acknowledgement that your audience members have intrinsic or immanent worth. You convey that you value your listeners when you allow all participants in the interaction to be heard. But valuing them means more than recognizing their right to participate in the conversation: it involves encouraging their participation—inviting them to share their perspectives with you and listening carefully when they do. When audience members' perspectives vary widely from yours, try to understand them by learning more about the individuals in your audience and trying to discover why they might have developed the perspectives they have. Making the effort to think from the standpoint of your audience members—trying to make vivid in your own mind their perspectives—also is a way of valuing them. When value is created in a speaking situation, audience members feel that you care about them, understand their ideas, and allow them to contribute in significant ways to the interaction.

Freedom, the third condition whose presence in an environment contributes to the possibility of transformation, is the power to choose or decide. You contribute to the creation of a sense of freedom when you create opportunities for others to develop and select their own options from alternatives they themselves have created. Freedom also is developed when you do not place restrictions on the interaction. Participants can bring any and all matters to the interaction for consideration; no subject matter is privileged subject matter, and all presuppositions can be challenged. If audience members do not make the choices you would like them to make, you do not ban their participation from the interaction, halt the interaction, or sever your relationship with them. They are free in the interaction to make their own choices and decisions.

If communication is to create an environment in which transformation may occur, it cannot deliberately exclude any perspectives. In fact, you want to encourage participants in the interaction to incorporate as many perspectives as possible to ensure that the greatest number of ideas is considered. The condition of openness, then, is the fourth characteristic of a potentially transformative environment. It involves genuine curiosity about and a deliberate seeking out of perspectives different from your own or from the standard view. It involves exploring carefully and thoughtfully these other perspectives and approaching the differences they represent with an attitude of appreciation and delight.

With our emphasis on presentational speaking as a means to create the conditions of safety, value, freedom, and openness and thus to invite transformation, we are privileging growth and change. We are suggesting that being open to being changed is desirable and is better than developing a rigid position and coming to a "correct" understanding of a subject and sticking to it. Our primary reason for this focus is that many of the problems facing the world today seem to be the result of people's beliefs that they hold the only right positions, which they try to impose on others. The conflicts among people in the former Yugoslavia, between the pro-choice and anti-abortion forces, and between loggers and environmentalists in the Pacific Northwest, for example, seem to be the result of such rigidity. On a more personal level, misunderstanding, conflicts, and severed relationships are often the result of an unwillingness to yield on positions and a lack of openness to those held by others. We believe understandings are more likely to develop, differences are more likely to be bridged, and creative and imaginative solutions are more likely to be generated when people are open to the possibility of transformation.

Because we have chosen to privilege the opportunity for transformation, the kind of speaking dealt with in this book may look very different from the kinds of speaking with which you are familiar. We are not interested in the kind of speaking that occurs when a speaker intimidates audience members, making them afraid to speak and humiliating them when they do; the environment that results from this type of presentation is not one in which individuals feel safe or valued. We are not interested in the kind of speaking that is designed to showcase the talents of the speaker and to enhance his status or ego; this kind of speaking devalues and is closed to the potential contributions of others involved and is not directed at encouraging an exchange of perspectives. The kind of speaking covered in this book also will not be relevant to those who engage in the kind of competitive speaking where the goal is to overpower others' positions by establishing the superiority of their own. This kind of speaking, again, does not create an environment in which others feel valued and free to hold their own perspectives. Although you may find yourself involved in speaking situations in which such communication occurs, we hope that your familiarity with and skill in using the model presented in this book will enable you to help convert those situations into ones of safety, value, freedom, and openness.

Rhetorical Analysis
Examines in Detail the Way Texts Work

by John J. Ruszkiewicz

Rhetorical analyses foster the kind of close reading that makes writers better thinkers. Moreover, they're everywhere in daily life, especially in politics and law. In fact, they're hard to avoid.

- An editorial in the college paper calls for yet another fee to support a get-out-the-vote initiative on campus. You respond with an op-ed of your own, pointing out the editor's factual errors and logical inconsistencies.

- As part of a course evaluation, you argue that the assigned history textbook inappropriately endorses a particular interpretation of contemporary European history rather than just stating facts and leaving it for readers to make judgments.

- In your blog, you post a paragraph-by-paragraph refutation of a review published by the *Los Angeles Times* of your favorite band's latest CD. You point to ample textual evidence that the reviewer is neither well-informed nor objective.

- You're pretty sure global warming is the real deal, but you find yourself wishing that news reporters wouldn't blame every spring tornado and summer thunderstorm on the phenomenon.

Understanding Rhetorical Analysis

You react to what others say or write all the time. Sometimes an advertisement, speech, or maybe a political anthem grabs you so hard that you want to take it apart to see how it works. Put those discoveries into words and you've composed a *rhetorical analysis*.

Rhetoric is the art of using language and media to achieve particular goals. A rhetorical analysis is an argument that takes a close look at the strategies of persuasion within a text; it lists and describes specific techniques that a writer, speaker, editor, or advertiser has employed and then assesses their effectiveness. You can take a rhetorical analysis one step further and respond to a particular argument by offering good reasons for agreeing or disagreeing with it. Such a detailed critique of a text is sometimes called a *critical analysis.*

When you write a rhetorical analysis, you'll do the following things.

Take words seriously. When you compose an analysis, whether admiring or critical, hold writers to a high standard because their ideas may have consequences. Good notions deserve to be identified and applauded. And bad ones should be ferreted out, exposed, and sent packing. Learning to discern one from the other takes practice—which is what rhetorical analyses provide.

Make strong claims about texts. Of course, you cannot make claims about texts until you know them inside out. The need for close examination may seem self-evident, but we blow through most of what we read (and see) without much thought. Serious critical or rhetorical analysis does just the opposite: It makes texts move like bullets in the movie *The Matrix*, their trajectories slowed and every motion magnified for careful study.

Mine texts for evidence. Not only should you read texts closely in preparing a rhetorical analysis: Use their words (and any other elements) as the evidence for your own claims. That's one of the goals of critical examinations of this sort: to find and cite what other readers of a text may have missed. Expect to use a lot of quotations in a rhetorical analysis.

ONLINE MAGAZINE

This polished and highly entertaining critical analysis is from the "Ad Report Card" series on Slate.com. Seth Stevenson goes after the famous Apple ad campaign comparing Macs and PCs, explaining how it misreads an important audience segment, and gets its facts wrong, too. Notice the personal point of view in this piece: Stevenson has no qualms about using his own experiences as grounds for dissing the ads. He explains exactly why.

Slate.com

Posted: Monday, June 19, 2006, at 6:29 A.M. E.T.
From: Seth Stevenson

Ad Report Card:
Mac Attack

Apple's mean-spirited new ad campaign

THE SPOT: *Two men stand side by side in front of a feature-less, white background. "Hello, I'm a Mac," says the guy on the right (who is much younger and dressed in jeans). "And I'm a PC," says the guy on the left (who wears dorky glasses, ill-fitting khakis, and a jacket and tie). The two men discuss the many advantages of using a Mac and seem to agree that Macs are "better" than PCs.*

Articles in this series open by describing text to be analyzed.

When I write about ads, I often face an obstacle: I'm not in the target demographic. Am I really in a position to judge whether, say, a Lexus ad is on the mark? The chances that I (driver of a 1996 Saturn with 105,000 miles on it) will buy a luxury sedan are essentially nil. Likewise, who am I to say if those adult-diaper spots are winning mind-share with senior citizens? Incontinence is a health issue that has (knock on wood) not yet hit my radar screen.

Written in a middle style, colloquial and personal: *Who am I to say.*

In the case of these Mac ads, however, I'm smack in the middle of the target demo. I'm a PC user, and I've often considered switching to an Apple. Thus, I feel equipped to say: These ads don't work on me. They are conceptually brilliant, beautifully executed, and highly entertaining. But they don't make me want to buy a Mac.

Explains why he is qualified to assess Mac ads.

Let's talk about the good news first. Directed by Phil Morrison (who also directed *Junebug*—my favorite film last year—and the recent VW ads featuring shocking car crashes), the campaign is a marvel of clarity and simplicity. No slogans. No video effects. No voice-overs. And lots of clean, white space. It's like a bath of cool mineral water when these ads come on after a string of garish, jam-packed spots for other products. (This bare-bones look is right in tune with Apple's consistently stripped-down

Lists rhetorical strategies that make ads attractive to viewers.

Stevenson, Seth. "Ad Report Card: Mac Attack" as appeared in *Slate*, June 19, 2006.

marketing approach.)

My problem with these ads begins with the casting. As the Mac character, Justin Long (who was in the forgettable movie *Dodgeball* and the forgettabler TV show *Ed*) is just the sort of unshaven, hoodie-wearing, hands-in-pockets hipster we've always imagined when picturing a Mac enthusiast. He's perfect. Too perfect. It's like Apple is parodying its own image while also cementing it. If the idea was to reach out to new types of consumers (the kind who aren't already evangelizing for Macs), they ought to have used a different type of actor.

Examines comparison at heart of ad's strategy: cool Mac dude vs. PC dweeb.

Meanwhile, the PC is played by John Hodgman— contributor to *The Daily Show* and *This American Life*, host of an amusing lecture series, and all-around dry-wit extraordinaire. Even as he plays the chump in these Apple spots, his humor and likability are evident. (Look at that hilariously perfect pratfall he pulls off in the spot titled "Viruses.") The ads pose a seemingly obvious question— Would you rather be the laid-back young dude or the portly old dweeb?—but I found myself consistently giving the "wrong" answer: I'd much sooner associate myself with Hodgman than with Long.

Explains why key rhetorical strategy in ad fails.

The writing may have something to do with this, too. Hodgman gets all the laugh lines! And Mr. Mac comes off as a smug little twit, who (in the spot titled "WSJ") just happens to carry around a newspaper that has a great review of himself inside. (Even Norman Mailer usually refrains from such crassness.)

The final straw, for me, is that the spots make unconvincing claims. The one titled "Network" has a funny bit where "that new digital camera from Japan" is represented by a Japanese woman in a minidress. While Hodgman has trouble talking with the woman, Long speaks Japanese and shares giggles with her because "everything just kind of works with a Mac." Now, I happen to have a digital camera from Japan, and it works just fine with my PC. It did from the moment I connected it. Similarly, the spot titled "Out of the Box" (again, a very funny visual meta-phor, with Hodgman and Long crouching in cardboard boxes) suggests that new PCs require tons of attention and alteration when you first fire them up. But I bought a new ThinkPad notebook just a few months ago, and it ran on all cylinders pretty much straight out of the gate. Why insult my intelligence by telling me something that I know isn't true?

Earns credibility by qualifying his own argument.

I suppose the answer is that some people don't know yet. I can see how these ads might be effective with inex-perienced computer users. If you're a first-time buyer, the idea that a Mac will make your life immeasurably easier sure does sound appealing. But if you're a PC user, these ads are more likely to irritate you than convert you.

Grade: C+. As usual, Apple hopes to shift the debate away from a battle over specs and value and toward a battle we can all understand: cool kid versus nerd. But these days, aren't nerds like John Hodgman the new cool kids? And isn't smug superiority (no matter how affable and casually dressed) a bit off-putting as a brand strategy?

Most rhetorical analyses don't include grades, but conclusion is specific and biting.

Exploring Purpose and Topic

Make a difference. Done right, rhetorical analyses can be as important as the texts they examine. They may change readers' opinions or keep an important argument going. They may also uncover rhetorical strategies and techniques worth imitating or avoiding.

When you write an angry letter to the editor complaining about bias in the news coverage, you don't fret much about defining a purpose or topic—they are given. But when responding to a course assignment and particularly when you can choose a text to analyze rhetorically, you've got to establish the boundaries. Given a choice, select a text to analyze with the following characteristics.

Choose a text you can work with. Find a gutsy piece that makes a claim you or someone else might actually disagree with. It helps if you have a stake in the issue and already know something about it. The text should also be of a manageable length that you can explore coherently within the limits of the assignment.

Choose a text you can learn more about. Some items won't make much sense out of context. So choose a text that you can research. It will obviously help to know when it was written or published, by whom, and where it first appeared. This information is just as important for visual texts, such as posters and advertisements, as for traditional speeches or articles.

Choose a text with handles. Investigate arguments that do interesting things. Maybe a speech uses lots of anecdotes or repetition to generate emotional appeals; perhaps a photoessay's commentary is more provocative than the images; or an ad arrests attention by its simplicity but is still full of cultural significance. You've got to write about the piece. Make sure it offers you interesting things to say.

Choose a text you know how to analyze. Stick to printed texts if you aren't sure how to write about ads or films or even speeches. But don't sell yourself short. You don't need highly technical terms to describe poor logic, inept design, or offensive strategies, no matter where they appear. And you can pick up the necessary vocabulary by reading models of rhetorical and critical analysis.

Understanding Your Audience

Some published rhetorical analyses are written to ready-made audiences already inclined to agree with the authors. Riled up by an offensive editorial or a controversial ad campaign, people these days, especially on the Web, may even seek and enjoy mean-spirited, over-the-top criticism. But the rhetorical and critical analyses you write for class should be relatively restrained because you won't be able to predict how your readers might feel about the arguments you are examining. So assume that you are writing for a diverse and thoughtful audience, full of readers who prefer reflective analysis to clever put-downs. You don't have to be dull or passionless. Just avoid the easy slide into rudeness.

Finding and Developing Materials

Before you analyze a text of any kind, do some background research. Discover what you can about its author, creator, publisher, sponsor, and so on. For example, it may be important to know that the TV commercial you want to understand better has aired only on sports networks or lifestyle programs on cable. Become familiar, too, with the contexts in which an argument occurs. If you reply to a *Wall Street Journal* editorial, know what news or events sparked that item and investigate the paper's editorial slant.

Read the piece carefully just for information first, highlighting names or allusions you don't recognize. Then look them up: There's very little you can't uncover quickly these days via a Web search. When you think you understand the basics, you are prepared to approach the text rhetorically. Pay attention to any standout aspects of the text you're analyzing—perhaps how it wins over wary readers through conciliatory language or draws on the life experiences of its author to frame its subject. You might look at any of the following elements.

Consider the topic or subject matter of the text. What is novel or striking about the topic? How well-defined is it? Could it be clearer? Is it important? Relevant? Controversial? Is the subject covered comprehensively or selectively? What is the level of detail? Does the piece make a point?

Consider the audiences of the text. To whom is the piece addressed? How is the text adapted to its audience? Who is excluded from the audience and how can you tell? What does the text offer its audience: information, controversy, entertainment? What does it expect from its audience?

Consider its author. What is the author's relationship to the material? Is the writer or creator personally invested or distant? Is the author an expert, a knowledgeable amateur, or something else? What does the author hope to accomplish?

Consider its medium or language. What is the medium or genre of the text: essay, article, editorial, advertisement, book excerpt, poster, video, podcast, and so on? How well does the medium suit the subject? How might the material look different in another medium? What is the level of the language: formal, informal, colloquial? What is the tone of the text—logical, sarcastic, humorous, angry, condescending? How do the various elements of design—such as arrangement, color, fonts, images, white space, audio, video, and so on—work in the text?

59

Consider its occasion. Why was the text created? To what circumstances or situations does it respond, and what might the reactions to it be? What problems does it solve or create? What pleasure might it give? Who benefits from the text?

Consider its contexts. What purposes do texts of this type serve? Do texts of this sort have a history? Do they serve the interests of specific groups or classes? Have they evolved over time? Does the text represent a new genre?

Consider its use of rhetorical appeals. Persuasive texts are often analyzed according to how they use three types of rhetorical appeal. Typically, a text may establish the character and credibility of its author (*ethos*); generate emotions in order to move audiences (*pathos*); and use evidence and logic to make its case (*logos*).

Ethos—the appeal to character—may be the toughest argumentative strategy to understand. Every text and argument is presented by someone or something, whether an individual, a group, or an institution. Audiences are usually influenced and swayed by writers or speakers who present themselves as knowledgeable, honest, fair-minded, and even likable. Here, for example, Susan Estrich injects herself into a column she wrote about the governor of California to reinforce her own appealing sense of fair play.

> What Schwarzenegger has accomplished in the past eight months, substantively, is remarkable. I'm a lifelong Democrat who was asked to serve on the Schwarzenegger transition team. I did. He also put together a coalition of Democrats and Republicans.
>
> —"Schwarzenegger's California Formula: Bipartisanship + Civility = Progress," *USA Today*, May 27, 2004

Pathos—the emotional appeal—is usually easy to detect. Look for ways that a text generates strong feelings to support its points or win over readers. The strategy is legitimate so long as an emotion fits the situation and doesn't manipulate audiences. For example, columnist Peggy Noonan routinely uses emotions to make her political points.

> We fought a war to free slaves. We sent millions of white men to battle and destroyed a portion of our nation to free millions of black men. What kind of nation does this? We went to Europe, fought, died, and won, and then taxed ourselves to save our enemies with the Marshall

Plan. What kind of nation does this? Soviet communism stalked the world and we were the ones who steeled ourselves and taxed ourselves to stop it. Again: What kind of nation does this? Only a very great one.

> —"Patriots, Then and Now," *Wall Street Journal*, March 30, 2006

Logos—the appeal to reason and evidence—is most favored in academic texts. Look carefully at the claims a text offers and whether they are supported by facts, data, testimony, and good reasons. What assumptions lie beneath the argument? Ask questions about evidence too. Does it come from reliable sources or valid research? Is it up-to-date? Has it been reported accurately and fully? Has due attention been given to alternative points of view and explanations? Has enough evidence been offered to make a valid point?

Creating a Structure

In a rhetorical analysis, you'll make a statement about how well the argumentative strategy of a piece works. Don't expect to come up with a thesis immediately or easily: You need to study a speech, editorial, or advertisement closely to figure out how it works and then think about its strengths and weaknesses. Draft a tentative thesis (or hypothesis) and then refine your words throughout the process of writing until they assert a claim you can prove.

Look for a complex and interesting thesis; don't just list some rhetorical features: *This ad has some good logical arguments and uses emotions and rhetorical questions.* Why would someone want to read (or write) a paper with such an empty claim? The following yields a far more interesting rhetorical analysis:

> The latest government antidrug posters offer good reasons for avoiding steroids but do it in a visual style so closely resembling typical health posters that most students will just ignore them.

Develop a structure. Once you have a thesis or hypothesis, try sketching a design based on a thesis/supporting reason/evidence plan. Focus on those features of the text that illustrate the points you wish to make. You don't have to discuss every facet of the text.

Noonan, Peggy. Excerpt from "Patriots, Then and Now" as appeared in *Wall Street Journal*, March 30, 2006.

*Introduction leading to a **claim***

- *First supporting reason + textual **evidence***
- *Second supporting reason + textual **evidence***
- *Additional supporting reasons + textual **evidence***

Conclusion

Under some circumstances, you might perform what amounts to a line-by-line or paragraph-by-paragraph deconstruction of a text. This structure—though not yet common in classrooms—shows up frequently online. Such analyses practically organize themselves, but your commentary must be smart, factually accurate, and stylish to keep readers on board.

*Introduction leading to a **claim***

- *First section/paragraph + detailed **analysis***
- *Next section/paragraph + detailed **analysis***
- *Additional section/paragraph + detailed **analysis***

Conclusion

In this example, political blogger Hugh Hewitt responds paragraph-by-paragraph to a letter from *New York Times* executive editor Bill Keller (June 25, 2006) justifying his newspaper's decision to reveal a top-secret antiterrorist spy program. Keller's remarks are below, followed immediately by Hewitt's critical analysis in italics.

Most Americans seem to support extraordinary measures in defense against this extraordinary threat, but some officials who have been involved in these programs have spoken to the *Times* about their discomfort over the legality of the government's actions and over the adequacy of oversight. We believe the *Times* and others in the press have served the public interest by accurately reporting on these programs so that the public can have an informed view of them.

Without disclosing the officials, we cannot be certain of their rank, their rancor, and their other agendas. We only know they are willing to break the law and their oaths. Mr. Keller's refusal to acknowledge this basic problem is more evidence of the deep dishonesty of his letter. He again asserts a "public interest" that is not his to judge as against

Keller, Bill. Excerpt from "Letter From Bill Keller on The Times's Banking Records Report" as appeared in the *New York Times*, June 25, 2006.

the laws passed by Congress, signed by presidents and interpreted by courts. But he doesn't argue why his judgment in this matter trumps that of the government and the people's elected representatives.

Choosing a Style and Design

The style of your textual analyses will vary depending on audience, but you always face one problem that can sometimes be helped by design: making the text you are analyzing more accessible to readers.

Consider a high style. Rhetorical and critical analyses you write in school will usually be formal and use a "high" style. Your tone should be respectful, your vocabulary as technical as the material requires, and your perspective impersonal—avoiding *I* and *you*. Such a style gives the impression of objectivity and seriousness. Unless an instructor gives you more leeway, use a formal style for critical analyses.

Consider a middle style. Oddly, rhetorical and critical analyses appearing in the public arena—rather than in the classroom—will usually be less formal and exploit the connection with readers that a middle style encourages. While still serious, such a style gives writers more options for expressing strong opinions and feelings (sometimes including anger, outrage, and contempt). In much public writing, you can detect a personal voice offering an opinion or advancing an agenda.

Make the text accessible to readers. A special challenge in any rhetorical analysis is to help readers understand the text you are scrutinizing. At a minimum, furnish basic information about the author, title, place of publication, and date, and briefly explain the context of the work.

When possible, also attach a photocopy of the article directly to your analysis or include a link to it if you are working online. But your analysis should still be written *as if readers do not have that text in hand*. One way to achieve that clarity is to summarize and quote selectively from the text as you examine it.

Annotate the text. When analyzing an image or a text available in digital form, consider attaching your comments directly to the item. Do this by simply inserting a copy of the image or article directly into your project and then using the design tools of your word processor to create annotations.

Hewitt, Hugh. Excerpt from "Mr. Keller Believes You Are Easily Confused" from http://www.hughhewitt.com/mr-keller-believes-you-are-easily-confused/, June 25, 2006.

Economic Citizenship and the Rhetoric of Gourmet Coffee

by Paula Mathieu

> *"You keep buying things, but you don't need them*
> *But as long as you're comfortable it feels like freedom."*
>
> —Billy Bragg

> *"To imagine a language is to imagine a form of life."*
>
> —Ludwig Wittgenstein

> *"We created the [gourmet coffee] business."*
>
> —Howard Schultz, Starbucks CEO

The power of global capitalism lies in its ability to define the boundaries in which citizens can act and effect change in their local communities.[1] As globalization signifies the interdependence of national governments, international trade organizations, and transnational business interests, the lines between local and global issues blur, making it unclear to whom citizens must appeal in order to effect change.[2] The most recent round of the General Agreement on Tariffs and Trade, for example, prohibits passing any local legislation that regulates business in a way that can be interpreted as a restriction to free trade. This means that if citizens in Illinois pass a local law banning certain pesticides from food, the World Trade Organization, not the people of Illinois, have the ultimate power to decide whether that law can stand.[3] Such trade agreements reshape traditional notions of citizenship by limiting the agency individuals can achieve through civic participation in electoral and legislative matters.

As citizens lose some of their traditional power, a new vision of citizenship becomes increasingly relevant. Saskia Sassen adopts the term *economic citizenship* to describe how globalization decreases the importance of national sovereignty and redefines citizenship in economic terms. Economic citizenship means accepting the task of defining political agency around the roles each of us plays in the cycle of global production and consumption. Many political acts we perform each day, in terms of our

Mathieu, Paula. "Economic Citizenship and the Rhetoric of Gourmet Coffee" as appeared in *Rhetoric Review* 18, No. 1, Autumn, 1999, Taylor and Francis. Ltd. http://www.informaworld.com

economic citizenship, occur not in the voting booths or even the state-house but in the stores, the workplace, and in our homes.

Economic citizens act politically by making critical choices as consumers and producers, by buying or refusing to buy, working or refusing to work, by writing and speaking out about trade agreements, IMF practices, and corporate behavior. Additionally, I would suggest, economic citizens act by critically examining and questioning the dominant narratives that are circulated in and about the economic system. James Berlin discusses a similar issue when he describes a need to interrogate "the insertion of myth between the realm of truth and the realm of ethical action" (55). Cultural narratives that "aestheticiz[e] politics," according to Berlin, often evade critique, allowing people to overlook contradictions in existing material conditions. Similarly, Paul Smith describes the present economic moment as marked by the "hyperextension of interpellative discourses and representations" (35). In other words, like Berlin, he sees the powerful role language and symbolic representations play in creating subjects who overlook gaps between the "news" about the economy and everyday realities. Powerful economic narratives naturalize a system of global exchange where trade and business priorities take precedence over other concerns, including the well-being of workers, consumers, and the environment.

One necessity of the global economy is continual economic growth; this requires businesses to create new customers and new products for customers to need.[4] New and often contradictory consumer needs are created, in real terms, all the time. Commodities that didn't exist until recently—such as gourmet coffee, cell phones, and sports-utility vehicles—are now things many swear they can't live without. We live in a country that sells both escalators and stair-masters. We drink gourmet coffee and take sleeping pills. We eat McDonald's and drink Slim-fast. This is a curious, if not sad, state of affairs.

Can rhetoric help by facilitating economic citizenship?

Citizenship and civic engagement have been longstanding concerns of rhetoric. Orators and rhetoricians as historically and ideologically diverse as Cicero, Quintilian, Hugh Blair, Margaret Fell, Sojourner Truth, Kenneth Burke, James Berlin, and Edward Schiappa have shared concerns about the relevance of rhetorical studies for developing active citizens. In "Intellectuals and the Place of Cultural Critique," Schiappa exhorts intellectuals to see themselves as active citizens, participating in public debates through newspaper writing and addressing public forums. For key figures in classical rhetoric, Schiappa notes, to be engaged in rhetoric was to be directly involved in pressing civic debates, and he encourages contemporary rhetoricians to see ourselves in that tradition.[5] He suggests that intellectuals should engage in cultural critique "not only [in] the classroom or academic books and journals, but also 'in the streets' and in other nonacademic public and private forums" (21). To avoid participating in public discourse and to work only in the classroom, Schiappa suggests, results in "'trickle-down' citizen participation" (23). In *Rhetorics, Poetics, Cultures*, James Berlin worries about how well education is preparing students to be "critical citizens of the nation" in the face of the drastic global economic and cultural shifts associated with postmodernity (52). He describes how restructuring financial markets and the shift toward a post-Fordist flexible system of production create a new climate in which we live and work. Berlin's work indicates that the rules of citizenship are changing, as rapidly as the economy is, and we need to be attuned to those shifts as teachers and as scholars.

Economics, to some extent, already figures in rhetorical investigations of political and public discourse (see for example Robert L. Brown and Carl Herndl's analysis of the John Birch Society or Richard Marback's exploration of the Joe Louis Memorial in Detroit). What I am suggesting is a shift of degree and not kind by focusing on the economic aspects of citizenship. What is changing is how completely the global economic sphere seeks to delineate and shape the political, as Berlin suggests (40–41). If rhetoric is the "ability to see the available means of persuasion" as Aristotle suggests, rhetorical analysis can be an act of citizenship by interrogating how economic forces seek to predetermine and limit the means available to citizens (1355a).

One aspect of economic citizenship worth considering is the roles language and persuasion play in defining habits of consumption. Cynthia Enloe, a political scientist, argues that scholars need to take the consumer-market relationship far more seriously than they usually do because it "not only mirrors changes in the global dynamics, it is helping to shape those dynamics" (197). I am not suggesting that narratives alone create or sustain consumer needs; rather they interact with complex and changing material conditions and engage consumers in a process of persuasion. Products like coffee and cell phones do provide certain tangible, material pleasures and conveniences to consumers. The social system itself can make some purchases—like a car or a caffeinated beverage—literally necessary to get through the working day. The problem, however, is that corporate narratives in the forms of PR and advertising offer myopic visions that magnify the positive attributes of a commodity and disconnect the consuming experience from alternative experiences, the material conditions that precipitate the need, how and by whom the product is produced, and how the profits are distributed. When we act as consumers, we assent, even if incompletely or momentarily, to such partial and fragmented narratives. They are comforting because they allow us not to look beyond the story to see the global picture.

This condition can be explained by introducing the concept of *scotosis*: rationalized acts of selective blindness that occur by allowing certain information to be discounted or unexamined. According to the *OED*, the etymology of its root word, *scotoma,* means "dizziness" and "to darken, to make dimsighted" (251).[6] *Scotosis* is a term that can help explain more fully the rhetorical process of interpellation as an ideological subject, in this case a consumer. One isn't duped, nor are false needs created. Rather, one is persuaded by the justifications offered within the narratives to remain, perhaps only momentarily or uncomfortably, within its parameters. It is thinking and acting within the frame offered. Nawal el Saadawi provides a good example of this type of blindness when discussing her training to become a doctor. She says she was drawn to medical school out of her passion for people, but once there she was taught to lose sight of whole people, instead to fragment them into pieces, to see spleens, kidneys, blood; this is an instance of scotosis. To suffer scotosis is to accept the rhetorical presence of a given narrative frame and act in the directions that frame suggests. It is analogous to looking in one direction without turning your head.[7]

I suggest that corporations circulate persuasive narratives that justify themselves, their products and the economic system. The stories are often "true," if one remains within the narrow parameters they set. Corporations seek to induce consumer scotosis in an effort to create new consumer needs. Analyzing the condition of scotosis is to look beyond the narratives offered and to name what is missing. It's an effort to broaden the cultural stories, and thus perspectives, about producers and consumers within the global capitalist framework. This is useful cultural work for economic citizens, as Herbert Marcuse's words remind us: "Naming the 'things that are absent' is breaking the spell of things that are; moreover it is the ingression of a different order of things into the established one" (68).

Rhetorical analysis as an effort to disrupt scotosis requires that certain questions be asked: How do narratives frame people as consumers? What needs do they promise to satisfy? What other needs do they deny? Where and how are the producers in these narratives portrayed? What material contradictions get ignored? What are consumers asked not to see, not to consider? What lies unspoken outside of these discourses? It is not enough to say *that* language creates narrow scripts for consumers and producers. Rhetorical analysis can interrogate the inducement of scotosis, which then sets the stage for critique, responses, and action.[8]

Scotosis at Work: The Narratives of Starbucks

"Coffee is one of the special things I have, instead of a social life."
—Joel Achenbach

The Seattle-based Starbucks Coffee Company is a major contributor to, if not entirely responsible for, the rise of a gourmet coffee culture in the United States. Starbucks' Chief Executive Officer, Howard Schultz, says that he can be personally thanked for the gourmet coffee craze: "I came back [from Italy] with the drink caffe latte in 1982. That word was not in existence in this town before we opened up our first coffee bar in April of 1984 in downtown Seattle. We created this business" (Gower 19). According to its shareholder report, Starbucks is the "leading retailer and roaster of specialty coffee in North America" (2). Since 1989 Starbucks' sales have increased more than 500 times, last year netting $996 million. Through an aggressive expansion policy, Starbucks has grown to more than 1,900 stores, mainly in metropolitan markets of North America (up from just 17 stores in 1987) (Starbucks, "The Company"). In 1994 Schultz boasted that his firm is creating a "Starbucks nation," expanding at a rate of four stores per week, and he accurately predicted that he would have "thousands and thousands" of Starbucks locations worldwide by the end of the decade (Gower 19).

Building a "Starbucks nation" requires creating a group of Starbucks consumers who are persuaded to act within the narratives that the company offers. Starbucks offers consumers "fanatical commitment to quality" (Starbucks, "Shareholder Report" 2), strict attention to detail and standardization, a unique language with which to talk about the products as well as elaborate narratives about a unique coffee experience. Starbucks is not the only gourmet coffee company that uses a specialized vocabulary, but it is the biggest and it was the first to do so on a mass scale.

So what do we buy when we buy a cup of Starbucks? One might be tempted to argue, "Just good coffee." But that position itself engages in scotosis, because it looks narrowly at the quality of the product (something the consumer somehow "deserves") and ignores the Starbucks worldview as well as the ramifications of its practices within the global economy. When we consume Starbucks, we consume justifying narratives along with the products. This is a similar argument to Shekhar Deshpande and Andy Kurtz's analysis of The Body Shop, a London-based cosmetic company. Deshpande and Kurtz argue that rather than the products, it is the discourse of "social responsibility" and "profits with principle" surrounding the Body Shop that legitimize it and make it profitable. They argue that the products consumed there are not only soap and shampoo but also discourses of liberal-politics. Like the Body Shop, Starbucks "produces as many explanations, justifications, and illustrations as it does primary goods" (Deshpande and Kurtz 38).

At Starbucks the justifying narratives can be found within the physical setup of the store, in the process of buying coffee, and within the vast amounts of literature it produces. The stores are generally located in urban or suburban high-traffic and high-income areas, and despite individual variations, are recognizably homogenous. Cherry-wood and brass accents set the scene, and at center stage in every store is a long coffee bar dominated by a "$7,000 dreaded espresso machine" (Van Matre 1). Behind it bustles an often-frantic, highly energetic staff of workers, called *baristas*; this term, which is Italian for "bartender," has become an industry standard for people who make espresso. The *baristas* wear matching uniforms consisting of green aprons and logoed baseball caps or visors. All orders are communicated and passed along verbally, in a system of call-and-response. The orders rapidly repeated back and forth take on a strange cadence, given the denseness of the terminology: "*doppio con panna*" "double tall skinny iced decaf no whip skim mocha." With all the scenery and action, set to the hiss and sputter of the espresso machine, a Starbucks store contains all the elements of a theatrical performance. In *A Primer for Daily Life*, Susan Willis describes how places of consumption often take on the look of a "postmodern museum" and a theater (17). She describes shopping places as stages for costumed employees to enact service:

Often, the employees' pert hats and aprons mimic the colors and patterns of the store's interior decor, making the [store] a stage for sales and the costumed employees the actors enacting service. . . . This is an instance where labor is truly rendered as performance, and hence, a commodity—customers consume the spectacle of work. Such spectacle stands in the place of any reference to the hundreds of laborers who cultivated, harvested, packed, shipped and marketed [the goods]. (17–18)

Thus, at Starbucks one need not even buy a cup of coffee, for one is a consumer the minute she walks in the door and comes face to face with its costumed employees and its chrome espresso bar—a consumer of the spectacle and the narratives created to surround the products. This sort of spectacle is one way scotosis is induced. Consumers are encouraged not to think of the people who plant, harvest, and transport coffee but instead to see only the performing *baristas* who take center stage, enacting the service of making coffee.

Deciding to make a purchase at Starbucks, one is faced with another inducement to scotosis in the form of Starbucks' specialized terminology. Starbucks offers its consumers an overwhelming array of drink choices; including all sizes and different options, the drink selections number in the dozens. Because many different drinks are available, one can entertain the illusion that a drink choice is tailored specifically to one's individual desires.

This narrative that much is available emphasizes a myth of "pseudo-individuality" to encourage standardization while maintaining the illusion of the autonomy of the individual, a claim Max Horkheimer and Theodor Adorno assert as endemic of the culture industry (154). They also argue that the presence of so many choices encourages total reliance on what is offered (142). Since Starbucks stresses so much choice within a fixed setting, to comply with what's offered, consumers must transform their desires. A need that may have begun as "I am sleepy," or "I am overworked," taken to Starbucks must be translated to, "I need a cup of coffee," and then further specialized to something like "I need a doppio almond espresso ristretto from Starbucks."

Given the number of minor variations, ordering a drink could easily turn into a lengthy process between consumer and *barista*. Such a dialogue would not be desirable to Starbucks since it could be time-consuming, and would also allow too much of the kind of "space" that both Marcuse and Adorno and Horkheimer describe as necessary to critically consider items outside the menu. To speed up the interaction, each drink choice has a "proper" name, which is a phrase with a correct word order, such as "Iced Grande Skim Hazelnut Latte." The Starbucks lexicon is used by the employees and taught to customers through verbal repetition and an assortment of brochures, which act as instructional literature. Drink names may contain upwards of five words, and there is a correct word order. Options are printed on the menu overhead; syntax is not. One must learn the "proper" word order from the coaching of the *baristas* and the repetition that follows. The drink names at Starbucks exemplify functionalized language as described by Marcuse: it is noun-based, and thus processes are frozen into things (84–88). Such cumbersome language, once repeated often enough, becomes just another "natural" part of the purchasing ritual. Marcuse suggests that "the ritualized concept is made immune against contradiction" (88).

Starbucks attempts to persuade consumers that drinking its coffee is a transcendent gourmet experience. The language and images of Starbucks bolster the assertion that its beverages are not merely coffee; rather they are made from incomparable ingredients and prepared to exacting standards. Therefore, the language used to describe the drinks must be completely different. This belief is reinforced by stamping one of two slogans on its disposable cups. One, "The Weather Changes Our Grind," tells customers that a variation in weather can drastically change the taste of a cup of coffee. At the same time, the message assures consumers that Starbucks adjusts its grinding technique in order to offer a consistent cup: "Our coffee preparation is so exacting that the grind of our coffee is constantly monitored. Even a change in weather can precipitate a change in our grind. It's our guarantee that your next cup of Starbucks will be as good as your last." How truthful or valid this statement is makes little difference; the message is consumed by people purchasing the coffee, by others standing with them at bus stops, and by anyone else faced with the cup once discarded as trash. The assurance that Starbucks will provide the drinker with a perfect cup of coffee in any weather lives on long past the actual drink. A second message gives espresso drinkers the "10 second rule" strictly followed by *baristas*. If a shot of espresso is not served within 10 seconds of brewing, it is poured out. Again, this message of efficiency, which actually valorizes wastefulness as a virtue, becomes an integral part of the product served by Starbucks.

More prevalent than the messages on its coffee cups is Starbucks' logo, a ubiquitous image that even passers-by recognize and consume. Willis describes logos as images first used in the 1930s and 1940s by the oil industry to demarcate roadside gas stations. Highway travelers, whether stopping or not, would consume the logo (58). Starbucks' logo is an ambiguous female Siren or mermaid. Her hair is long, her body is curvy, and her mouth is open. Her arms are spread out to her side, and what appears to be her tail is spread wide, disappearing behind her crowned head. Willis contends that "if logos are predominantly graphic abstractions, they allow the consumer to interpret them according to his or her fantasies" (53). This sexualized logo is a form of visual rhetoric, appearing on store signs and disposable cups as a constant reminder of the company and its products, perhaps appealing to the majority-male Starbucks' repeat customers (Gower 22).

Through extended narratives found in its brochures, Starbucks addresses its drinkers' libidos in a technical way, by drawing from the languages of science and technology at the same time as sex, art, and fantasy. The language, and the drinks, speak of unbridled pleasure that is absolutely, scientifically the most pleasurable of all. These brochures emphasize the company's paradoxical marketing approach: to portray the making of great coffee as a precarious combination of scientific exactness and uncontrolled passion.

One brochure, "Espresso: What You Need to Know," borrows heavily from the discourses of technology and science. Technological terms such as *standardization, high-pressure commercial quality units, rate,* and *capabilities* communicate a sense of machinery and exactness. This meticulousness is carried over into day-to-day interactions within Starbucks. At every locale the espresso machine is the focal point around which the coffee bar is built. Because of the "10 Second Rule," employees are expected to work in an assembly-line fashion with machine-like consistency and speed. According to one Starbucks employee, corporate representatives randomly and secretly pose as customers, purchasing drinks to assure consistency; they check that the *baristas* use the proper drink names, and, with a concealed thermometer, they measure the exact temperature of the drink (Lofton). Espresso beans, if ground but not brewed within one hour, are thrown away. A tendency to transform waste into need is a characteristic of consumerist "one-dimensional" society, according to Marcuse (9). Before Starbucks ever made such rigid freshness claims, pouring or throwing out good coffee would have been considered a wasteful procedure, rather than a sign of careful brewing. But once proclaimed as a motto, which is reproduced on cups and brochures, such efficiency is written into the narrative of what consumers "need" and thus are asked to demand.

Closely related to the technological language (and procedures), the "Espresso: What You Need to Know" brochure contains numerous references to science and medicine. The very title assumes the dire, medical tone more commonly associated with an informational brochure on venereal-disease prevention than one for a coffee shop. Other examples of medical language include "the right dose," "extraction," "method," "variables," "experiment," "optimum temperature," "results," and "critical." By detailing the meticulous steps involved in coffee brewing, Starbucks spins a narrative that a successful cup is always elusive. The company promises, however, that following the instructions carefully will improve one's "chances of achieving good results." Good results, as defined by Starbucks, depend on strict attention to a confusing array of variables: bean type, roast, grind, "dosage," equipment, and even climate changes. Since "The Weather Changes Our Grind," is never backed up with information about how Starbucks adjusts for climate changes, it reminds consumers that they can never match Starbucks' exacting standards. Coffee is positioned no longer as a drink, but as a drug that must be administered by skilled professionals in its proper "dose."[9] The company can then justify its elaborate rituals and higher prices all in the name of good science, and firmly establish its authority. To either learn all the nuances of brewing, or to avoid the hassles and buy brewed coffee from the pros, one must defer to the knowledge of the *baristas* and to the awkward and confusing language they speak.

Starbucks' discourse, crucially, does not rely on the language of technology and science alone. At the same time as emphasizing strict brewing procedures, Starbucks promises how sensual and refined an experience drinking its coffee will be. To capture this element of eroticism and connoisseurship, Starbucks echoes language commonly used to describe sexuality, wine-tasting, art, philosophy, and European imperialism. As an erotic experience, espresso-drinking is presented as a momentary thrill, one which will leave the drinker almost painfully wanting more. This is achieved by the use of phrases like "savored momentarily," "burst of flavor sensed throughout the mouth," "fleeting flavor," and "rewarding the drinker." Marcuse, Adorno, and Horkheimer all discuss how eroticism can be manipulatively used as a means of "(controlled) satisfaction"

(Marcuse 75), sexual pleasure that has been reduced to "a masochistic semblance" (Horkheimer and Adorno 140).

In addition to being an erotic thrill, gourmet coffee is portrayed as a pleasure to be appreciated by aficionados with highly refined taste. Europe, especially Italy, is referred to time and again as a romantic world of connoisseurs who should be emulated. The basis for Starbucks' language is Italian: *Barista, doppio, chiaro, ristretto, machiatto,* and *con panna* are all Italian-based drink names while sizes are short, tall, or *grande*. References are made to the "authentic," "Italian coffee culture," "aficionados," "in France and Italy," "Milan and Turin." Throughout many brochures, coffee-drinking is compared to wine connoisseurship. "The World of Coffee" includes a glossary of coffee-tasting terminology, with terms reminiscent of wine-tasting, like "earthy," "briny," "mellow," "tangy" and even "winy—a desirable flavor reminiscent of fine red wine." To drink Starbucks and to speak the language allows the consumer to define himor herself as someone with refined tastes, without requiring the massive costs of fine art or wine collecting. It allows consumers to partake in a fast-food version of a European connoisseur tradition. According to Pierre Bourdieu, command of language is one of the key elements that allows a person the distinction of connoisseurship: "Through his [sic] mastery of a verbal accompaniment, preferably technical, archaic and esoteric, which separates informed tasting from mere passive consumption, the connoisseur shows himself worthy of symbolically appropriating the rarities he had the material needs of acquiring" (279).

While coffee consumption is portrayed as an act of connoisseurship, Starbucks' narratives romanticize coffee production. Its descriptions encourage consumers to ignore or exoticize the people who plant, grow, and harvest the coffee, by erasing them or by invoking imperialistic[10] images to describe the relationship between Starbucks and the rest of the world. In "The World of Coffee," Starbucks describes its coffee as "exotic … coffee with unusual aromatic and flavor notes … [c]offees from East Africa and Indonesia often have such characteristics." What makes the coffee exotic is that it was grown in such an "exotic" place. The brochure, "The Story of Good Coffee from the Pacific Northwest," details the company's purchasing practices as, "Buying the best the world has to offer." There it's "the world," not specific people in specific countries who grow and provide coffee.

Willis argues that US companies regularly portray grower nations in fetishized ways: "… the Third World is … a cornucopia spilling out a steady supply of ordinary foodstuffs for North American supermarkets" (48). This attitude is especially prevalent in the Starbucks brochure that focuses on "Dave Olsen ... [who] travels the world in search of the best beans. He knows the name of a country means something, but not everything.... Each variety of coffee has distinctive regional characteristics, which may vary from season to season much like fine wine grapes do" (Starbucks, "World of Coffee"). Countries, in and of themselves, mean very little to Dave or US consumers. People don't seem to exist there at all. All that matters is the quality of the resource that can be taken from each country.

"The World of Coffee" brochure catalogues coffees by country of origin while referring to a highly stylized map. The coffee from each country is numbered, mapped, and divided by location as "The Americas," "East African," and "Indonesian." Visual logos portray each country: Arabian Mocha Sanani is depicted by a man on a camel, Kenya is represented by a large elephant, and Ethiopia by a dark woman in a patterned head scarf. The location of each country is marked with a number on a map drawn to resemble those of colonialist explorers of the seventeenth century. Willis argues that to consumers such nostalgic labels become a chic element of consumption (52). Within the text descriptions, Sulawesi coffee is described as being grown in "the former Dutch colony known as Celebes." The great taste of estate Java coffee is directly credited to colonization: "Great coffee has been cultivated in Java ever since the Dutch first transplanted trees there in 1696." Not surprisingly, use of the passive voice leaves unanswered the question, cultivated by whom?

In the world of these brochures, countries exist merely as storehouses of commodities, which seem to be planted, tended, and harvested without the labor of individuals. Erased from this narrative are those who pick the coffee in countries such as Brazil, where almost two-thirds of the people are undernourished, and where workers make a day wage sufficient to buy only a moderate portion of beans (Stolcke 226). Such erasure encourages consumers to believe, as Jean Baudrillard proclaims, that being poor means, effectively, not to exist (Faigley 210).

When depicting coffee producers, Starbucks presents romanticized images while promoting its own work with aid organizations like CARE. Starbucks donates two dollars to CARE from the purchase of a special "CARE sampler" of coffees from Kenya, Guatemala, Sumatra, and Java. The company also boasts other financial donations to global charities as well as donation of its "old" coffee beans to local charities. The advertisement of these donation practices, as well as a health-care package available to part-time employees at its retail stores, allows Starbucks to create a reputation as an ethical, global-friendly coffee purveyor. While retail workers deserve health care, Starbucks undoubtedly benefits from its provision of benefits and charity work as a form of self-promotion:

> This two dollar contribution, in addition to Starbucks ongoing annual grant, will help bring clean drinking water and a healthful future to the people of Indonesia and Guatemala; as well as environmental and health education to Kenyan children. As one of CARE's major contributors, we're able to support these vital programs, and we invite you to join us. Together, we can help the people in these coffee-producing countries, and show our appreciation for the years of pleasure their coffee has shown us.

Starbucks shows its "appreciation for the years of pleasure their coffee has shown" not by seeking to pay workers on coffee plantations a subsistent wage but rather by donating to an aid organization. In other words, the company need not concern itself with the economic conditions of its global business operations as long as it donates money to a charity. At the same time, it allows the company to present an image to its consumers as a politically committed enterprise. Consumers are thus encouraged to indulge in connoisseur fantasies while remaining exempt from any guilt.

To summarize, the narratives presented by the Starbucks Coffee Company include spoken and written texts as well as logos and other visual images. They surround its products with claims that equate consumption with connoisseurship by borrowing from scientific and sensual discourses. At the same time, these narratives distort a consumer's view of the acts of production—both by exaggerating the role of *barista* as a performative spectacle and erasing the conditions of non-US laborers who grow and harvest coffee. These narratives not only justify inflated prices for their products, they also invite consumers to view the experience of buying coffee through the myopic lenses they provide.

This case study is an effort to explore how corporations create discourses of consumption and, in doing so, examines just one aspect of economic citizenship. Other questions warrant consideration: What real human needs are not being met that, in their place, corporations promise to fulfill them in the form of a commodity? What are consumers saying about what they buy and what it means? What are the stories of producers? What do they say about their work?

77

Not to explore these other questions is a mistake, according to Adorno, who sternly reminds would-be cultural critics that examining consumer needs is a worthless enterprise if in doing so one loses sight of the overall system that fosters consumption: "Whenever cultural criticism complains of 'materialism,' it furthers the belief that the sin lies in man's [sic] desire for consumer goods, and not in the organization of the whole which withholds these goods from man: for the cultural critic, the sin is satiety not hunger" (24–25). In other words, the problem is not a desire for a good cup of coffee, but in the way that desire is written into scripts in a global capitalist system that encourages consumer scotosis. Scotosis is rhetorical, in that the narratives create a persuasive worldview within which it is easy and comforting to remain.

Rhetorical analysis, therefore, as an aspect of economic citizenship, can explore how corporate scripts encourage the beliefs that all human needs can be satisfied within the commodity form and that the unpleasant realities of the commodity system are either nonexistent or inconsequential. To combat this scotosis, it is necessary to go outside the frames, take off the blinders, and consider ways of desiring differently. As John Tomlinson writes, "people have other desires: for health, security, freedom from anxiety, and for autonomy (particularly in the way they spend their time). It is by no means clear that capitalist culture delivers these 'goods' with the same efficiency it delivers consumer goods" (131).

Focusing on discourses of consumption and production, rhetoricians can begin to explore the realm of economic citizenship—how we act and interact in a world of producers and consumers. By resisting conditions of scotosis, we can analyze, teach, and speak out (as Schiappa advises) about the ways discourses of consumption and production are justifying changes in our world. We can also boycott, strike, and protest. Voices in journals, newspapers, and in classrooms can seek to envision more humane practices for the global marketplace in which we live. Like the needs explored here, meaningful alternatives cannot be desired by people until they are articulated.

Notes

1   My deepest thanks to James Sosnoski, Jamie Owen Daniel, C. Mark Hurlbert, Eve Wiederhold, Jeff Purdue, and Charles E. Lee for their careful feedback on earlier drafts. Thanks also to *RR* reviewers Stuart C. Brown and Gregory Clark for their insightful and useful responses.

2 For arguments on globalization, see among others, Saskia Sassen's *Losing Control: Sovereignty in an Age of Globalization*, William Greider's *One World, Ready or Not: The Manic Logic of Global Capitalism*, Richard Longworth's *Global Squeeze: The Coming Crisis for First World Nations*, and Jerry Mander and Edward Goldsmith's edited collection *The Case Against the Global Economy, and For a Turn Toward the Local*.

3 For a discussion of this issue, see "GATT, NAFTA, and the Subversion of the Democratic Process" by Ralph Nader and Lori Wallach (in Mander and Goldsmith).

4 See Paul Wachtel's *The Poverty of Affluence* for a critique of the psychological dependence on the value of growth.

5 For other recent treatment of the public responsibilities of rhetoricians, see for example, Peter Mortenson and Elizabeth Ervin.

6 *Scotosis* was introduced to me by James Sosnoski, who references this term in *Token Professionals and Master Critics: A Critique of Orthodoxy in Literary Studies* (237). He uses it to describe the tendency (among orthodox critics and others) not to let oneself know what one doesn't know (179). Bernard Lonergan named this act *scotosis* in *Insight: A Study of Human Understanding*. Insight, according to Lonergan, is the "apprehension of relations," while oversight is an effort to engage in a "flight from understanding" (xi–xiii). Scotosis is an example of a flight from understanding, a rationalized act of ruling out certain information or viewpoints from one's consideration. According to Lonergan, there is a willfulness to one's acts of scotosis—we allow certain blindspots to exist—yet the actual process of ruling out information is an unconscious and largely emotional response (191–92).

7 Scotosis, as an integral part of accepting a subject position, is necessary to act in the world, thus certain blindspots are inevitable in all individuals. It's unavoidable that "American consumer" is a partially blind position; the problem arises when alternative visions do not carry equal sway (like that of a Brazilian coffee grower) and when the position of consumer is one that can be occupied all the time.

   This description is informed by Althusser's discussion of the process of interpellation into ideology. According to Althusser, as one is hailed, "Hey you," one begins to engage in behaviors that maintain one's place as an ideological subject. I also inform my understanding of scotosis with Gramsci's view of hegemony (12): it has a rhetorical component, in that subjects are persuaded of benefits to self by engaging in certain choices or behaviors. (Richard Ohmann argues similarly when investigating how advertising works in *Selling Culture*.)

8   This article is part of a larger work in which I analyze justifying narratives related to economic culture and consider how rhetoric and composition can offer useful analytic and pedagogical responses to economic globalization. I see this essay as a continuation of the long tradition of rhetorical analysis of consumer culture, both within and outside the discipline of rhetoric. I owe much to the history of cultural studies, beginning alternately with Antonio Gramsci's discussions of the importance of everyday life and the Frankfort School's attention to the culture industry, especially Adorno and Marcuse. These traditions were elaborated by the Birmingham's Centre for Contemporary Cultural Studies. The tradition of cultural studies continues to influence American academics in English departments, especially in areas of composition studies. James Berlin's composition pedagogy at Purdue largely emphasized analyses of cultural binaries and asked students to understand how language constructed them as subjects. Patricia Harkin refined this tradition after Berlin's death (see Mathieu et al.). In the discipline of rhetoric, Kenneth Burke paid close attention to rhetorical analyses of current political issues (e.g., his analysis of Hitler's *Battle*) as well as the way corporate culture created its own "good conscience" (he explores this in *Attitudes Toward History*).

9   By relying on the discourse of medicine and science, Starbucks echoes the historical tradition of coffee. When introduced to sixteenth-century Europe, coffee was hailed for its medicinal value as a virtual panacea (Schivelbusch 19). In the seventeenth century when it replaced beer as the European morning drink of choice, it was lauded for its ability to make workers more alert and efficient. Historian Wolfgang Schivelbusch calls coffee an "ideologically freighted drink" that helped society make the transition into the modern industrial age (38): "[C]offee functioned as a historically significant drug. It spread through the body and achieved chemically and pharmacologically what rationalism and the Protestant ethic sought to fulfill spiritually and ideologically . . . . The result was a body which functioned in accord

with the new demands—a rationalistic, middle-class, forward-looking body" (39).

10 In *Keywords*, Raymond Williams distinguishes between the original definition of "imperialism" as a form of government and its evolution to refer to an economic practice. The discourse of Starbucks relies on nostalgic references to periods of colonial exploration (through graphics and language choice). At the same time, Starbucks seeks to appropriate the riches of raw materials from the supplier countries and to present such appropriations as a right of Western consumers. Williams refers to this economic form of imperialism as "neo-imperialism" and "neo-colonialism" (132).

Works Cited

Achenbach, Joel. Commentary. *Morning Edition*. Natl. Public Radio. WBEZ, Chicago. 11 Feb. 1999.

Adorno, Theodor. *Prisms*. 1967. Trans. Samuel and Shierry Weber. Cambridge: MIT, 1981.

Althusser, Louis. *Lenin and Philosophy*. London: New Left, 1971.

Aristotle. *On Rhetoric: A Theory of Civic Discourse*. Trans. George Kennedy. New York: Oxford UP, 1991.

Berlin, James. *Rhetorics, Poetics, Cultures: Refiguring College English Studies*. Urbana, IL: NCTE, 1996.

Bourdieu, Pierre. *Distinction: A Social Critique of the Judgement of Taste*. Trans. Richard Nice. Cambridge: Harvard UP, 1984.

Burke, Kenneth. *Attitudes Toward History*. Los Altos, CA: Hermes, 1959.

———. *On Symbols and Society*. Chicago: U of Chicago P, 1989.

Bragg, Billy. "North Sea Bubble." *Don't Try This at Home* Electra Records, Los Angeles. 1982.

Brown, Robert L., and Carl Herndl. "Beyond the Realm of Reasoning: Understanding the Extreme Environmental Rhetoric of the John Birch Society." *Green Culture: Environmental Rhetoric in Contemporary America*. Ed. Carl Herndl and Stuart C. Brown. Madison: U of Wisconsin P, 1996. 213–35.

Deshpande, Shekhar, and Andy Kurtz. "Trade Tales." *Mediations* 18:1 (1994): 33–52.

Enloe, Cynthia. *Bananas, Beaches and Bases*: *Making Feminist Sense of International Politics*. Berkeley: U of California P, 1990.

Ervin, Elizabeth. "Encouraging Civic Participation Among First-Year Writing Students, or Why Composition Class Should be More Like a Bowling Team." *Rhetoric Review* 15 (Spring 1997): 382–99.

Faigley, Lester. *Fragments of Rationality: Postmodernity and the Subject of Composition*. Pittsburgh: U of Pittsburgh P, 1992.

Gower, Timothy. "Starbucks Nation: A Caffeinated Juggernaut Gives Competitors the Jitters." *Seattle Weekly*. 10 Aug. 1994: 22.

Gramsci, Antonio. *Selections from the Prison Notebooks*. 1971. New York: International, 1997.

Greider, William. *One World, Ready or Not: The Manic Logic of Global Capitalism*. New York: Simon, 1997.

Horkheimer, Max, and Theodor Adorno. *Dialectic of Enlightenment*. 1944. Trans. John Cumming. New York: Continuum, 1991.

Jameson, Fredric. *The Political Unconscious*: *Narrative as a Socially Symbolic Act*. Ithaca, NY: Cornell UP, 1982.

Lofton, Kimberly. Personal Interview. 27 July 1994.

Lonergan, Bernard. *Insight: A Study of Human Understanding*. 1957. London: Darton, 1983.

Longworth, Richard C. *Global Squeeze*: *The Coming Crisis to First-World Nations*. Chicago: Contemporary, 1998.

Marback, Richard. "Detroit and the Closed Fist: Toward a Theory of Material Rhetoric." *Rhetoric Review* 17 (Fall 1998): 74–92.

Marcuse, Herbert. *One-Dimensional Man: Studies in the Ideology of Advanced Industrial Society*. 1964. Boston: Beacon, 1991.

Mathieu, Paula, James J. Sosnoski, and David Zauhar. "Cultural Studies." *Theorizing Composition*. Ed. Mary Lynch Kennedy. Westport, CT: Greenwood, 1998. 62–72.

Mortenson, Peter. "Going Public." *College Composition and Communication* 50 (Dec. 1998): 182–205.

Nader, Ralph, and Lori Wallach. "GATT, NAFTA and the Subversion of the Democratic Process." *The Case Against the Global Economy*: *And For a Turn Toward the Local*. Ed. Jerry Mander and Edward Goldsmith. San Francisco: Sierra Club, 1996.

Ohmann, Richard. *Selling Culture: Magazines, Markets, and Class at the Turn of the Century.* London: Verso. 1996.

Saadawi, Nawal El. Lecture. University of Illinois at Chicago. Chicago. 25 Mar. 1998.

Sassen, Saskia. *Losing Control? Sovereignty in an Age of Globalization.* New York, Columbia UP, 1996.

Schiappa, Edward. "Intellectuals and the Place of Cultural Critique." *Rhetoric, Cultural Studies, and Literacy: Selected Papers from the 1994 Conference of the Rhetoric Society of America.* Ed. John Frederick Reynolds. Hillside, NJ: Erlbaum, 1995. 21–28.

Schivelbusch, Wolfgang. *Tastes of Paradise: A Social History of Spices, Stimulants, and Intoxicants.* 1980. Trans. David Jacobson. New York: Vintage, 1992.

Smith, Paul. "Visiting the Banana Republic." *Universal Abandon?* Ed. Andrew Ross. Minneapolis: U of Minnesota P. 1988. 112–36.

Sosnoski, James J. *Token Professional and Master Critics: A Critique of Orthodoxy in Literary Studies.* New York: SUNY. 1994.

Starbucks Coffee Company. *The Company.* 1 Apr. 1999. http://www.starbucks.com/company.

———.*Espresso: What You Need to Know.* n.p.

———. *The Good Story of Coffee from the Pacific Northwest*, n.p.

———. *The World of Coffee*, n.p.

———.*CARE.* n.p.

———. 1993 *Report to Shareholders*, n.p.

Stolcke, Verena. *Coffee Planters, Workers and Wives.* New York: St. Martin's, 1988.

Tomlinson, John. *Cultural Imperialism.* Baltimore: John Hopkins UP, 1991.

Van Matre, Lynn. "The Espresso Express: How Starbucks Turns Trainees Who Don't Know Beans about Coffee into Full-Fledged Baristas." *Chicago Tribune.* 24 January 1994. D: 1–3.

Wachtel, Paul. *The Poverty of Affluence: A Psychological Portrait of an American Way of Life.* New York: Free, 1983.

Williams, Raymond. *Keywords: A Vocabulary of Culture and Society.* London: Croon Helm, 1976.

Willis, Susan. *A Primer for Everyday Life.* London: Routledge, 1991.

Paula Mathieu is a doctoral candidate in Language, Literacy, and Rhetoric at the University of Illinois at Chicago. Her work has appeared in Works and Days, *and she is a member of the editorial collective for that journal. Additionally, she runs a computer learning center and writers group in Chicago for homeless men and women.*

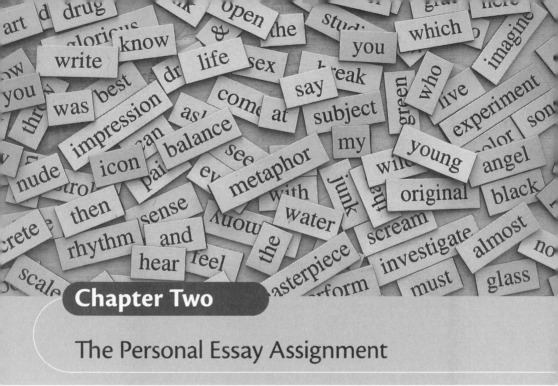

Chapter Two

The Personal Essay Assignment

Assignment Overview

Personal Essay

One feature of academic inquiry is the way scholars view a subject through different lenses. For example, using their discipline's methods and concepts, anthropologists and psychologists both study adolescence, but from different perspectives. One may study a culture's adulthood rites while the other may focus on emotional development. Essays can also be a mode of inquiry. The personal essay in particular combines first person experience with interpretation and reflection. The writer can narrate, portray and describe, as well as offer insights and reflections that shape how a reader understands the subject.

Content and Audience

Write a personal essay that explores and explains some aspect of the transition to adulthood that young people make in the twenty-first century. The essay should document and interpret your experience as it represents or clashes with previous eras, your culture, or your community. In the other essays you will write for this course, you will use research to collect data that supports your arguments. For the personal essay, your experience is the source of your data and the basis for your claim.

While crafting your essay, you may want to explore the following questions:

- What rites of passage marked your transition from childhood to adulthood; what causes and conditions gave rise to those transitions; what are their roots and how did they work?

- How did you express change during this time through your loyalties, actions and self-image? What did these choices represent? What are the roots of their significance?

- How were your values, tastes, principles and beliefs transformed? Why are these particular transformations significant to the transition you are exploring here?

- What roles did popular culture, historical events, education, neighborhood or family play in your emergence as an adult and how did they influence that transition?

- How does the transition alter a person's place in the world?

You might consider these questions through these lenses:

- Ethics and values
- Religion and spirituality
- Cultural inheritance and choice
- Identities and identifications
- Loyalties and loves
- Education and schooling
- Passages and adulthood rites
- Sex and gender roles
- Media and popular culture

We do ask you to avoid one particular topic, college admission and/or arrival at college. If you choose to write on romantic relationships, please check in with your instructor as you begin.

Your audience is the Binghamton University first-year community: students and faculty with diverse backgrounds, beliefs, and interests. How you develop your essay must take this audience into account.

Organization and Format

One challenge of the personal essay is how to best structure it to make your point clear. Our readings illustrate several ways to arrange a personal essay. Through the process of critical reading, composing and revision, along with the process of consultation with your teacher and your classmates, you'll work to discover an organization that suits what you are trying to show and explain to your audience.

Your final draft should be no fewer than four full pages and no more than five, and must be formatted according to MLA style.

● INVENTION: Identifying Problems and Questions

In this first activity, you'll practice a crucial first step of almost every writing project, especially new ones: identifying problems you'll have to solve and questions or concerns you want answered, either immediately or along the way.

Some questions and concerns can be addressed right away. Others may only be addressed through the process of working on your essays, as examples emerge and you gain experience with the topic. You'll return to your questions as your essay develops. The importance of some may fade with time. This is true of your first ideas as well. Some that look good today may not look so good tomorrow; some that seem like nonstarters today can suddenly make fabulous sense in a week or two.

Instructions

1. Break into groups.

2. Review the assignment sheet and consider the following issues. Be as detailed as you can be in your questions and responses.

    •   What questions do you have about what you are being asked to do?

    •   Have you written or read anything like this kind of essay before, either for school, in workshops outside school, or for yourself? Have you written anything that might be similar to this kind of essay?

    •   If you have written or read anything similar to this kind of essay, what were the features of the essay that were important, what were the goals of that essay, and what did you do? Who did you do it for? What was the purpose of writing it and what did a successful product look like?

- With only the knowledge that you have now, collaborate and come up with ten possible ideas or angles on the assignment. Ten may seem like a lot, but if you hang in there past the first things that come to mind to the things that maybe could fit and maybe not, good ideas, even unexpected ones, can emerge. But you have to be there to discover them.

3. Reconvene as a class and combine your material.

Notes

When you meet, don't rely on a "scribe" to write everything down for everyone. Each person needs to take notes on what his or her colleagues in the group say. This extends to when other groups report back to the class. Listening to how people talk about the topic and the question at hand will help you find and refine an idea. The more closely you engage with your colleagues, the more likely you are to find just the right thing to write about.

INVENTION: Using Research to Come Up with Ideas

Since your personal essays ask you to reflect on your experience in the context of how adulthood, maturity, or some other experience of adolescence is defined in our culture today, you might stir up some ideas if you read about how your generation is studied, reported on and discussed. You can pose some important questions to get writing started: *What can I add to this? Is there a voice or experience missing? Can I confirm or elaborate upon something already talked about? What are my immediate thoughts or feelings when I read this?*

Your teacher will assign three to five articles for you to read. Complete the following tasks related to these readings to prepare for class.

1. Based on what you read, compose a portrait of the generation born between 1981 and 2000 as it appears here. What are its characteristics and features? What are the historical and cultural circumstances that seem to shape it?

2. Do you see yourself in this portrait or see others in it? What's missing from it? What would you want to add? Write a portrait of your generation as you see it, using your own experience and what you observe in your friends, classmates, neighborhoods and high schools as evidence.

● INVENTION: **Writing Prompts**

Since your experience forms the basis for this paper, you need to investigate your experience. Use the following "invitations" to write as a means to explore the assignment topic. For this to work, you'll want to suspend the need to produce perfect prose or to judge every thought before it hits the page. You should think expansively but also observe closely. Your overall purpose is to consider the topic from many angles.

Try at least four prompts, typed or in longhand. Set your own time limits to work. If getting started writing is a struggle for you, you might simply make a deal with yourself to work on a prompt for fifteen minutes. If you find you're stuck during those fifteen minutes, choose another prompt. When the time is up, take a break, and return later for another fifteen minutes. Continue with the previous prompt or choose another. Do four sets of fifteen minutes one after the other or spread them out over days. But try at least four, and do your best to use writing to "think through" your ideas.

1. The musician Brian Eno and his collaborator Peter Schmidt developed a creativity exercise to help in the recording studio. They turned them into a deck of cards called Oblique Strategies. The decks are expensive, but a free version exists online at http://stoney.sb.org/eno/oblique.html. It's sort of a game. When you are stuck, you use it to suggest another direction. The directions are generated at random. Think about the assignment topic. Go to the link and "choose" a strategy and follow the directions. Even if they sound strange, find a way to follow it. That's part of the point—when we're stuck we sometimes need to change direction suddenly or incorporate something new. Choose one if you're not stuck and follow the instructions. So that you can see the value of the strategy you choose, record it at the top of the writing you do.

2. The following two archives explore "coming of age" at different times. The *Time* magazine link has a section "In the archives" which is organized by decade. The second link is a set of photographs. Compare your experience today to what you discover in the archives. http://www.time.com/time/sponsoredarchive/landing/0,31909,2023426,00.html http://www.jamelshabazz.com/js_bitd.html

3. Set a timer for fifteen minutes. Start at the top of a page and write your autobiography. You must begin with your birth and arrive at the present at the bottom of the page. When you're finished, look at number nine (don't look now) and complete the exercise.

4. Create a timeline of your life. On that timeline put all the significant events of your life. No one will look at this but you. Be as exhaustive as you want to be. Write an annotation of each event. An annotation is a brief description of a thing or event that explains what it is and why it is important.

5. Return to your timeline. Add historical events, along with events in your community or country that were important and may have had an impact on your life.

6. Choose one or more of the questions on the assignment sheet. Assume the identity of someone you know and write an answer as if you were that person. Do it again. Then, in your own voice, speculate on how you'd answer one of the topics.

7. Three things: Choose three things that you'd want to pass on to others that show something about what you love, think is fun, honors or amazes you. Describe those things for a stranger. They can be movies, books, places, times, foods, restaurants, events—whatever moves you. Choose three and describe.

8. Create a list of rules and advice you'd pass on to a younger self (as if you could get a younger self to pay attention) about the years between fourteen and eighteen.

9. When you've completed your page-long autobiography, read it over. List what surprises you that you left out and included. Write on one of those things.

10. Draw a circle that fills one sheet of paper, lined or unlined. Fill it with symbols that represent your values, relationships, passions, interests and commitments. Simple drawings and words can stand in for things. Then, compose a document which explains it to a stranger. Repeat the exercise for yourself five years ago.

11. Someone once described dreams by comparing the dreamer to a traveler who returns to his childhood home after years away and finds he can't understand the language. The place is both strange and familiar. Mind you, the comparison was made in a time of wooden ships and overland travel by beast. Leaving might mean for good, or for a very long time with no contact in between. Imagine you are that traveler returned to the place you were a child. Send a letter home.

12. The assignment asks you to consider coming of age. Observe "coming of age" by making an inventory of your possessions or your room. Choose a drawer, your wallet, your bag, your iPod, or the bookmarks or history on your browser. Take a moment to consider what you believe this inventory says about you.

13. Create a list of coming of age artifacts for exhibit composed of songs from your collection, YouTube links, articles, literature, photographs and articles of clothing that you consider representative of "coming of age" right now. Write up an explanation of them in the voice of an academic treating them as artifacts, then switch and write from the perspective of the creator of the list.

14. Create an imaginary panel of five experts on the topic "Coming of Age in the Twenty-First Century." It can include people you know, experts, teachers, celebrities. You can get anyone you want. Write a letter that explains to them what the panel will explore and why they were invited.

● INVENTION: **Defining a Conversation and Your Place in It**

Overview: Each of these activities are methods for searching out what might become an idea for an essay, or a starting point for thinking through an idea. The goal of this activity is to define some of the concepts, issues, and ideas that will be important to your reflection on "Coming of Age in the Twenty-First Century."

Instructions

Part I: Generate Ideas and Associations

As a class, generate a list of ideas, events, things, or aspects of adolescence, coming of age, or adulthood in the twenty-first century. This list will be a starting point for ideas you might choose to reflect upon in your essay. Try grouping some of what you generate and giving names to those groups. Try choosing a single idea, event, thing or aspect and generate more ideas and associations from it.

Part II: Make Assertions and Create Definitions

Sometimes, if you put two ideas or things next to one another, you don't only learn what makes them different from each other; you learn what makes them distinct, unique, in and of themselves. Make several sentences for each of these oppositions that express something about them. You can generate your own oppositions based on part I. The only rule is the following: each sentence must contain both words.

Childhood/Adulthood	Adulthood/Adolescence
Maturity/Adolescence	Coming of age/Childhood
Adulthood/Coming of age	Coming of age/Parents
Adolescence/Technology	Boyhood/Manhood
Girlhood/Womanhood	

Part III: Investigating Ideas

Answer these questions using any concept that might be useful to explore for this essay, such as adolescence, manhood, womanhood, the idea of adulthood, maturity, culture, generation, or coming of age. Ask yourself three questions. You can make three columns or three separate lists.

Since your essay is particularly interested in the unique aspects or impact of coming of age, or ways that adolescence changes you, or makes change possible, the third question might be particularly important. You can even begin by asking these questions of yourself—the "X" below can be "I."

> If X is a thing made up of parts, what would those parts be?
>
> If X is part of something larger, what would those things be?
>
> If X changes over time, how does it change?

Try to be concrete and specific when you can. Be attentive to differences in culture, class, gender, and place, for example. Ask yourself if X is the same for everyone and, if not, how is it different.

Once you've compiled lists on one or more concepts, look at how you fit into it simply by putting "my" in front of the concept. Or look at how the people you come from fit into it by putting a different word in front of it.

For example,

> If my adolescence is a thing made up of parts, what would they be?
>
> If my adolescence is a part of something larger, what would those larger categories be?
>
> If my adolescence has changed over time, how has it changed?

or

> If a suburban adolescence is a thing made up of parts, what would those parts be?
>
> If a suburban adolescence is part of something larger, what would those larger categories be?
>
> If a suburban adolescence changes over time, how does it change?

Part IV: Summarize Thoughts and Questions

Review the notes you've taken and the ideas you've investigated. Write some exploratory paragraphs that define the direction of your thinking or speculate on approaches you might take to the assignment. Try simply coming with answers to the question, "What might I write about?" Attempt to define some of the key concepts that are a part of this essay assignment. You can identify one from the work you've just done, or you can try some of the key ideas from the assignment sheet, such as coming of age, adolescence, and so on. You might try writing a paragraph that explores a concept, such as "adolescence and culture," "adolescence and sexuality," or "adolescence and values."

INVENTION: **Constructing a Playlist, Activity One**

Throughout this term, when you think about what you are writing, you'll also think about your audience (who you are writing for) and the purpose of your writing (what you would like an audience to think about or do). Imagining an audience for your personal essay can help you decide what you need to write about, what your audience needs to know, and what you would like the audience to reflect on or understand. Sharing your ideas with a group of people can also help you figure out where your idea fits, or inspire you to weigh in on an aspect of the topic you might not have considered.

Rather than think about your "Coming of Age" essay as "only" for the teacher, try this "thought experiment." Imagine that you and your class have been invited to write for an online journal called *Playlist*. The concept of this journal is that each issue is like a playlist on iTunes in that it revolves around one major theme. Each essay is like a track that explores or elaborates upon the theme. This Playlist's theme is "Coming of Age" in the Twenty-First Century.

Your assignment sheet describes the kinds of topics this *Playlist* wants. It also describes an audience made up of first-year writing students and faculty. Your goal for this exercise is to come up with the contents of the *Playlist*. Each student in class will offer an idea.

Your classmates comprise part of the audience for your *Playlist*. Your goal now is to learn what interests them and what they think about the experience of "Coming of Age in the Twenty-First Century." A simple thing to do is to ask people questions and learn what they think.

Instructions

1. Divide into groups.

2. As a group, choose two questions from the following list.

3. Write those questions on a piece of paper so you can take notes on the answers you get.

4. Your teacher will decide on a time limit. When your teacher tells you to begin, circulate around the class and interview at least two people. Take notes on their answers.

5. Reconvene as a group and compare notes on your inquiry.

6. Report your findings to your classmates. Take notes on what you learn from them.

Questions for the Interview *(Choose two your group wants to learn about):*

- How do you think the way you view your generation differs from the way your generation is viewed by others? That can include family, the new media, film and so on.

- How would you define "coming of age," "childhood," or "adulthood" (choose one)?

- Are there specific rites of passage, official or unofficial, that mark transitions in young people's lives today? What are they and why are they important?

- How does your culture, community, or society define and view the period of time between childhood and adulthood? What do they believe should go on during that time?

- What should mark the end of it? How do you view that same period of time?

- What particular challenges face your generation? What challenges faced previous generations? What challenges will face your generation's children?

Put All Your Responses to the Following in Writing

If you haven't yet, answer the questions you asked your classmates. Put your answers in writing.

Summarize what you've learned from your group members and offer any explanations for the answers you received, such as why certain answers might be common or why some answers were different.

Answer this question: *As a reader, what would I want to learn from or read in a magazine devoted to the topic of "Coming of Age in the Twenty-First Century?"* Remember that the assignment sheet tells you that, along with faculty, you are a part of the intended audience for the essay. Think about what you want to read and what you think other people should learn more about, even if those things aren't part of your direct experience. Think about gaps, blind spots, controversies, common or unique experiences.

Propose three ideas for essays that you might write. Try to think of a title, or a question you want to answer, or name a topic. Write a brief description of what the essay could include and what you want the audience to understand. These ideas don't have to be "good" ideas. They just need to be ideas. To write something that matters to you, you need to risk not knowing exactly where you'll end up. And if you have more than one choice, it's likely you'll make a stronger decision by practicing some ideas than if you commit to one idea without exploring any others.

● INVENTION: **Constructing a Playlist, Activity Two**

Continue this "experiment" by imagining that you need a draft of the contents for this issue of *Playlist*. Each member of the class contributes a title for his or her "coming of age" essay. Writers often create "working" titles for pieces still under construction.

1. In a group, share the ideas you generated for "Constructing a *Playlist*, Activity One." Then, offer your essay ideas to the class, including a title and a brief summary of the proposed essay and how it fits. On the board, your teacher will, title by title, put the issue of *Playlist* together. As the class adds something to the Playlist, write that title down. At the end of class, you should have a preliminary idea of what your Playlist will look like.

2. Once you have a preliminary list, review it. Ask, "What's missing?' and "What would I like to hear more about?" and "What do we have a lot of?"

3. Provide each entry on the Playlist with a tag. Online content, such as articles, are tagged to make searching easy. The tag puts content in a group of like things. An essay called "Not Every Man is a Soldier," about how someone developed his own idea of what it was to become a man might be tagged as follows: *masculinity, boyhood versus manhood, gender roles, adulthood* and *childhood*. By typing the key word masculinity into the search bar on a site, all essays with that tag come up. This way, if you wanted to see all the essays published that concerned the theme of masculinity you could type "masculinity" or click the tag at the end of an article or essay. Tag the titles in the Playlist.

● REVISION: **Reading as a Writer**

In the exercise *Identifying Problems and Questions* you wondered what your essay should sound like, how it should be structured, and how to write an essay that uses your own experience to talk about ideas that are significant to an audience, like the way that breaking away from parental values is an important part of coming of age, or how adolescence gives you a chance to choose a course of action based on your own values and how your response to those choices contributes to the kind of adult you might become.

To help you understand the kinds of choices you can make as writer of a personal essay, you'll have a chance to read personal essays that have been published. You've already read "Reflection," which has given you an idea of how to approach writing this essay. Keep the ideas you encountered in "Reflection" in mind, especially those about choosing a theme or topic and organizing your essay, as you answer the following questions. Use these questions for each of the essays you read so that you can compare the ways that different authors use the genre to explore their topics.

Instructions

1. You can choose one or two elements to follow closely or note your impressions of several of them. Follow your teacher's directions in this regard, but do keep one thing in mind: Be ready to point to something in the text that shows how you have identified the following ideas going on in the essay. Consider the following:

- How the piece is structured and how the parts connect
- How scene, narrative, dialogue, description, portrait and other craft elements are used
- How the beginning and end differ
- When the writer reveals how she interprets or judges events
- How the writer relates to the reader
- How you would characterize the writer's voice
- How the writer's mind, her way of thinking and seeing unfolds
- How characters besides the author appear and are used

2. These personal essays use many of the elements of a novel or a short story, and yet the authors introduce ideas about politics, anthropology, culture, and literature. They talk about their own feelings, thoughts and perceptions, but they also talk about how they are influenced by history, politics, tradition, and cultural events. How does the writer blend personal experience and thoughts about his or her place in larger events or his or her relationship to broader ideas? If the essay fits into larger questions, how would you describe them?

3. What would the writers of these essays have to do if they wanted to write an academic essay on the same topic or an opinion piece written for a newspaper?

● REVISION: "Zero Draft" Workshop

In an upcoming class, your "peer review draft" will be due. It'll have the proper heading, page numbers, an appropriate title, and have the "feel" of the essay coming together but it won't be "polished." You'll save time to make changes before you submit it. A "zero draft" is even more tentative than a peer review draft. It may be a collection of notes, lists, outlines, and sketches assembled in a folder, or a very rough draft that falls short of the page requirement or exceeds it. A zero draft helps you make some decisions that clarify your purpose so you can create a peer review draft that gets you the answers you need. Do the following exercise for class. Be prepared to share the results.

The editor-in-chief of *Playlist* has asked you to write a letter that updates him on the progress of the essay.

This letter should be 350 to 500 words long.

The letter should be broken up into the following parts:

- In the first part, tell the editor the essay's working title, where you think it fits into the issue, and what you think will be interesting about it to the audience for the issue.

- In the second part, offer the editor a picture of what you are working on. Describe how you think the essay will begin, what it will contain, what ideas you want to explore or express, and how you think it might end.

- The third part should share any concerns about how the piece is working.

- Finally, attach three pages of your essay. They can be any three pages. If any part needs a context, supply it. (For example, "This part of the essay shows how music defines sexuality" or "Here is the opening, along with the middle two pages of the essay").

Instructions

- Convene in a group.

- Each member should read her letter to the group.

- When the writer has read the letter, each member of the group should take a moment and jot down some thoughts in response to it. Consider the following: How do you think it fits within the assignment? Are you trying some of the same things? How would you handle the questions and concerns the writer has? What do you think stands out about this description of the piece? What would you expect to see or hope to see?

- When everyone has had a chance to share thoughts, move on to the next writer and repeat the process.

REVISION: General Guidelines for Peer Review

Although a peer review draft is not read by your teacher and your draft may still be rough and have an unfinished feel, put the draft you submit in the format required by the syllabus and teacher, including giving the essay a title, double-spacing your work, and using Times New Roman 12 font.

For each group session, choose a facilitator to keep conversation on track. Choose a timekeeper to alert the group to time left. Choose new people for these roles each new session.

Review the instructions for a day's work at the beginning of a session so you can ask for clarification.

Avoid getting bogged down on one student's essay by going back and forth over one issue or perceived problem.

Writers can stay silent when their essay receives feedback. You needn't defend or explain. Take observations in, note them, and note how you feel or what you think when you hear them.

Writers should answer the day's assigned questions, too. This may be the first time you've heard your essay aloud.

Don't try to "solve problems" or "fix" someone's essay. There will be time for editing help later.

Don't spend time correcting grammar or punctuation. There will be time for proofreading later.

Try not to approach listening to someone's essay in terms of what you would do with the same topic. Try to listen in terms of what the writer is trying to accomplish. Focus on what you would like more of and what you see the writer doing, rather than your own tastes or preferences.

When you reply to a writer, make one goal for a response to be able to point to a specific place in an essay that does what you say it does. Specific details help writers see what they do well and where they need to change.

Often, people think peer review is most important for hearing what people have to say about their work. In fact, peer review is as important for the opportunity it gives you to hear how other writers approach a similar task. Learn from how others approach the assignment and use what you learn to plan your revision.

Although it's encouraging to tell writers how much you relate to or like what they've written, remember that you must also listen to help writers see what works and what might not work for readers who don't have the advantage of a similar experience. That's why it's not enough to say you really like something; try to describe why it works so well.

REVISION: "Listening for" Exercise

For peer review to work, it helps to have a sense of what to listen *for*. Consider your peer review group a "writers' group," a group of colleagues who help each other produce essays that can appear in the issue of *Playlist*. You might find that you like an essay, but find it doesn't quite do what the assignment asks of it. So despite your affection for the piece, you may have to say, "I didn't hear you address that part of the assignment that asks us to interpret our experience in the context of a shared experience." To help, you must be of "two minds:" listen for what the writer is trying to accomplish and listen for how the essay fits the assignment. To help this process, we can define what to "listen for," so that you can use your knowledge of the assignment and the genre of the personal essay to help you assist your colleagues.

Take time to review this list of things to "listen for:"

- How does the essay use the writer's experience and observations of the world?

- How does it respond to what the assignment asks for?

- How does it define terms the writer uses and explain their importance to the reader?

- Does the writer anticipate what the reader may or may not know and write with the reader's likely familiarity or unfamiliarity with the writer's experience in mind?

- Does it offer an appropriately detailed portrayal of the writer's experience?

- Does it portray the subject of the essay from the perspective of the individual and the perspective of the world she lives in?

- Does she explore how these perspectives clash or coincide?

- Does the essay meaningfully meet the page length requirement by elaborating and explaining the writers claims and experiences?

Now add to this list. Start in groups and, then, as a class, compile a list you can refer to for peer review. To help you come up with ideas, try considering what to listen for from the following perspectives:

- The author and what she hopes to accomplish.

- Features of the text, such as use of language and organization.

- The audience, what they know, and what they expect.

- The time and place the writer and audience lives in and impact of the cultural moment, historical moment, and institutional setting (composing the essay for a teacher to read).

REVISION: "Coming of Age" Peer Review

Keep your assignment sheet and you "things to listen for" sheet handy. Look them over. You might choose something from the "things to listen for" list to guide your listening, especially things you are thinking about for your essay.

Instructions

1. Distribute papers. Someone other than the writer reads aloud.

2. When the reader finishes, take three minutes to write up your responses using the list below to guide you. The writer should do this as well. Try to be concrete. Think of it this way: you want to be able to point to a part of the essay where what you describe does or doesn't take place.

    - What strikes you as the "hot" parts of the essay—things that stand out to you?

    - Use the "things to listen for" list as a reference and describe what you heard in terms of one or more of those "things."

    - Think of at least one thing you want more of. Compose a statement that begins "I'd like to hear more about..." or "I'd like to see more..." or "I'd more explanation or description of..."

3. Share what you've written. Move on to the next writer.

4. When your group has finished, writers should review what they've heard and said. Then, in writing, answer the following: "Based on what I have learned today about my essay and what I've seen in other people's essays, what do I think I need to do to revise?" If there is time, discuss your answers with your group. If there is more time, begin the work of revision.

REVISION: Characteristics of ABCD Writing Workshop

Your teacher uses "The Characteristics of ABCD Writing" to comment on your essay. She'll use those characteristics to describe where your essay falls on a grading spectrum. They will also help guide how she offers direction for revision so that you and she share a common language when working on your essay. You and your teacher will continue this all semester for each assignment. Your teacher also carries on a similar dialogue with her colleagues each week in a Pedagogy Group. In these groups, teachers read and grade student essays and talk about their choices so they can come to a shared understanding of the "Characteristics," and ensure that all Writing 111 classes share a vision of competence and excellence.

The "Characteristics of ABCD Writing" are statements that identify features of essays at certain grades. Your teacher will be concrete about how your essay demonstrates various characteristics and point you towards revising your essay. You can use the "Characteristics" to identify the strengths and weaknesses of a particular essay.

The process of working with the "Characteristics" is one part of a process that mirrors what we face throughout our writing lives, whether we are in creative, professional or academic settings. We gather information about "what works" through several sources. We read and analyze examples and seek input from colleagues. We submit our work to others as well so their feedback can help us revise. We also seek out experienced practitioners to describe what is expected and what falls short. We must manage this process of learning what is right for a situation and make adjustments based on what we learn.

Instructions

1. After your teacher has reviewed the portfolio process and the characteristics, read them over again. Then, reread your peer review draft.

2. Use the "Characteristics" to describe the strengths and weaknesses of your essay. Remember, you may find characteristics under different grades. For example, you may feel that the content of your essay meets the demands of the assignment at an "A" level, but also see that the organization of your essay makes the essay difficult to follow. Make a list and be concrete.

3. Jot down any questions that come to mind or ideas you have to solve a problem you notice. You may write "Under the 'C' characteristics, it describes…" "In my essay I…" "Maybe I can…"

4. Convene with a group of students and discuss what your essay looked like when you began to see it within the context of the "Characteristics." Note if there are common concerns or questions.

5. Keep this list. When you receive your teacher's feedback on your essay, compare how you understood the characteristics with how your teacher explains them.

● REVISION: Edit and Proofread

When you edit and proofread, you turn your attention to close textual concerns, such as spelling, grammatical errors, whether sentences and transitions are as clear as they can be, or whether the text is clear of typos. Below are some "must do" suggestions and tips to help you prepare to submit your essay.

Review assignment guidelines. Be sure to review assignment guidelines so that you are aware of page length and other requirements.

Review format guidelines. Check the syllabus for type size and font. Essays in this class use MLA. There are instructions for MLA format in Easy Writer. You can also find an example of a correctly formatted paper in MLA with guidelines at the following link: http://owl.english.purdue. edu/owl/resource/747/01/

Give your essay a title. Your heading may include the assignment name, but the assignment name is different than a title. Give your essay a title appropriate to its content.

Get help with new computer functions. If you do not know how to paginate or use the headers and footers on your computer, give yourself time and ask a colleague for help.

Edit. Once you have more or less decided on the content and form of your essay, you can attend to the sound of specific sentences and transitions. Go over your essay a sentence and a paragraph at a time and ask yourself if the sentences are clear and if the relationships between paragraphs are clear. Though people are now used to doing this on the computer, it is often useful to print the essay out, make edits by hand, and then input them.

Proofread. When you proofread, you look for surface errors such as typos, misspellings, and dropped words. You also check for any grammatical errors. You can run spell and grammar check, but do your own proofreading after, since spell check can lead to embarrassing typos. Again, people are used to doing this on a computer, but it can help to print it out, make your corrections, and then input those corrections. Some people even read an essay sentence by sentence from the end to the beginning to make sure they don't get caught up in the flow of the essay and miss something.

Share the task. Arrange with someone, maybe someone from the class, to swap papers with for editing and proofreading.

Listen to the text. Download text-to-speech software and listen to your paper. Some computers come with software preloaded. The company NaturalSoft offers a free version of its software that suits editing and proofreading purposes. Simply listen to your paper read back to you, pause, and make changes as you go.

● REVISION: Reader-Response Comment Sheet

Please place the following identifying information at the top of a piece of loose-leaf paper and clearly label your responses "Step 1," Step 2," etc. If you find you're repeating yourself, you may want to reference a previous response.

For the Writer: Before distributing your paper to peers, write out the specific kind of feedback you are looking for on your draft. Use the space in the heading of your paper to do so.

For the Reader: As you read your colleague's draft, challenge yourself to offer constructive feedback and to engage in the process with integrity. Label your responses "Step #1, #2," etc.

STEP #1: Read the essay completely through (without commenting on it) once. Give feedback on the issues the writer has identified.

STEP #2: Read the essay again, asking facilitative questions. In other words, ask questions that push the writer to think further or to consider something in a new light. (Why or how might some people pose counterarguments? What does the writer still need to consider?)

STEP #3: Focus on the introductory paragraph. Does it catch your attention? If so, tell the writer specifically why it is working. If not, make a concrete suggestion that might make the introduction stronger.

STEP #4: Read for a thesis statement. If you find one, note a) what paragraph you found it in; and b) whether or not it is clear. Then, restate the thesis in your own language. If you do not find a thesis statement or it is unclear, brainstorm one that might be appropriate for the paper.

STEP #5: As you read further, list the points that the writer makes in support of the argument. Comment on whether these points are clear, logical, etc. Is the writer's voice in control of the essay, or are sources dominating it? While source integration is important, let the writer know if you do not hear his or her voice in the paper, or don't hear it enough. Also, let the writer know if sources are integrated properly: are sources clearly introduced with author credentials, title, source context/summary, in-text citations and Works Cited entries?

STEP #6: Look for places where the writer needs to consider alternate points of view or interpretations. Can you think of ways in which some readers might disagree with the writer that he or she doesn't address? How would you engage such readers? Do you think that the writer fairly represents a range of views or interpretations? List your advice here.

STEP #7: Comment on the structure and organization of the essay. Are paragraphs or sections introduced with clear topic sentences that relate back to the thesis? Are transitions effective and clear? Make specific suggestions if you have any advice on how to develop more effective organizational strategies.

STEP #8: Do you see repeated punctuation or grammar errors? List here what those are and the paragraphs where the writer might find them.

STEP #9: Reflect on the "Characteristics of ABCD Writing." What is the most important piece of advice you would give the writer considering these evaluation criteria? What do you think is strongest about the paper in its present stage in regard to these evaluation criteria? Be specific when answering both questions.

STEP #10: List here any additional evaluation criteria your instructor may ask you to consider.

● REFLECTION: **Personal Essay Cover Letter**

Guidelines: Approximately 200 Words

Please consider the following questions in the format of an informal letter to your instructor. You are not obligated to discuss all of these questions; instead, answer the three or four that will give your instructor the best insight into your work and your experience with this assignment. Instructors will use this statement to guide their feedback, so do your best to reflect on both the strengths and weaknesses of your project.

Before You Write Your Cover Letter

Prior to putting pen to paper, consider your most recent draft of the Personal Essay carefully.

Question 1: Getting Started

Explain how you went about starting the assignment. How did the invention activities shape your thinking, and which seemed the most fruitful for you as a writer? Did you jump in and plan your essay from top to bottom? Or did you start in some other way?

Question 2: Focusing

What is your purpose with the essay? If you have a traditional thesis, paraphrase it again here. If you have a less traditional focus statement, how did you develop it, and where is it in your essay?

Question 3: Revising

During peer review, what advice did you seek from your classmates? What specific concerns and praise did they offer? What revision decisions did you decide to make and implement?

Question 4: What's Working Well? What's Not?

What are you happiest with in this essay? Did you try a particular rhetorical technique that seemed to work for you? Did your classmates confirm that technique's success? What's not working at this point? Were there any techniques that you tried that didn't seem to work?

Question 5: Goals for Future Revision

When planning for your final portfolio, what priorities will you set for revision? What are your specific goals for improvement?

Question 6: Characteristics of ABCD Writing

Take a few minutes to reflect on the Characteristics of ABCD Writing. Which of the criteria do you feel most confident about? Which one are you the least confident about? Why?

Related Readings

Reflections

by Richard Bullock

Sometimes we write essays just to think about something—to speculate, ponder, probe; to play with an idea, develop a thought; or simply to share something. Reflective essays are our attempt to think something through by writing about it and to share our thinking with others. If such essays make an argument, it is about things we care or think about more than about what we believe to be "true." Have a look at one example by Jonathan Safran Foer, a novelist who lives in Brooklyn. This essay originally appeared on the Op-Ed page of the *New York Times* in 2006.

My Life as a Dog

by Jonathan Safran Foer

For the last twenty years, New York City parks without designated dog runs have permitted dogs to be off-leash from 9 p.m. to 9 a.m. Because of recent complaints from the Juniper Park Civic Association in Queens, the issue has been revisited. On December 5, the Board of Health will vote on the future of off-leash hours.

Retrievers in elevators, Pomeranians on No. 6 trains, bull mastiffs crossing the Brooklyn Bridge ... it is easy to forget just how strange it is that dogs live in New York in the first place. It is about as unlikely a place for dogs as one could imagine, and yet 1.4 million of them are among us. Why do we keep them in our apartments and houses, always at some expense and inconvenience? Is it even possible, in a city, to provide a good life for a dog, and what is a "good life"? Does the health board's vote matter in ways other than the most obvious?

I adopted George (a Great Dane/Lab/pit/greyhound/ridgeback/whatever mix—a.k.a. Brooklyn shorthair) because I thought it would be fun. As it turns out, she is a major pain an awful lot of the time.

She mounts guests, eats my son's toys (and occasionally tries to eat my son), is obsessed with squirrels, lunges at skateboarders and Hasids,[1] has the savant-like ability to find her way between the camera lens and subject of every photo taken in her vicinity, backs her tush into the least interested person in the room, digs up the freshly planted, scratches the newly bought, licks the about-to-be-served, and occasionally relieves herself on the wrong side of the front door. Her head is resting on my foot as I type this. I love her.

Our various struggles—to communicate, to recognize and accommodate each other's desires, simply to coexist—force me to interact with something, or rather someone, entirely "other." George can respond to a handful of words, but our relationship takes place almost entirely outside of language. She seems to have thoughts and emotions, desires and fears. Sometimes I think I understand them; often I don't. She is a mystery to me. And I must be one to her.

Of course our relationship is not always a struggle. My morning walk with George is very often the highlight of my day—when I have my best thoughts, when I most appreciate both nature and the city, and in a deeper sense, life itself. Our hour together is a bit of compensation for the burdens of civilization: business attire, email, money, etiquette, walls, and artificial lighting. It is even a kind of compensation for language. Why does watching a dog be a dog fill one with happiness? And why does it make one feel, in the best sense of the word, human?

It is children, very often, who want dogs. In a recent study, when asked to name the ten most important "individuals" in their lives, 7- and 10-year-olds included two pets on average. In another study, 42 percent of 5-year-olds spontaneously mentioned their pets when asked, "Whom do you turn to when you are feeling, sad, angry, happy, or wanting to share a secret?" Just about every children's book in my local bookstore has an animal for its hero. But then, only a few feet away in the cookbook section, just about every cookbook includes recipes for cooking animals. Is there a more illuminating illustration of our paradoxical relationship with the nonhuman world?

In the course of our lives, we move from a warm and benevolent relationship with animals (learning responsibility through caring for our pets, stroking and confiding in them) to a cruel one (virtually all

---

1   Hasids: a Jewish sect whose members dress distinctively. [Editor's note]

animals raised for meat in this country are factory farmed—they spend their lives in confinement, dosed with antibiotics and other drugs).

How do you explain this? Is our kindness replaced with cruelty? I don't think so. I think in part it's because the older we get, the less exposure we have to animals. And nothing facilitates indifference or forgetfulness so much as distance. In this sense, dogs and cats have been very lucky: they are the only animals we are intimately exposed to daily.

Folk parental wisdom and behavioral studies alike generally view the relationships children have with companion animals as beneficial. But one does not have to be a child to learn from a pet. It is precisely my frustrations with George, and the inconveniences she creates, that reinforce in me how much compromise is necessary to share space with other beings.

The practical arguments against off-leash hours are easily refuted. One doesn't have to be an animal scientist to know that the more a dog is able to exercise its "dogness"—to run and play, to socialize with other dogs—the happier it will be. Happy dogs, like happy people, tend not to be aggressive. In the years that dogs have been allowed to run free in city parks, dog bites have decreased 90 percent. But there is another argument that is not so easy to respond to: some people just don't want to be inconvenienced by dogs. Giving dogs space necessarily takes away space from humans.

We have been having this latter debate, in different forms, for ages. Again and again we are confronted with the reality—some might say the problem—of sharing our space with other living things, be they dogs, trees, fish, or penguins. Dogs in the park are a present example of something that is often too abstracted or far away to gain our consideration.

The very existence of parks is a response to this debate: earlier New Yorkers had the foresight to recognize that if we did not carve out places for nature in our cities, there would be no nature. It was recently estimated that Central Park's real estate would be worth more than $500 billion. Which is to say we are half a trillion dollars inconvenienced by trees and grass. But we do not think of it as an inconvenience. We think of it as balance.

Living on a planet of fixed size requires compromise, and while we are the only party capable of negotiating, we are not the only party at the table. We've never claimed more, and we've never had less. There has never been less clean air or water, fewer fish or mature trees. If we are not simply ignoring the situation, we keep hoping for (and expecting) a technological solution that will erase our destruction, while allowing us to continue to live without compromise. Maybe zoos will be an adequate replacement for wild animals in natural habitats. Maybe we will be able to recreate the Amazon somewhere else. Maybe one day we will be able to genetically engineer dogs that do not wish to run free. Maybe. But will those futures make us feel, in the best sense of the word, human?

I have been taking George to Prospect Park twice a day for more than three years, but her running is still a revelation to me. Effortlessly, joyfully, she runs quite a bit faster than the fastest human on the planet. And faster, I've come to realize, than the other dogs in the park. George might well be the fastest land animal in Brooklyn. Once or twice every morning, for no obvious reason, she'll tear into a full sprint. Other dog owners can't help but watch her. Every now and then someone will cheer her on. It is something to behold.

A vote regarding off-leash hours for dogs sparks Foer's reflection on the relationship between dogs and humans. He begins by thinking about his relationship with his own dog, then goes on to consider the paradoxical nature of our treatment of animals in general. From there, he moves into a larger discussion of the compromises we make to "share space with other beings." Finally, he brings his reflection back to the personal, describing the joy of watching his dog be herself, off-leash.

Key Features /Reflections

A topic that intrigues you. A reflective essay has a dual purpose: to ponder something you find interesting or puzzling and to share your thoughts with an audience. Your topic may be anything that interests you. You might write about someone you have never met and are curious about, an object or occurrence that makes you think, a place where you feel comfortable or safe. Your goal is to explore the meaning that the person, object, event, or place has for you in a way that will interest others. One way to do that is by making connections between your personal experience and more general ones that readers may share. Foer writes about his experience with his dog, but in so doing he raises questions and offers insights about the way everyone relates to others, human and nonhuman alike.

Some kind of structure. A reflective essay can be structured in many ways, but it needs to be structured. It may seem to wander, but all its paths and ideas should relate, one way or another. The challenge is to keep your readers' interest as you explore your topic and to leave readers satisfied that the journey was pleasurable, interesting, and profitable. Foer brings his essay full-circle, introducing the vote on the off-leash law in his opening, then considering our complex relationship with dogs, and, after suggesting some of the compromises we make to share our world with other nonhuman living things, closing with an indelible image of the joy that freedom from a leash brings.

Specific details. You'll need to provide specific details to help readers understand and connect with your subject, especially if it's an abstract or unfamiliar one. Foer offers a wealth of details about his dog: "She mounts guests, eats my son's toys (and occasionally tries to eat my son), is obsessed by squirrels, lunges at skateboarders and Hasids." Anecdotes can bring your subject to life: "Once or twice every morning, for no obvious reason, she'll tear into a full sprint. Other dog owners can't help but watch her. Every now and then someone will cheer her on." Reflections may be about causes, such as why dogs make us feel more human; comparisons, such as when Foer compares animals as pets and as food; and examples: "virtually all animals raised for meat in this country are factory farmed."

A questioning, speculative tone. In a reflective essay, you are working toward answers, not providing them neatly organized and ready for consumption. So your tone is usually tentative and open, demonstrating a willingness to entertain, accept, and reject various ideas as your essay progresses from beginning to end. Foer achieves this tone by looking at people's relationships with dogs from several different perspectives as well as by asking questions for which he provides no direct answers.

A Brief Guide to Writing Reflections

Deciding on a Topic

Choose a subject you want to explore. Write a list of things that you think about, wonder about, find puzzling or annoying. They may be big things—life, relationships—or little things—quirks of certain people's behavior, curious objects, everyday events. Try CLUSTERING one or more of those things, or begin by FREEWRITING to see what comes to mind as you write.

Considering the Rhetorical Situation

Purpose. What's your goal in writing this essay? To introduce a topic that interests you? Entertain? Provoke readers to think about something? What aspects of your subject do you want to ponder and reflect on?

Audience. Who is the audience? How familiar are they with your subject? How will you introduce it in a way that will interest them?

Stance. What is your attitude toward the topic you plan to explore? Questioning? Playful? Critical? Curious? Something else?

Media/Design. Will your essay be a print document? An oral presentation? Will it be posted on a website? Would it help to have any visuals?

Generating Ideas and Text

Explore your subject in detail. Reflections often include descriptive details. Foer, for example, DESCRIBES the many ways he encounters dogs in New York: "Retrievers in elevators, Pomeranians on No. 6 trains, bull mastiffs crossing the Brooklyn Bridge." Those details provide a base for the speculations to come. You may also make your point by DEFINING, COMPARING, even CLASSIFYING. Virtually any organizing pattern will help you explore your subject.

Back away. Ask yourself why your subject matters: why is it important or intriguing or significant? You may try LISTING or OUTLINING possibilities, or you may want to start DRAFTING to see where the writing takes your thinking. Your goal is to think on paper (or screen) about your subject, to play with its possibilities.

Think about how to keep readers with you. Reflections may seem loose or unstructured, but they must be carefully crafted so that readers can follow your train of thought. It's a good idea to sketch out a rough THESIS to help focus your thoughts. You may not include the thesis in the essay itself, but every part of the essay should in some way relate to it.

Ways of Organizing a Reflective Essay

Reflective essays may be organized in many ways because they mimic the way we think, associating one idea with another in ways that make sense but do not necessarily form a "logical" progression. In general, you might consider organizing a reflection using this overall strategy:

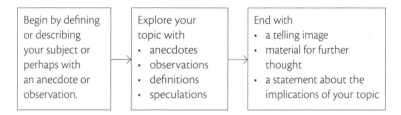

Begin by defining or describing your subject or perhaps with an anecdote or observation. → Explore your topic with
- anecdotes
- observations
- definitions
- speculations

→ End with
- a telling image
- material for further thought
- a statement about the implications of your topic

Another way to organize this type of essay is as a series of brief reflections that together create an overall impression:

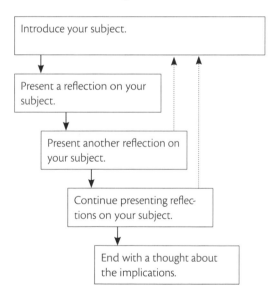

Introduce your subject.

Present a reflection on your subject.

Present another reflection on your subject.

Continue presenting reflections on your subject.

End with a thought about the implications.

Writing Autobiography

by bell hooks

To me, telling the story of my growing-up years was intimately connected with the longing to kill the self I was without really having to die. I wanted to kill that self in writing. Once that self was gone—out of my life forever—I could more easily become the me of me. It was clearly the Gloria Jean of my tormented and anguished childhood that I wanted to be rid of, the girl who was always wrong, always punished, always subjected to some humiliation or other, always crying, the girl who was to end up in a mental institution because she could not be anything but crazy, or so they told her. She was the girl who sat a hot iron on her arm pleading with them to leave her alone, the girl who wore her scar as a brand marking her madness. Even now I can hear the voices of my sisters saying, "mama make Gloria stop crying." By writing the autobiography, it was not just this Gloria I would be rid of, but the past that had a hold on me, that kept me from the present. I wanted not to forget the past but to break its hold. This death in writing was to be liberatory.

Until I began to try and write an autobiography, I thought that it would be a simple task, this telling of one's story. And yet I tried year after year, never writing more than a few pages. My inability to write out the story I interpreted as an indication that I was not ready to let go of the past, that I was not ready to be fully in the present. Psychologically, I considered the possibility that I had become attached to the wounds and sorrows of my childhood, that I held to them in a manner that blocked my efforts to be self-realized, whole, to be healed. A key message in Toni Cade Bambara's novel *The Salt Eaters*, which tells the story of Velma's suicide attempt, her breakdown, is expressed when the healer asks her, "Are you sure sweetheart, that you want to be well?"

There was very clearly something blocking my ability to tell my story. Perhaps it was remembered scoldings and punishments when mama heard me saying something to a friend or stranger that she did not think should be said. Secrecy and silence—these were central issues. Secrecy about family, about what went on in the domestic household was a bond between us—was part of what made us family. There was a dread one felt about breaking that bond. And yet I could not grow inside the atmosphere of secrecy that had pervaded our lives and the lives of other families about us. Strange that I had always challenged the secrecy, always let something slip that should not be known growing up, yet as a writer staring into the solitary space of paper, I was bound, trapped in the fear that a bond is lost or broken in the telling. I did not want to be the traitor, the teller of family secrets—and yet I wanted to be a writer. Surely, I told myself, I could write a purely imaginative work—a work that would not hint at personal private realities. And so I tried. But always there were the intruding traces, those elements of real life however disguised. Claiming the freedom to grow as an imaginative writer was connected for me with having the courage to be open, to be able to tell the truth of one's life as I had experienced it in writing. To talk about one's life—that I could do. To write about it, to leave a trace—that was frightening.

The longer it took me to begin the process of writing autobiography, the further removed from those memories I was becoming. Each year, a memory seemed less and less clear. I wanted not to lose the vividness, the recall and felt an urgent need to begin the work and complete it. Yet I could not begin even though I had begun to confront some of the reasons I was blocked, as I am blocked just now in writing this piece because I am afraid to express in writing the experience that served as a catalyst for that block to move.

I had met a young black man. We were having an affair. It is important that he was black. He was in some mysterious way a link to this past that I had been struggling to grapple with, to name in writing. With him I remembered incidents, moments of the past that I had completely suppressed. It was as though there was something about the passion of contact that was hypnotic, that enabled me to drop barriers and thus enter fully, rather reenter those past experiences. A key aspect seemed to be the way he smelled, the combined odors of cigarettes, occasionally alcohol, and his body smells. I thought often of the phrase "scent of memory," for it was those smells that carried me back. And there were specific occasions when it was very evident that the experience of being in his company was the catalyst for this remembering.

Two specific incidents come to mind. One day in the middle of the afternoon we met at his place. We were drinking cognac and dancing to music from the radio. He was smoking cigarettes (not only do I not smoke, but I usually make an effort to avoid smoke). As we held each other dancing those mingled odors of alcohol, sweat, and cigarettes led me to say, quite without thinking about it, "Uncle Pete." It was not that

I had forgotten Uncle Pete. It was more that I had forgotten the childhood experience of meeting him. He drank often, smoked cigarettes, and always on the few occasions that we met him, he held us children in tight embraces. It was the memory of those embraces—of the way I hated and longed to resist them—that I recalled.

Another day we went to a favorite park to feed ducks and parked the car in front of tall bushes. As we were sitting there, we suddenly heard the sound of an oncoming train—a sound that startled me so that it evoked another long-suppressed memory: that of crossing the train tracks in my father's car. I recalled an incident where the car stopped on the tracks and my father left us sitting there while he raised the hood of the car and worked to repair it. This is an incident that I am not certain actually happened. As a child, I had been terrified of just such an incident occurring, perhaps so terrified that it played itself out in my mind as though it had happened. These are just two ways this encounter acted as a catalyst, breaking down barriers, enabling me to finally write this long-desired autobiography of my childhood.

Each day I sat at the typewriter and different memories were written about in short vignettes. They came in a rush, as though they were a sudden thunderstorm. They came in a surreal, dreamlike style that made me cease to think of them as strictly autobiographical because it seemed that myth, dream, and reality had merged. There were many incidents that I would talk about with my siblings to see if they recalled them. Often we remembered together a general outline of an incident but the details were different for us. This fact was a constant reminder of the limitations of autobiography, of the extent to which autobiography is a very personal storytelling—a unique recounting of events not so much as they have happened but as we remember and invent them. One memory that I would have sworn was "the truth and nothing but the truth" concerned a wagon that my brother and I shared as children. I remembered that we played with this toy only at my grandfather's house, that we shared it, that I would ride it and my brother would push me. Yet one facet of the memory was puzzling—I remembered always returning home with bruises or scratches from this toy. When I called my mother, she said there had never been any wagon, that we had shared a red wheelbarrow, that it had always been at my grandfather's house because there were sidewalks on that part of town. We lived in the hills where there were no sidewalks. Again I was compelled to face the fiction that is a part of all retelling, remembering. I began to think of the work I was doing as both fiction and autobiography.

It seemed to fall in the category of writing that Audre Lorde, in her auto-biographically based work *Zami*, calls bio-mythography. As I wrote, I felt that I was not as concerned with accuracy of detail as I was with evoking in writing the state of mind, the spirit of a particular moment.

The longing to tell one's story and the process of telling is symbolically a gesture of longing to recover the past in such a way that one experiences both a sense of reunion and a sense of release. It was the longing for release that compelled the writing but concurrently it was the joy of reunion that enabled me to see that the act of writing one's autobiography is a way to find again that aspect of self and experience that may no longer be an actual part of one's life but is a living memory shaping and informing the present. Autobiographical writing was a way for me to evoke the particular experience of growing up southern and black in segregated communities. It was a way to recapture the richness of southern black culture. The need to remember and hold to the legacy of that experience and what it taught me has been all the more important since I have since lived in predominately white communities and taught at predominately white colleges. Black southern folk experience was the foundation of the life around me when I was a child; that experience no longer exists in many places where it was once all of life that we knew. Capitalism, upward mobility, assimilation of other values have all led to rapid disintegration of black folk experience or in some cases the gradual wearing away of that experience.

Within the world of my childhood, we held on to the legacy of a distinct black culture by listening to the elders tell their stories. Autobiography was experienced most actively in the art of telling one's story. I can recall sitting at Baba's (my grandmother on my mother's side) at 1200 Broad Street—listening to people come and recount their life experience. In those days, whenever I brought a playmate to my grandmother's house, Baba would want a brief outline of their autobiography before we would begin playing. She wanted not only to know who their people were but what their values were. It was sometimes an awesome and terrifying experience to stand answering these questions or witness another playmate being subjected to the process and yet this was the way we would come to know our own and one another's family histories. It is the absence of such a tradition in my adult life that makes the written narrative of my girlhood all the more important. As the years pass and these glorious memories grow much more vague, there will remain the clarity contained within the written words.

Conceptually, the autobiography was framed in the manner of a hope chest. I remembered my mother's hope chest, with its wonderful odor of cedar, and thought about her taking the most precious items and placing them there for safekeeping. Certain memories were for me a similar treasure. I wanted to place them somewhere for safekeeping. An autobiographical narrative seemed an appropriate place. Each particular incident, encounter, experience had its own story, sometimes told from the first person, sometimes told from the third person. Often I felt as though I was in a trance at my typewriter, that the shape of a particular memory was decided not by my conscious mind but by all that is dark and deep within me, unconscious but present. It was the act of making it present, bringing it into the open, so to speak, that was liberating.

From the perspective of trying to understand my psyche, it was also interesting to read the narrative in its entirety after I had completed the work. It had not occurred to me that bringing one's past, one's memories together in a complete narrative would allow one to view them from a different perspective, not as singular isolated events but as part of a continuum. Reading the completed manuscript, I felt as though I had an overview not so much of my childhood but of those experiences that were deeply imprinted in my consciousness. Significantly, that which was absent, left out, not included also was important. I was shocked to find at the end of my narrative that there were few incidents I recalled that involved my five sisters. Most of the incidents with siblings were with me and my brother. There was a sense of alienation from my sisters present in childhood, a sense of estrangement. This was reflected in the narrative. Another aspect of the completed manuscript that is interesting to me is the way in which the incidents describing adult men suggest that I feared them intensely, with the exception of my grandfather and a few old men. Writing the autobiographical narrative enabled me to look at my past from a different perspective and to use this knowledge as a means of self-growth and change in a practical way.

In the end I did not feel as though I had killed the Gloria of my childhood. Instead I had rescued her. She was no longer the enemy within, the little girl who had to be annihilated for the woman to come into being. In writing about her, I reclaimed that part of myself I had long ago rejected, left uncared for, just as she had often felt alone and uncared for as a child. Remembering was part of a cycle of reunion, a joining of fragments, "the bits and pieces of my heart" that the narrative made whole again.

Memory and Imagination

by Patricia Hampl

When I was seven, my father, who played the violin on Sundays with a nicely tortured flair which we considered artistic, led me by the hand down a long, unlit corridor in St. Luke's School basement, a sort of tunnel that ended in a room of pianos. There many little girls and a single sad boy were playing truly tortured scales and arpeggios in a mash of troubled sound. My father gave me over to Sister Olive Marie, who did look remarkably like an olive.

Her oily face gleamed as if it had just been rolled out of a can and laid on the white plate of her broad, spotless wimple. She was a small, plump woman; her body and the small window of her face seemed to interpret the entire alphabet of olive: her face was a sallow green olive placed upon the jumbo ripe olive of her black habit. I trusted her instantly and smiled, glad to have my hand placed in the hand of a woman who made sense, who provided the satisfaction of being what she was: an Olive who looked like an olive.

My father left me to discover the piano with Sister Olive Marie so that one day I would join him in mutually tortured piano-violin duets for the edification of my mother and brother who sat at the table meditatively spooning in the last of their pineapple sherbet until their part was called for: they put down their spoons and clapped while we bowed, while the sweet ice in their bowls melted, while the music melted, and we all melted a little into each other for a moment.

But first Sister Olive must do her work. I was shown middle C, which Sister seemed to think terribly important. I stared at middle C and then glanced away for a second. When my eye returned, middle C was gone, its slim finger lost in the complicated grasp of the keyboard. Sister Olive struck it again, finding it with laughable ease. She emphasized the importance of middle C, its central position, a sort of North Star of sound. I remember thinking, "Middle C is the belly button of the piano," an insight whose originality and accuracy stunned me with pride. For the first time in my life I was astonished by metaphor. I hesitated to tell the kindly Olive for some reason; apparently I understood a true metaphor is a risky business, revealing of the self. In fact, I have never, until this moment of writing it down, told my first metaphor to anyone.

Sunlight flooded the room; the pianos, all black, gleamed. Sister Olive, dressed in the colors of the keyboard, gleamed; middle C shimmered with meaning and I resolved never—never—to forget its location: it was the center of the world.

Then Sister Olive, who had had to show me middle C twice but who seemed to have drawn no bad conclusions about me anyway, got up and went to the windows on the opposite wall. She pulled the shades down, one after the other. The sun was too bright, she said. She sneezed as she stood at the windows with the sun shedding its glare over her. She sneezed and sneezed, crazy little convulsive sneezes, one after another, as helpless as if she had the hiccups.

"The sun makes me sneeze," she said when the fit was over and she was back at the piano. This was odd, too odd to grasp in the mind. I associated sneezing with colds, and colds with rain, fog, snow and bad weather. The sun, however, had caused Sister Olive to sneeze in this wild way, Sister Olive who gleamed benignly and who was so certain of the location of the center of the world. The universe wobbled a bit and became unreliable. Things were not, after all, necessarily what they seemed. Appearance deceived: here was the sun acting totally out of character, hurling this woman into sneezes, a woman so mild that she was named, so it seemed, for a bland object on a relish tray.

I was given a red book, the first Thompson book, and told to play the first piece over and over at one of the black pianos where the other children were crashing away. This, I was told, was called practicing. It sounded alluringly adult, practicing. The piece itself consisted mainly of middle C, and I excelled, thrilled by my savvy at being able to locate that central note amidst the cunning camouflage of all the other white keys before me. Thrilled too by the shiny red book that gleamed, as the pianos did, as Sister Olive did, as my eager eyes probably did. I sat at the formidable machine of the piano and got to know middle C intimately, preparing to be as tortured as I could manage one day soon with my father's violin at my side.

But at the moment Mary Katherine Reilly was at my side, playing something at least two or three lessons more sophisticated than my piece. I believe she even struck a chord. I glanced at her from the peasantry of single notes, shy, ready to pay homage. She turned toward me, stopped playing, and sized me up.

Sized me up and found a person ready to be dominated. Without introduction she said, "My grandfather invented the collapsible opera hat."

I nodded, I acquiesced, I was hers. With that little stroke it was decided between us—that she should be the leader, and I the sidekick. My job was admiration. Even when she added, "But he didn't make a penny from it. He didn't have a patent"—even then, I knew and she knew that this was not an admission of powerlessness, but the easy candor of a master, of one who can afford a weakness or two.

With the clairvoyance of all fated relationships based on dominance and submission, it was decided in advance; that when the time came for us to play duets, I should always play second piano, that I should spend my allowance to buy her the Twinkies she craved but was not allowed to have, that finally, I should let her copy from my test paper, and when confronted by our teacher, confess with convincing hysteria that it was I, I who had cheated, who had reached above myself to steal what clearly belonged to the rightful heir of the inventor of the collapsible opera hat...

There must be a reason I remember that little story about my first piano lesson. In fact, it isn't a story, just a moment, the beginning of what could perhaps become a story. For the memoirist, more than for the fiction writer, the story seems already *there*, already accomplished and fully achieved in history ("in reality," as we naively say). For the memoirist, the writing of the story is a matter of transcription.

That, anyway, is the myth, but no memoirist writes for long without experiencing an unsettling disbelief about the reliability of memory, a hunch that memory is not, after all, *just* memory. I don't know why I remembered this fragment about my first piano lesson. I don't, for instance, have a single recollection of my first arithmetic lesson, the first time I studied Latin, the first time my grandmother tried to teach me to knit. Yet these things occurred too, and must have their stories.

It is the piano lesson that has trudged forward, clearing the haze of forgetfulness, showing itself bright with detail more than thirty years after the event. I did not choose to remember the piano lesson. It was simply there, like a book that has always been on the shelf, whether I ever read it or not, the binding and title showing as I skim across the contents of my life. On the day I wrote this fragment I happened to take that memory, not some other, from the shelf and paged through it. I found more detail, more event, perhaps a little more entertainment than I had expected, but the memory itself was there from the start. Waiting for me.

Or was it? When I reread what I had written just after I finished it, I realized that I had told a number of lies. I *think* it was my father who took me the first time for my piano lesson—but maybe he only took me to meet my teacher and there was no actual lesson that day. And did I even know then that he played the violin—didn't he take up his violin again much later, as a result of my piano playing; and not the reverse? And is it even remotely accurate to describe as "tortured" the musicianship of a man who began every day by belting out "Oh What a Beautiful Morning" as he shaved?

More: Sister Olive Marie did sneeze in the sun, but was her name Olive? As for her skin tone—I would have sworn it was olive-like; I would have been willing to spend the better part of an afternoon trying to write the exact description of imported Italian or Greek olive her face suggest-ed: I wanted to get it right. But now, were I to write that passage over, it is her intense black eyebrows I would see, for suddenly they seem the central fact of that face, some indicative mark of her serious and patient nature. But the truth is, I don't remember the woman at all. She's a sneeze in the sun and a finger touching middle C. That, at least, is steady and clear.

Worse: I didn't have the Thompson book as my piano text. I'm sure of that because I remember envying children who did have this wonderful book with its pictures of children and animals printed on the pages of music.

As for Mary Katherine Reilly. She didn't even go to grade school with me (and her name isn't Mary Katherine Reilly—but I made that change on purpose). I met her in Girl Scouts and only went to school with her later, in high school. Our relationship was not really one of leader and follower; I played first piano most of the time in duets. She certainly never copied anything from a test paper of mine: she was a better student, and cheating just wasn't a possibility with her. Though her grandfather (or someone in her family) did invent the collapsible opera hat and I remem-ber that she was proud of that fact, she didn't tell me this news as a deft move in a childish power play.

So, what was I doing in this brief memoir? Is it simply an example of the curious relation a fiction writer has to the material of her own life? Maybe. That may have some value in itself. But to tell the truth (if anyone still believes me capable of telling the truth), I wasn't writing fiction, I was writing memoir—or was trying to. My desire was to be accurate. I wished to embody the myth of memoir to write as an act of dutiful transcription.

Yet clearly the work of writing narrative caused me to do something very different from transcription. I am forced to admit that memoir is not a matter of transcription, that memory itself is not a warehouse of finished stories, not a static gallery of framed pictures. I must admit that I invented. But why?

Two whys: why did I invent, and then, if a memoirist must inevitably invent rather than transcribe, why do I—why should anybody—write memoir at all?

I must respond to these impertinent questions because they, like the bumper sticker I saw the other day commanding all who read it to QUESTION AUTHORITY, challenge my authority as a memoirist and as a witness.

It still comes as a shock to realize that I don't write about what I know: I write in order to find out what I know. Is it possible to convey to a reader the enormous degree of blankness, confusion, hunch and uncertainty lurking in the act of writing? When I am the reader, not the writer, I too fall into the lovely illusion that the words before me (in a story by Mavis Gallant, an essay by Carol Bly, a memoir by M. F. K. Fisher), which *read* so inevitably, must also have been *written* exactly as they appear, rhythm and cadence, language and syntax, the powerful waves of the sentences laying themselves on the smooth beach of the page one after another faultlessly.

But here I sit before a yellow legal pad, and the long page of the preceding two paragraphs is a jumble of crossed-out lines, false starts, confused order. A mess. The mess of my mind trying to find out what it wants to say. This is a writer's frantic, grabby mind, not the poised mind of a reader ready to be edified or entertained.

I sometimes think of the reader as a cat, endlessly fastidious, capable, by turns, of mordant indifference and riveted attention, luxurious, re-cumbent, and ever poised. Whereas the writer is absolutely a dog, panting and moping, too eager for an affectionate scratch behind the ears, lunging frantically after any old stick thrown in the distance.

The blankness of a new page never fails to intrigue and terrify me. Some times, in fact, I think my habit of writing on long yellow sheets comes from an atavistic fear of the writer's stereotypic "blank white page." At least when I begin writing, my page isn't utterly blank; at least it has a wash of color on it, even if the absence of words must finally be faced on a yellow sheet as truly as on a blank white one. Well, we all have our ways of whistling in the dark.

If I approach writing from memory with the assumption that I know what I wish to say, I assume that intentionality is running the show. Things are not that simple. Or perhaps writing is even more profoundly simple, more telegraphic and immediate in its choices than the grating wheels and chugging engine of logic and rational intention. The heart, the guardian of intuition with its secret, often fearful intentions, is the boss, its commands are what a writer obeys—often without knowing it. Or, I do.

That's why I'm a strong adherent of the first draft. And why it's worth pausing for a moment to consider what a first draft really is. By my lights, the piano lesson memoir is a first draft. That doesn't mean it exists here exactly as I first wrote it. I like to think I've cleaned it up from the first time I put it down on paper. I've cut some adjectives here, toned down the hyperbole there, smoothed transition, cut a repetition—that sort of housekeeperly tidying-up. But the piece remains a first draft because I haven't yet gotten to know it, haven't given it a chance to tell me anything. For me, writing a first draft is a little like meeting someone for the first time. I come away with a wary acquaintanceship, but the real friendship (if any) and genuine intimacy—that's all down the road. Intimacy with a piece of writing, as with a person, comes from paying attention to the revelations it is capable of giving, not by imposing my own preconceived notions, no matter how well-intentioned they might be.

I try to let pretty much anything happen in a first draft. A careful first draft is a failed first draft. That may be why there are so many inaccuracies in the piano lesson memoir: I didn't censor, I didn't judge. I kept moving. But I would not publish this piece as a memoir on its own in its present state. It isn't the "lies" in the piece that give me pause, though a reader has a right to expect a memoir to be as accurate as the writer's memory can make it. No, it isn't the lies themselves that makes the piano lesson memoir a first draft and therefore "unpublishable."

The real trouble: the piece hasn't yet found its subject; it isn't yet about what it wants to be about. Note: what *it* wants, not what I want. The difference has to do with the relation a memoirist—any writer, in fact—has to unconscious or half-known intentions and impulses in composition.

Now that I have the fragment down on paper, I can read this little piece as a mystery which drops clues to the riddle of my feelings, like a culprit who wishes to he apprehended. My narrative self (the culprit who has invented) wishes to be discovered by my reflective self, the self who wants to understand and make sense of a half-remembered story about a nun sneezing in the sun....

We only store in memory images of value. The value may be lost over the passage of time (I was baffled about why I remembered that sneezing nun, for example), but that's the implacable judgment of feeling: *this*, we say somewhere deep within us, is something I'm hanging on to. And of course, often we cleave to things because they possess heavy negative charges. Pain likes to be vivid.

Over time, the value (the feeling) and the stored memory (the image) may become estranged. Memoir seeks a permanent home for feeling and image, a habitation where they can live together in harmony. Naturally, I've had a lot of experiences since I packed away that one from the basement of St. Luke's School; that piano lesson has been effaced by waves of feeling for other moments and episodes. I persist in believing the event has value—after all, I remember it—but in writing the memoir I did not simply relive the experience. Rather, I explored the mysterious relationship between all the images I could round up and the even more impacted feelings that caused me to store the images safely away in memory. Stalking the relationship, seeking the congruence between stored image and hidden emotion—that's the real job of memoir.

By writing about that first piano lesson, I've come to know things I could not know otherwise. But I only know these things as a result of reading this first draft. While I was writing, I was following the images, letting the details fill the room of the page and use the furniture as they wished. I was their dutiful servant—or thought I was. In fact, I was the faithful retainer of my hidden feelings which were giving the commands.

I really did feel, for instance, that Mary Katherine Reilly was far superior to me. She was smarter, funnier, more wonderful in every way—that's how I saw it. Our friendship (or she herself) did not require that I become her vassal, yet perhaps in my heart that was something I wanted; I wanted a way to express my feeling of admiration. I suppose I waited until this memoir to begin to find the way.

Just as, in the memoir, I finally possess that red Thompson book with the barking dogs and bleating lambs and winsome children. I couldn't (and still can't) remember what my own music book was, so I grabbed the name and image of the one book I could remember. It was only in reviewing the piece after writing it that I saw my inaccuracy. In pondering this "lie," I to see what I was up to: I was getting what I wanted. At last.

The truth of many circumstances and episodes in the past emerges for the memoirist through details (the red music book, the fascination with a nun's name and gleaming face), but these details are not merely information, not flat facts. Such details are not allowed to lounge. They must work. Their work is the creation of symbol. But it's more accurate to call it the *recognition* of symbol. For meaning is not "attached" to the detail by the memoirist; meaning is revealed.

That's why a first draft is important. Just as the first meeting (good or bad) with someone who later becomes the beloved is important and is often reviewed for signals, meanings, omens, and indications.

Now I can look at that music book and see it not only as "a detail," but for what it is, how it *acts*. See it as the small red door leading straight into the dark room of my childhood longing and disappointment. That red book *becomes* the palpable evidence of that longing. In other words, it becomes symbol. There is no symbol, no life-of-the-spirit in the general or the abstract. Yet a writer wishes—indeed all of us wish—to speak about profound matters that are, like it or not, general and abstract. We wish to talk to each other about life and death, about love, despair, loss, and innocence. We sense that in order to live together we must learn to speak of peace, of history, of meaning and values. Those are a few.

We seek a means of exchange, a language which will renew these ancient concerns and make them wholly and pulsingly ours. Instinctively, we go to our store of private images and associations for our authority to speak of these weighty issues. We find, in our details and broken and obscured images, the language of symbol. Here memory impulsively reaches out its arms and embraces imagination. That is the resort to invention. It isn't a lie, but an act of necessity, as the innate urge to locate personal truth always is.

All right. Invention is inevitable. But why write memoir? Why not call it fiction and be done with all the hashing about, wondering where memory stops and imagination begins? And if memoir seeks to talk about "the big issues," about history and peace, death and love—why not leave these reflections to those with expert and scholarly knowledge? Why let the common or garden variety memoirist into the club? I'm thinking again of that bumper sticker: why Question Authority?

My answer, of course, is a memoirist's answer. Memoir must be written because each of us must have a created version of the past. Created: that is, real, tangible, made of the stuff of a life lived in place and in history. And the down side of any created thing as well: we must live with a version that attaches us to our limitations, to the inevitable subjectivity, of our points of view. We must acquiesce to our experience and our gift to transform experience into meaning and value. You tell me your story, I'll tell you my story.

If we refuse to do the work of creating this personal version of the past, someone else will do it for us. That is a scary political fact. "The struggle of man against power," a character in Milan Kundera's novel *The Book of Laughter and Forgetting* says, "is the struggle of memory against forgetting." Me refers to willful political forgetting, the habit of nations and those in power (Question Authority!) to deny the truth of memory in order to disarm moral and ethical power. It's an efficient way of controlling masses of people. It doesn't even require much bloodshed, as long as people are entirely willing to give over their personal memories. Whole histories can be rewritten. As Czeslaw Milosz said in his 1980 Nobel Prize lecture, the number of books published that seek to deny the existence of the Nazi death camps now exceeds one hundred.

What is remembered is what *becomes* reality. If we "forget" Auschwitz, if we "forget" My Lai, what then do we remember? And what is the purpose of our remembering? If we think of memory naively, as a simple story, logged like a documentary in the archive of the mind, we miss its beauty but also its function. The beauty of memory rests in its talent for rendering detail, for paying homage to the senses, its capacity to love the particles of life, the richness and idiosyncrasy or our existence. The function of memory, on the other hand, is intensely personal and surprisingly political.

Our capacity to move forward as developing beings rests on a healthy relation with the past. Psychotherapy, that widespread method of mental health, relies heavily on memory and on the ability to retrieve and organize images and events from the personal past. We carry our wounds and perhaps even worse, our capacity to wound, forward with us. If we learn not only to tell our stories but to listen to what our stories tell us—to write the first draft and then return for the second draft—we are doing the work of memoir.

Memoir is the intersection of narration and reflection, of story-telling and essay-writing. It can present its story *and* reflect and consider the meaning of the story. It is a peculiarly open form, inviting broken and incomplete images, half-recollected fragments, all the mass (and mess) of detail. It offers to shape this confusion—and in shaping, of course it necessarily creates a work of art, not a legal document. But then, even legal documents are only valiant attempts to consign the truth, the whole truth and nothing but the truth to paper. Even they remain versions.

141

Locating touchstones—the red music book, the olive Olive, my father's violin playing—is deeply satisfying. Who knows why? Perhaps we all sense that we can't grasp the whole truth and nothing but the truth of our experience. Just can't be done. What can be achieved, however, is a version of its swirling, changing wholeness. A memoirist must acquiesce to selectivity, like any artist. The version we dare to write is the only truth, the only relationship we can have with the past. Refuse to write your life and you have no life. At least, that is the stern view of the memoirist.

Personal history, logged in memory, is a sort of slide projector flashing images on the wall of the mind. And there's precious little order to the slides in the rotating carousel. Beyond that confusion, who knows who is running the projector? A memoirist steps into this darkened room of flashing, unorganized images and stands blinking for a while. Maybe for a long while. But eventually, as with any attempt to tell a story, it is necessary to put something first, then something else. And so on, to the end. That's a first draft. Not necessarily the truth, not even *a* truth sometimes, but the first attempt to create a shape.

The first thing I usually notice at this stage of composition is the appalling inaccuracy of the piece. Witness my first piano lesson draft. Invention is screamingly evident in what I intended to be transcription. But here's the further truth: I feel no shame. In fact, it's only now that my interest in the piece truly quickens. For I can see what isn't there, what is shyly hugging the walls, hoping not to be seen. I see the filmy shape of the next draft. I see a more acute version of the episode or—this is more likely—an entirely new piece rising from the ashes of the first attempt.

The next draft of the piece would have to be a true re-vision, a new seeing of the materials of the first draft. Nothing merely cosmetic will do—no rouge buffing up the opening sentence, no glossy adjective to lift a sagging line, nothing to attempt covering a patch of gray writing. None of that. I can't say for sure, but my hunch is the revision would lead me to more writing about my father (why was I so impressed by that ancestral inventor of the collapsible opera hat? Did I feel I had nothing as remarkable in my own background? Did this make me feel inadequate?). I begin to think perhaps Sister Olive is less central to this business than she is in this draft. She is meant to be a moment, not a character.

And so I might proceed, if I were to undertake a new draft of the memoir. I begin to feel a relationship developing between a former self and me.

And, even more compelling, a relationship between an old world and me. Some people think of autobiographical writing as the precious occupation of a particularly self-absorbed person. Maybe, but I don't buy that. True memoir is written in an attempt to find not only a self but a world.

The self-absorption that seems to be the impetus and embarrassment of autobiography turns into (or perhaps always was) a hunger for the world. Actually it begins as hunger for *a* world, one gone or lost, effaced by time or a more sudden brutality. But in the act of remembering, the personal environment expands, resonates beyond itself, beyond its "subject," into the endless and tragic recollection that is history.

We look at old family photographs in which we stand next to black, boxy Fords and are wearing period costumes, and we do not gaze fascinated because there we are young again, or there we are standing, as we never will again in life, next to our mother. We stare and drift because there we are...historical. It is the dress, the black car that dazzle us now and draw us beyond our mother's bright arms which once caught us. We reach into the attractive impersonality of something more significant than ourselves. We write memoir, in other words. We accept the humble position of writing a version rather than "the whole truth."

I suppose I write memoir because of the radiance of the past—it draws me back and back to it. Not that the past is beautiful. In our communal memoir, in history, the death camps *are* back there. In intimate life too, the record is usually pretty mixed. "I could tell you stories..." people say and drift off, meaning terrible things have happened to them.

But the past is radiant. It has the light of lived life. A memoirist wishes to touch it. No one owns the past, though typically the first act of new political regimes, whether of the left or the right, is to attempt to re-write history, to grab the past and make it over so the end comes out right. So their power looks inevitable.

No one owns the past, but it is a grave error (another age would have said a grave sin) not to inhabit memory. Sometimes I think it is all we really have. But that may be a trifle melodramatic. At any rate, memory possesses authority for the fearful self in a world where it is necessary to have authority in order to Question Authority.

There may be no more pressing intellectual need in our culture than for people to become sophisticated about the function of memory. The political implications of the loss of memory are obvious. The authority of memory is a personal confirmation of selfhood. To write one's life is to live it twice, and the second living is both spiritual and historical, for a

143

memoir reaches deep within the personality as it seeks its narrative form and also grasps the life-of-the-times as no political treatise can.

Our most ancient metaphor says life is a journey. Memoir is travel writing, then, notes taken along the way, telling how things looked and what thoughts occurred. But I cannot think of the memoirist as a tourist. This is the traveller who goes on foot, living the journey, taking on mountains, enduring deserts, marveling at the lush green places. Moving through it all faithfully, not so much a survivor with a harrowing tale to tell as a pilgrim, seeking, wondering.

Reading My Way Out of South L.A.

by Mike Rose

Mike Rose (b. 1944) grew up in South Los Angeles, an area populated by working-class immigrants like his Italian parents. Early in his schooling he was channeled into "vocational education," and school became a place of boredom, frustration, and very little learning. He was eventually reclassified as "college material" and suddenly found himself at Loyola University, without the background and learning skills expected of a college student. Rose went on to become a poet, a teacher, and associate director of UCLA Writing Programs, he is currently a professor of education at UCLA. He has won awards from the National Academy of Education, the National Council of Teachers of English (NCTE), and the John Simon Guggenheim Memorial Foundation. His works include textbooks, two books on writer's block, Perspectives on Literacy *(1988), and* Lives on the Boundary: The Struggles and Achievements of America's Underprepared *(1989), a widely acclaimed account of disadvantaged students. In this excerpt from* Lives on the Boundary, *Rose describes how his reading outside of the classroom enriched his life and provided fodder for his fantasies.*

Some people who manage to write their way out of the working class describe the classroom as an oasis of possibility. It became their intellectual playground, their competitive arena. Given the richness of my memories of this time, it's funny how scant are my recollections of school. I remember the red brick building of St. Regina's itself, and the topography of the playground: the swings and basketball courts and peeling benches. There are images of a few students: Erwin Petschaur, a muscular German boy with a strong accent; Dave Sanchez, who was good in math; and Sheila Wilkes, everyone's curly-haired heartthrob. And there are two nuns: Sister Monica, the third-grade teacher with beautiful hands for whom I carried a candle and who, to my dismay, had wedded herself to Christ; and Sister Beatrice, a woman truly crazed, who would sweep into class, eyes wide, to tell us about the Apocalypse.

All the hours in class tend to blend into one long, vague stretch of time. What I remember best, strangely enough, are the two things I couldn't understand and over the years grew to hate: grammar lessons and mathematics. I would sit there watching a teacher draw her long horizontal line and her short, oblique lines and break up sentences and put adjectives here and adverbs there and just not get it, couldn't see the reason for it, turned off to it. I would hide by slumping down in my seat and page through my reader, carried along by the flow of sentences in a story. She would test us, and I would dread that, for I always got Cs and Ds. Mathematics was a bit different. For whatever reasons, I didn't learn early math very well, so when it came time for more complicated operations, I couldn't keep up and started daydreaming to avoid my inadequacy. This was a strategy I would rely on as I grew older. I fell further and further behind. A memory: The teacher is faceless and seems very far away. The voice is faint and is discussing an equation written on the board. It is raining, and I am watching the streams of water form patterns on the windows.

I realize now how consistently I defended myself against the lessons I couldn't understand and the people and events of South L.A. that were too strange to view head-on. I got very good at watching a blackboard with minimum awareness. And I drifted more and more into a variety of protective fantasies. I was lucky in that although my parents didn't read or write very much and had no more than a few books around the house, they never debunked my pursuits. And when they could, they bought me what I needed to spin my web.

One early Christmas they got me a small chemistry set. My father brought home an old card table from the secondhand store, and on that table I spread out my test tubes, my beaker, my Erlenmeyer flask, and my gas-generating apparatus. The set came equipped with chemicals, minerals, and various treated papers—all in little square bottles. You could send away to someplace in Maryland for more, and I did, saving pennies and nickels to get the substances that were too exotic for my set, the Junior Chemcraft: Congo red paper, azurite, glycerine, chrome alum, cochineal—this from female insects!—tartaric acid, chameleon paper, logwood. I would sit before my laboratory and play for hours. My father rested on the purple couch in front of me watching wrestling or *Gunsmoke* while I measured powders or heated crystals or blew into solutions that my breath would turn red or pink. I was taken by the blends of names and by the colors that swirled through the beaker. My equations were visual and phonetic. I would hold a flask up to the hall light, imagining the veils of a million atoms dancing. Sulfur and alcohol hung in the air. I wanted to shake down the house.

One day my mother came home from Coffee Dan's with an awful story. The teenage brother of one of her waitress friends was in the hospital. He had been fooling around with explosives in his garage "where his mother couldn't see him," and something happened, and "he blew away part of his throat. For God's sake, be careful," my mother said. "Remember poor Ada's brother." Wow! I thought. How neat! Why couldn't my experiments be that dangerous? I really lost heart when I realized that you could probably eat the chemicals spread across my table.

I knew what I had to do. I saved my money for a week and then walked with firm resolve past Walt's Malts, past the brake shop, across Ninetieth Street, and into Palazolla's market. I bought a little bottle of Alka-Seltzer and ran home. I chipped up the wafers and mixed them into a jar of white crystals. When my mother came home, dog tired, and sat down on the edge of the couch to tell me and Dad about her day, I gravely poured my concoction into a beaker of water, cried something about the unexpected, and ran out from behind my table. The beaker foamed ominously. My father swore in Italian. The second time I tried it, I got something milder— in English. And by my third near-miss with death, my parents were calling my behavior cute. Cute! Who wanted cute? I wanted to toy with the disaster that befell Ada Pendleton's brother. I wanted all those wonderful colors to collide in ways that could blow your voice box right off.

But I was limited by the real. The best I could do was create a toxic antacid. I loved my chemistry set—its glassware and its intriguing labels— but it wouldn't allow me to do the things I wanted to do. St. Regina's had an all-purpose room, one wall of which was lined with old books—and one of those shelves held a row of plastic-covered space novels. The sheen of their covers was gone, and their futuristic portraits were dotted with erasures and grease spots like a meteor shower of the everyday. I remember the rockets best. Long cylinders outfitted at the base with three slick fins, tapering at the other end to a perfect conical point, ready to pierce out of the stratosphere and into my imagination: X-fifteens and Mach 1, the dark side of the moon, the Red Planet, Jupiter's Great Red Spot, Saturn's rings—and beyond the solar system to swirling wisps of galaxies, to stardust.

I would check out my books two at a time and take them home to curl up with a blanket on my chaise lounge, reading, sometimes, through the weekend, my back aching, my thoughts lost between galaxies. I became the hero of a thousand adventures, all with intricate plots and the triumph of good over evil, all many dimensions removed from the dim walls of the living room. We were given time to draw in school, so, before long, all this worked itself onto paper. The stories I was reading were reshaping themselves into pictures. My father got me some butcher paper from Palazolla's, and I continued to draw at home. My collected works rendered the Horsehead Nebula, goofy space cruisers, robots, and Saturn. Each had its crayon, a particular waxy pencil with mood and meaning: rust and burnt sienna for Mars, yellow for the Sun, lime and rose for Saturn's rings, and bright red for the Jovian spot. I had a little sharpener to keep the points just right. I didn't write any stories; I just read and drew. I wouldn't care much about writing until late in high school.

The summer before the sixth grade, I got a couple of jobs. The first was at a pet store a block or so away from my house. Since I was still small, I could maneuver around in breeder cages, scraping the heaps of parakeet crap from the tin floor, cleaning the water troughs and seed trays. It was pretty awful. I would go home after work and fill the tub and soak until all the fleas and bird mites came floating to the surface, little Xs in their multiple eyes. When I heard about a job selling strawberries door-to-door, I jumped at it. I went to work for a white-haired Chicano named Frank. He would carry four or five kids and dozens of crates of strawberries in his ramshackle truck up and down the avenues of the better neighborhoods: houses with mowed lawns and petunia beds. We'd work all day for seventy-five cents, Frank dropping pairs of us off with two crates each, then picking us up at preassigned corners. We spent lots of time together, bouncing around on the truck bed redolent with strawberries or sitting on a corner, cold, listening for the sputter of Frank's muffler. I started telling the other kids about my books, and soon it was my job to fill up that time with stories.

Reading opened up the world. There I was, a skinny bookworm drawing the attention of street kids who, in any other circumstances, would have had me for breakfast. Like an epic tale-teller, I developed the stories as I went along, relying on a flexible plot line and a repository of heroic events. I had a great time. I sketched out trajectories with my finger on Frank's dusty truck bed. And I stretched out each story's climax, creating cliff-hangers like the ones I saw in the Saturday serials. These stories created for me a temporary community.

It was around this time that fiction started leading me circuitously to a child's version of science. In addition to the space novels, St. Regina's library also had half a dozen books on astronomy—*The Golden Book of the Planets* and stuff like that—so I checked out a few of them. I liked what I read and wheedled enough change out of my father to enable me to take the bus to the public library. I discovered star maps, maps of lunar seas, charts upon charts of the solar system and the planetary moons: Rhea, Europa, Callisto, Miranda, Io. I didn't know that most of these moons were named for women—I didn't know classical mythology—but I would say their names to myself as though they had a woman's power to protect: Europa, Miranda, Io…. The distances between stars fascinated me, as did the sizes of the big telescopes. I sent away for catalogs. Then prices fascinated me too. I wanted to drape my arm over a thousand-dollar scope and hear its motor drive whirr. I conjured a twelve-year-old's life of the astronomer: sitting up all night with potato chips and the stars, tracking the sky for supernovas, humming "Earth Angel" with the Penguins. What was my mother to do but save her tips and buy me a telescope?!

It was a little reflecting job, and I solemnly used to carry it out to the front of the house on warm summer nights, to find Venus or Alpha Centauri or trace the stars in Orion or lock onto the moon. I would lay out my star maps on the concrete, more for their magic than anything else, for I had trouble figuring them out. I was no geometer of the constellations; I was their balladeer. Those nights were very peaceful. I was far enough away from the front door and up enough from the sidewalk to make it seem as if I rested on a mound of dark silence, a mountain in Arizona, perhaps, watching the sky alive with points of light. Poor Freddie, toothless Lester whispering promises about making me feel good, the flat days, the gang fights—all this receded, for it was now me, the star child, lost in an eyepiece focused on a reflecting mirror that cradled, in its center, a shimmering moon.

Consider the Source

1. Compare Rose's classroom memories with his recollections of his chemistry experiments at home. How do specific details contribute to his descriptions?

2. Explain what Rose means when he says, "I was limited by the real." How does reading free him from the "real"?

3. What kind of reading does Rose indulge in? Why do you suppose he selected the books he chose?

4. List the various characterizations Rose gives of himself. Which ones come from books?

On Being a Cripple

by Nancy Mairs

"To escape is nothing. Not to escape is nothing."　　—Louise Bogan

The other day I was thinking of writing an essay on being a cripple. I was thinking hard in one of the stalls of the women's room in my office building, as I was shoving my shirt into my jeans and tugging up my zipper. Preoccupied, I flushed, picked up my book bag, took my cane down from the hook, and unlatched the door. So many movements unbalanced me, and as I pulled the door open I fell over backward, landing fully clothed on the toilet seat with my legs splayed in front of me: the old beetle-on-its-back routine. Saturday afternoon, the building deserted, I was free to laugh aloud as I wriggled back to my feet, my voice bouncing off the yellowish tiles from all directions. Had anyone been there with me, I'd have been still and faint and hot with chagrin. I decided that it was high time to write the essay.

First, the matter of semantics. I am a cripple. I choose this word to name me. I choose from among several possibilities, the most common of which are "handicapped" and "disabled." I made the choice a number of years ago, without thinking, unaware of my motives for doing so. Even now, I'm not sure what those motives are, but I recognize that they are complex and not entirely flattering. People—crippled or not—wince at the word "cripple," as they do not at "handicapped" or "disabled." Perhaps I want them to wince. I want them to see me as a tough customer, one to whom the fates/gods/viruses have not been kind, but who can face the brutal truth of her existence squarely. As a cripple, I swagger.

But, to be fair to myself, a certain amount of honesty underlies my choice. "Cripple" seems to me a clean word, straightforward and precise. It has an honorable history, having made its first appearance in the Lindisfarne Gospel in the tenth century. As a lover of words, I like the accuracy with which it describes my condition: I have lost the full use of my limbs. "Disabled," by contrast, suggests any incapacity, physical or mental. And I certainly don't like "handicapped," which implies that I

Mairs, Nancy. "On Being a Cripple" from *Plaintext* by Nancy Mairs. © 1986 The Arizona Board of Regents. Reprinted by permission of the University of Arizona Press.

have deliberately been put at a disadvantage, by whom I can't imagine (my God is not a Handicapper General), in order to equalize chances in the great race of life. These words seem to me to be moving away from my condition, to be widening the gap between word and reality. Most remote is the recently coined euphemism "differently abled," which partakes of the same semantic hopefulness that transformed countries from "unde-veloped" to "underdeveloped," then to "less developed," and finally to "developing" nations. People have continued to starve in those countries during the shift. Some realities do not obey the dictates of language.

Mine is one of them. Whatever you call me, I remain crippled. But I don't care what you call me, so long as it isn't "differently abled," which strikes me as pure verbal garbage designed, by its ability to describe anyone, to describe no one. I subscribe to George Orwell's thesis that "the slovenliness of our language makes it easier for us to have foolish thoughts." And I refuse to participate in the degeneration of the language to the extent that I deny that I have lost anything in the course of this calamitous disease; I refuse to pretend that the only differences between you and me are the various ordinary ones that distinguish any one person from another. But call me "disabled" or "handicapped" if you like. I have long since grown accustomed to them; and if they are vague, at least they hint at the truth. Moreover, I use them myself. Society is no readier to accept crippledness than to accept death, war, sex, sweat, or wrinkles. I would never refer to another person as a cripple. It is the word I use to name only myself.

I haven't always been crippled, a fact for which I am soundly grateful. To be whole of limb is, I know from experience, infinitely more pleasant and useful than to be crippled; and if that knowledge leaves me open to bitterness at MY loss, the physical soundness I once enjoyed (though I did not enjoy it half enough) is well worth the occasional stab of regret. Though never any good at sports, I was a normally active child and young adult. I climbed trees, played hopscotch, jumped rope, skated, swam, rode my bicycle, sailed. I despised team sports, spending some of the wretched-est afternoons of my life, sweaty and humiliated, behind a field-hockey stick and under a basketball hoop. I tramped alone for miles along the bri-dle paths that webbed the woods behind the house I grew up in. I swayed through countless dim hours in the arms of one man or another under the scattered shot of light from mirrored balls, and gyrated through countless more as Tab Hunter and Johnny Mathis gave way to the Rolling Stones, Creedence Clearwater Revival, Cream. I walked down the aisle. I pushed baby carriages, changed tires in the rain, marched for peace.

When I was twenty-eight I started to trip and drop things. What at first seemed my natural clumsiness soon became too pronounced to shrug off. I consulted a neurologist, who told me that I had a brain tumor. A battery of tests, increasingly disagreeable, revealed no tumor. About a year and a half later I developed a blurred spot in one eye. I had, at last, the episodes "disseminated in space and time" requisite for a diagnosis: multiple sclerosis. I have never been sorry for the doctor's initial misdiagnosis, however. For almost a week, until the negative results of the tests were in, I thought that I was going to die right away. Every day for the past nearly ten years, then, has been a kind of gift. I accept all gifts.

Multiple sclerosis is a chronic degenerative disease of the central nervous system, in which the myelin that sheathes the nerves is somehow catcn away and scar tissue forms in its place, interrupting the nerves' signals. During its course, which is unpredictable and uncontrollable, one may lose vision, hearing, speech, the ability to walk, control of bladder and/or bowels, strength in any or all extremities, sensitivity to touch, vibration, and/or pain, potency, coordination of movements—the list of possibilities is lengthy and, yes, horrifying. One may also lose one's sense of humor. That's the easiest to lose and the hardest to survive without.

In the past ten years, I have sustained some of these losses. Characteristic of MS are sudden attacks, called exacerbations, followed by remissions, and these I have not had. Instead, my disease has been slowly progressive. My left leg is now so weak that I walk with the aid of a brace and a cane; and for distances I use an Amigo, a variation on the electric wheelchair that looks rather like an electrified kiddie car. I no longer have much use of my left hand. Now my right side is weakening as well. I still have the blurred spot in my right eye. Overall, though, I've been lucky so far. My world has, of necessity, been circumscribed by my losses, but the terrain left me has been ample enough for me to continue many of the activities that absorb me: writing, teaching, raising children and cats and plants and snakes, reading, speaking publicly about MS and depression, even playing bridge with people patient and honorable enough to let me scatter cards every which way without sneaking a peek.

Lest I begin to sound like Pollyanna, however, let me say that I don't like having MS. I hate it. My life holds realities—harsh ones, some of them—that no right-minded human being ought to accept without grumbling. One of them is fatigue. I know of no one with MS who does not complain of bone-weariness; in a disease that presents an astonishing variety of symptoms, fatigue seems to be a common factor. I wake up in the morning feeling the way most people do at the end of a bad day, and I take it from there. As a result, I spend a lot of time in extremis and, impatient with limitation, I tend to ignore my fatigue until my body breaks down in some way and forces rest. Then I miss picnics, dinner parties, poetry readings, the brief visits of old friends from out of town. The offspring of a puritanical tradition of exceptional venerability, I cannot view these lapses without shame. My life often seems a series of small failures to do as I ought.

I lead, on the whole, an ordinary life, probably rather like the one I would have led had I not had MS. I am lucky that my predilections were already solitary, sedentary, and bookish—unlike the world-famous French cellist I have read about, or the young woman I talked with one long afternoon who wanted only to be a jockey. I had just begun graduate school when I found out something was wrong with me, and I have remained, interminably, a graduate student. Perhaps I would not have if I'd thought I had the stamina to return to a full-time job as a technical editor; but I've enjoyed my studies.

In addition to studying, I teach writing courses. I also teach medical students how to give neurological examinations. I pick up freelance editing jobs here and there. I have raised a foster son and sent him into the world, where he has made me two grandbabies, and I am still escorting my daughter and son through adolescence. I go to Mass every Saturday. I am a superb, if messy, cook. I am also an enthusiastic laundress, capable of sorting a hamper full of clothes into five subtly differentiated piles, but a terrible housekeeper. I can do italic writing and, in an emergency, bathe an oil-soaked cat. I play a fiendish game of Scrabble. When I have the time and the money, I like to sit on my front steps with my husband, drinking Amaretto and smoking a cigar, as we imagine our counterparts in Leningrad and make sure that the sun gets down once more behind the sharp childish scrawl of the Tucson Mountains.

This lively plenty has its bleak complement, of course, in all the things I can no longer do. I will never run again, except in dreams, and one day I may have to write that I will never walk again. I like to go camping, but I can't follow George and the children along the trails that wander out of a campsite through the desert or into the mountains. In fact, even on the level I've learned never to check the weather or try to hold a coherent conversation: I need all my attention for my wayward feet. Of late, I have begun to catch myself wondering how people can propel themselves without canes. With only one usable hand, I have to select my clothing with care not so much for style as for ease of ingress and egress, and even so, dressing can be laborious. I can no longer do fine stitchery, pick up babies, play the piano, braid my hair. I am immobilized by acute attacks of depression, which may or may not be physiologically related to MS but are certainly its logical concomitant.

These two elements, the plenty and the privation, are never pure, nor are the delight and wretchedness that accompany them. Almost every pickle that I get into as a result of my weakness and clumsiness—and I get into plenty—is funny as well as maddening and sometimes painful. I recall one May afternoon when a friend and I were going out for a drink after finishing up at school. As we were climbing into opposite sides of my car, chatting, I tripped and fell, flat and hard, onto the asphalt parking lot, my abrupt departure interrupting him in mid-sentence. "Where'd you go?" he called as he came around the back of the car to find me hauling myself up by the door frame. "Are you all right?" Yes, I told him, I was fine, just a bit rattly, and we drove off to find a shady patio and some beer. When I got home an hour or so later, my daughter greeted me with "What have you done to yourself?" I looked down. One elbow of my white turtleneck with the green froggies, one knee of my white trousers, one white kneesock were blood-soaked. We peeled off the clothes and inspected the damage, which was nasty enough but not alarming. That part wasn't funny: The abrasions took a long time to heal, and one got a little infected. Even so, when I think of my friend talking earnestly, suddenly, to the hot thin air while I dropped from his view as though through a trap door, I find the image as silly as something from a Marx Brothers movie.

I may find it easier than other cripples to amuse myself because I live propped by the acceptance and the assistance and, sometimes, the amusement of those around me. Grocery clerks tear my checks out of my checkbook for me, and sales clerks find chairs to put into dressing rooms when I want to try on clothes. The people I work with make sure I teach at times when I am least likely to be fatigued, in places I can get to, with the materials I need. My students, with one anonymous exception (in an end-of-the-semester evaluation), have been unperturbed by my disability. Some even like it. One was immensely cheered by the information that I paint my own fingernails; she decided, she told me, that if I could go to such trouble over fine details, she could keep on writing essays. I suppose I became some sort of bright-fingered muse. She wrote good essays, too.

The most important struts in the framework of my existence, of course, are my husband and children. Dismayingly few marriages survive the MS test, and why should they? Most twenty-two- and nineteen-year-olds, like George and me, can vow in clear conscience, after a childhood of chicken pox and summer colds, to keep one another in sickness and in health so long as they both shall live. Not many are equipped for catastrophe: the dismay, the depression, the extra work, the boredom that a degenerative disease can insinuate into a relationship. And our society, with its emphasis on fun and its association of fun with physical performance, offers little encouragement for a whole spouse to stay with a crippled partner. Children experience similar stresses when faced with a crippled parent, and they are more helpless, since parents and children can't usually get divorced. They hate, of course, to be different from their peers, and the child whose mother is tacking down the aisle of a school auditorium packed with proud parents like a Cape Cod dinghy in a stiff breeze jolly well stands out in a crowd. Deprived of legal divorce, the child can at least deny the mother's disability, even her existence, forgetting to tell her about recitals and PTA meetings, refusing to accompany her to stores or church or the movies, never inviting friends to the house. Many do.

But I've been limping along for ten years now, and so far George and the children are still at my left elbow, holding tight. Anne and Matthew vacuum floors and dust furniture and haul trash and rake up dog droppings and button my cuffs and bake lasagna and Toll House cookies with just enough grumbling so I know that they don't have brain fever. And far from hiding me, they're forever dragging me by racks of fancy clothes or through teeming school corridors, or welcoming gaggles of friends while I'm wandering through the house in Anne's filmy pink babydoll pajamas. George generally calls before he brings someone home, but he does just as many dumb thankless chores as the children. And they all yell at me, laugh at some of my jokes, write me funny letters when we're apart—in short, treat me as an ordinary human being for whom they have some use. I think they like me. Unless they're faking....

Faking. There's the rub. Tugging at the fringes of my consciousness always is the terror that people are kind to me only because I'm a cripple. My mother almost shattered me once, with that instinct mothers have—blind, I think, in this case, but unerring nonetheless—for striking blows along the fault-lines of their children's hearts, by telling me, in an attack on my selfishness, "We all have to make allowances for you, of course, because of the way you are." From the distance of a couple of years, I have to admit that I haven't any idea just what she meant, and I'm not sure that she knew either. She was awfully angry. But at the time, as the words thudded home, I felt my worst fear, suddenly realized. I could bear being called selfish: I am. But I couldn't bear the corroboration that those around me were doing in fact what I'd always suspected them of doing, professing fondness while silently putting up with me because of the way I am. A cripple. I've been a little cracked ever since.

Along with this fear that people are secretly accepting shoddy goods comes a relentless pressure to please—to prove myself worth the burdens I impose, I guess, or to build a substantial account of goodwill against which I may write drafts in times of need. Part of the pressure arises from social expectations. In our society, anyone who deviates from the norm had better find some way to compensate. Like fat people, who are expected to be jolly, cripples must bear their lot meekly and cheerfully. A grumpy cripple isn't playing by the rules. And much of the pressure is self-generated. Early on I vowed that, if I had to have MS, by God I was going to do it well. This is a class act, ladies and gentlemen. No tears, no recriminations, no faintheartedness.

One way and another, then, I wind up feeling like Tiny Tim, peering over the edge of the table at the Christmas goose, waving my crutch, piping down God's blessing on us all. Only sometimes I don't want to play Tiny Tim. I'd rather be Caliban, a most scurvy monster. Fortunately, at home no one much cares whether I'm a good cripple or a bad cripple as long as I make vichyssoise with fair regularity. One evening several years ago, Anne was reading at the dining-room table while I cooked dinner. As I opened a can of tomatoes, the can slipped in my left hand and juice spattered me and the counter with bloody spots. Fatigued and infuriated, I bellowed, "I'm so sick of being crippled!" Anne glanced at me over the top of her book. "There now," she said, "do you feel better?" "Yes," I said, "yes, I do." She went back to her reading. I felt better. That's about all the attention my scurviness ever gets.

Because I hate being crippled, I sometimes hate myself for being a cripple. Over the years I have come to expect—even accept—attacks of violent self-loathing. Luckily, in general our society no longer connects deformity and disease directly with evil (though a charismatic once told me that I have MS because a devil is in me) and so I'm allowed to move largely at will, even among small children. But I'm not sure that this revision of attitude has been particularly helpful. Physical imperfection, even freed of moral disapprobation, still defies and violates the ideal, especially for women, whose confinement in their bodies as objects of desire is far from over. Each age, of course, has its ideal, and I doubt that ours is any better or worse than any other. Today's ideal woman, who lives on the glossy pages of dozens of magazines, seems to be between the ages of eighteen and twenty-five; her hair has body, her teeth flash white, her breath smells minty, her underarms are dry; she has a career but is still a fabulous cook, especially of meals that take less than twenty minutes to prepare; she does not ordinarily appear to have a husband or children; she is trim and deeply tanned; she jogs, swims, plays tennis, rides a bicycle, sails, but does not bowl; she travels widely, even to out-of-the-way places like Finland and Samoa, always in the company of the ideal man, who possesses a nearly identical set of characteristics. There are a few exceptions. Though usually white and often blonde, she may be black, Hispanic, Asian, or Native American, so long as she is unusually sleek. She may be old, provided she is selling a laxative or is Lauren Bacall. If she is selling a detergent, she may be married and have a flock of strikingly messy children. But she is never a cripple.

Like many women I know, I have always had an uneasy relationship with my body. I was not a popular child, largely, I think now, because I was peculiar: intelligent, intense, moody, shy, given to unexpected actions and inexplicable notions and emotions. But as I entered adolescence, I believed myself unpopular because I was homely: my breasts too flat, my mouth too wide, my hips too narrow, my clothing never quite right in fit or style. I was not, in fact, particularly ugly, old photographs inform me, though I was well off the ideal; but I carried this sense of self-alienation with me into adulthood, where it regenerated in response to the depredations of MS. Even with my brace I walk with a limp so pronounced that, seeing myself on the videotape of a television program on the disabled, I couldn't believe that anything but an inchworm could make progress humping along like that. My shoulders droop and my pelvis thrusts forward as I try to balance myself upright, throwing my frame into a bony S. As a result of contractures, one shoulder is higher that the other and I carry one arm bent in front of me, the fingers curled into a claw. My left arm and leg have wasted into pipe-stems, and I try always to keep them covered. When I think about how my body must look to others, especially to men, to whom I have been trained to display myself, I feel ludicrous, even loathsome.

At my age, however, I don't spend much time thinking about my appearance. The burning egocentricity of adolescence, which assures one that all the world is looking all the time, has passed, thank God, and I'm generally too caught up in what I'm doing to step back, as I used to, and watch myself as though upon a stage. I'm also too old to believe in the accuracy of self-image. I know that I'm not a hideous crone, that in fact, when I'm rested, well dressed, and well made up, I look fine. The self-loathing I feel is neither physically nor intellectually substantial. What I hate is not me but a disease.

I am not a disease.

And a disease is not—at least not single-handedly—going to determine who I am, though at first it seemed to be going to. Adjusting to a chronic incurable illness, I have moved through a process similar to that outlined by Elizabeth Kubler-Ross in On Death and Dying. The major difference—and it is far more significant than most people recognize—is that I can't be sure of the outcome, as the terminally ill cancer patient can. Research studies indicate that, with proper medical care, I may achieve a "normal" life span. And in our society, with its vision of death as the ultimate evil, worse even than decrepitude, the response to such news is, "Oh well, at least you're not going to die." Are there worse things than dying? I think that there may be.

I think of two women I know, both with MS, both enough older than I to have served me as models. One took to her bed several years ago and has been there ever since. Although she can sit in a high-backed wheelchair, because she is incontinent she refuses to go out at all, even though incontinence pants, which are readily available at any pharmacy, could protect her from embarrassment. Instead, she stays at home and insists that her husband, a small quiet man, a retired civil servant, stay there with her except for a quick weekly foray to the supermarket. The other woman, whose illness was diagnosed when she was eighteen, a nursing student engaged to a young doctor, finished her training, married her doctor, accompanied him to Germany when he was in the service, bore three sons and a daughter, now grown and gone. When she can, she travels with her husband; she plays bridge, embroiders, swims regularly; she works, like me, as a symptomatic-patient instructor of medical students in neurology. Guess which woman I hope to be.

At the beginning, I thought about having MS almost incessantly. And because of the unpredictable course of the disease, my thoughts were always terrified. Each night I'd get into bed wondering whether I'd get out again the next morning, whether I'd be able to see, to speak, to hold a pen between my fingers. Knowing that the day might come when I'd be physically incapable of killing myself, I thought perhaps I ought to do so right away, while I still had the strength. Gradually I came to understand that the Nancy who might one day lie inert under a bedsheet, arms and legs paralyzed, unable to feed or bathe herself, unable to reach out for a gun, a bottle of pills, was not the Nancy I was at present, and that I could not presume to make decisions for that future Nancy, who might well not want in the least to die. Now the only provision I've made for the future Nancy is that when the time comes—and it is likely to come in the form of pneumonia, friend to the weak and the old—I am not to be treated with machines and medications. If she is unable to communicate by then, I hope she will be satisfied with these terms.

Thinking all the time about having MS grew tiresome and intrusive, especially in the large and tragic mode in which I was accustomed to considering my plight. Months and even years went by without catastrophe (at least without one related to MS), and really I was awfully busy, what with George and children and snakes and students and poems, and I hadn't the time, let alone the inclination, to devote myself to being a disease. Too, the richer my life became, the funnier it seemed, as though there were some connection between largesse and laughter, and so my tragic stance began to waver until, even with the aid of a brace and a cane, I couldn't hold it for very long at a time.

After several years I was satisfied with my adjustment. I had suffered my grief and fury and terror, I thought, but now I was at ease with my lot. Then one summer day I set out with George and the children across the desert for a vacation in California. Part way to Yuma I became aware that my right leg felt funny. "I think I've had an exacerbation," I told George. "What shall we do?" he asked. "I think we'd better get the hell to California," I said, "because I don't know whether I'll ever make it again." So we went on to San Diego and then to Orange, up the Pacific Coast Highway to Santa Cruz, across to Yosemite, down to Sequoia and Joshua Tree, and so back over the desert to home. It was a fine two-week trip, filled with friends and fair weather, and I wouldn't have missed it for the world, though I did in fact make it back to California two years later. Nor would there have been any point in missing it, since in MS, once the symptoms have appeared, the neurological damage has been done, and there's no way to predict or prevent that damage.

The incident spoiled my self-satisfaction, however. It renewed my grief and fury and terror, and I learned that one never finishes adjusting to MS. I don't know now why I thought one would. One does not, after all, finish adjusting to life, and MS is simply a fact of my life—not my favorite fact, of course—but as ordinary as my nose and my tropical fish and my yellow

Mazda station wagon. It may at any time get worse, but no amount of worry or anticipation can prepare me for a new loss. My life is a lesson in losses. I learn one at a time.

And I had best be patient in the learning, since I'll have to do it like it or not. As any rock fan knows, you can't always get what you want. Particularly when you have MS. You can't, for example, get cured. In recent years researchers and the organizations that fund research have started to pay MS some attention even though it isn't fatal; perhaps they have begun to see that life is something other than a quantitative phenomenon, that one may be very much alive for a very long time in a life that isn't worth living. The researchers have made some progress toward understanding the mechanism of the disease: It may well be an autoimmune reaction triggered by a slow-acting virus. But they are nowhere near its prevention, control, or cure. And most of us want to be cured. Some, unable to accept incurability, grasp at one treatment after another; no matter how bizarre: megavitamin therapy, gluten-free diet, injections of cobra venom, hypothermal suits, lymphocytopharesjs, hyperbaric chambers. Many treatments are probably harmless enough, but none are curative.

The absence of a cure often makes MS patients bitter toward their doctors. Doctors are, after all, the priests of modern society, the new shamans, whose business is to heal, and many an MS patient roves from one to another, searching for the "good" doctor who will make him well. Doctors too think of themselves as healers, and for this reason many have trouble dealing with MS patients, whose disease in its intransigence defeats their aims and mocks their skills. Too few doctors, it is true, treat their patients as whole human beings, but the reverse is also true. I have always tried to be gentle with my doctors, who often have more at stake in terms of ego than I do. I may be frustrated, maddened, depressed by the incurability of my disease, but I am not diminished by it, and they are. When I push myself up from my seat in the waiting room and stumble toward them, I incarnate the limitation of their powers. The least I can do is refuse to press on their tenderest spots.

This gentleness is part of the reason that I'm not sorry to be a cripple. I didn't have it before. Perhaps I'd have developed it anyway—how could I know such a thing?—and I wish I had more of it, but I'm glad of what I have. It has opened and enriched my life enormously. This sense that my frailty and need must be mirrored in others, that in searching for and shaping a stable core in a life wrenched by change and loss, change and loss, I must recognize the same process, under individual conditions, in the lives around me. I do not deprecate such knowledge, however I've come by it.

All the same, if a cure were found, would I take it? In a minute. I may be a cripple, but I'm only occasionally a loony and never a saint. Anyway, in my brand of theology God doesn't give bonus points for a limp. I'd take a cure; I just don't need one. A friend who also has MS startled me once by asking, "Do you ever say to yourself, 'Why me, Lord?'" "No, Michael, I don't," I told him, "because whenever I try, the only response I can think of is 'Why not?'" If I could make a cosmic deal, whom would I put in my place? What in my life would I give up in exchange for sound limbs and a thrilling rush of energy? No one. Nothing. I might as well do the job myself. Now that I'm getting the hang of it.

Black Men in Public Spaces

by Brent Staples (1986)

My first victim was a woman—white, well dressed, probably in her early twenties. I came upon her late one evening on a deserted street in Hyde Park, a relatively affluent neighborhood in an otherwise mean, impoverished section of Chicago. As I swung onto the avenue behind her, there seemed to be a discreet, uninflammatory distance between us. Not so. She cast back a worried glance. To her, the youngish black man—a broad six feet two inches with a beard and billowing hair, both hands shoved into the pockets of a bulky military jacket—seemed menacingly close. After a few more quick glimpses, she picked up her pace and was soon running in earnest. Within seconds she disappeared into a cross street.

That was more than a decade ago. I was twenty-two years old, a graduate student newly arrived at the University of Chicago. It was in the echo of that terrified woman's footfalls that I first began to know the unwieldy inheritance I'd come into—the ability to alter public space in ugly ways. It was clear that she thought herself the quarry of a mugger, a rapist, or worse. Suffering a bout of insomnia, however, I was stalking sleep, not defenseless wayfarers. As a softy who is scarcely able to take a knife to a raw chicken—let alone hold it to a person's throat—I was surprised, embarrassed, and dismayed all at once. Her flight made me feel like an accomplice in tyranny. It also made it clear that I was indistinguishable from the muggers who occasionally seeped into the area from the surrounding ghetto. That first encounter, and those that followed, signified that a vast, unnerving gulf lay between nighttime pedestrians—particularly women—and me. And I soon gathered that being perceived as dangerous is a hazard in itself. I only needed to turn a corner into a dicey situation, or crowd some frightened, armed person in a foyer somewhere, or make an errant move after being pulled over by a policeman. Where fear and weapons meet—and they often do in urban America—there is always the possibility of death.

In that first year, my first away from my hometown, I was to become thoroughly familiar with the language of fear. At dark, shadowy intersections in Chicago, I could cross in front of a car stopped at a traffic light and

Staples, Brent. "Black Men in Public Spaces," 1986. Reprinted by permission of the author.

163

elicit the thunk, thunk, thunk, thunk of the driver—black, white, male, or female—hammering down the door locks. On less traveled streets after dark, I grew accustomed to but never comfortable with people who crossed to the other side of the street rather than pass me. Then there were the standard unpleasantries with police, doormen, bouncers, cabdrivers, and others whose business is to screen out troublesome individuals before there is any nastiness.

I moved to New York nearly two years ago and I have remained an avid night walker. In central Manhattan, the near-constant crowd cover minimizes tense one-on-one street encounters. Elsewhere—visiting friends in SoHo, where sidewalks are narrow and tightly spaced buildings shut out the sky—things can get very taut indeed.

Black men have a firm place in New York mugging literature. Norman Podhoretz in his famed (or infamous) 1963 essay, "My Negro Problem— And Ours," recalls growing up in terror of black males; they "were tougher than we were, more ruthless," he writes—and as an adult on the Upper West Side of Manhattan, he continues, he cannot constrain his nervousness when he meets black men on certain streets. Similarly, a decade later, the essayist and novelist Edward Hoagland extols a New York where once "Negro bitterness bore down mainly on other Negroes." Where some see mere panhandlers, Hoagland sees "a mugger who is clearly screwing up his nerve to do more than just ask for money." But Hoagland has "the New Yorker's quick-hunch posture for broken-field maneuvering," and the bad guy swerves away.

I often witness that "hunch posture," from women after dark on the warrenlike streets of Brooklyn where I live. They seem to set their faces on neutral and, with their purse straps strung across their chests bandolier style, they forge ahead as though bracing themselves against being tackled. I understand, of course, that the danger they perceive is not a hallucination. Women are particularly vulnerable to street violence, and young black males are drastically overrepresented among the perpetrators of that violence. Yet these truths are no solace against the kind of alienation that comes of being ever the suspect, against being set apart, a fearsome entity with whom pedestrians avoid making eye contact.

It is not altogether clear to me how I reached the ripe old age of twenty-two without being conscious of the lethality nighttime pedestrians attributed to me. Perhaps it was because in Chester, Pennsylvania, the small, angry industrial town where I came of age in the 1960s, I was scarcely noticeable against a backdrop of gang warfare, street knifings, and murders.

I grew up one of the good boys, had perhaps a half-dozen fistfights. In retrospect, my shyness of combat has clear sources.

Many things go into the making of a young thug. One of those things is the consummation of the male romance with the power to intimidate. An infant discovers that random flailings send the baby bottle flying out of the crib and crashing to the floor. Delighted, the joyful babe repeats those motions again and again, seeking to duplicate the feat. Just so, I recall the points at which some of my boyhood friends were finally seduced by the perception of themselves as tough guys. When a mark cowered and surrendered his money without resistance, myth and reality merged—and paid off. It is, after all, only manly to embrace the power to frighten and intimidate. We, as men, are not supposed to give an inch of our lane on the highway; we are to seize the fighter's edge in work and in play and even in love; we are to be valiant in the face of hostile forces.

Unfortunately, poor and powerless young men seem to take all this nonsense literally. As a boy, I saw countless tough guys locked away; I have since buried several, too. They were babies, really—a teenage cousin, a brother of twenty-two, a childhood friend in his midtwenties—all gone down in episodes of bravado played out in the streets. I came to doubt the virtues of intimidation early on. I chose, perhaps even unconsciously, to remain a shadow—timid, but a survivor.

The fearsomeness mistakenly attributed to me in public places often has a perilous flavor. The most frightening of these confusions occurred in the late 1970s and early 1980s when I worked as a journalist in Chicago. One day, rushing into the office of a magazine I was writing for with a deadline story in hand, I was mistaken for a burglar. The office manager called security and, with an ad hoc posse, pursued me through the labyrinthine halls, nearly to my editor's door. I had no way of proving who I was. I could only move briskly toward the company of someone who knew me.

Another time I was on assignment for a local paper and killing time before an interview. I entered a jewelry store on the city's affluent Near North Side. The proprietor excused herself and returned with an enormous red Doberman pinscher straining at the end of a leash. She stood, the dog extended toward me, silent to my questions, her eyes bulging nearly out of her head. I took a cursory look around, nodded, and bade her good night. Relatively speaking, however, I never fared as badly as another black male journalist. He went to nearby Waukegan, Illinois, a couple of summers ago to work on a story about a murderer who was born there.

Mistaking the reporter for the killer, police hauled him from his car at gunpoint and but for his press credentials would probably have tried to book him. Such episodes are not uncommon. Black men trade tales like this all the time.

In "My Negro Problem—And Ours," Podhoretz writes that the hatred he feels for blacks makes itself known to him through a variety of avenues—one being his discomfort with that "special brand of paranoid touchiness" to which he says blacks are prone. No doubt he is speaking here of black men. In time, I learned to smother the rage I felt at so often being taken for a criminal. Not to do so would surely have led to madness—via that special "paranoid touchiness" that so annoyed Podhoretz at the time he wrote the essay.

I began to take precautions to make myself less threatening. I move about with care, particularly late in the evening. I give a wide berth to nervous people on subway platforms during the wee hours, particularly when I have exchanged business clothes for jeans. If I happen to be entering a building behind some people who appear skittish, I may walk by, letting them clear the lobby before I return, so as not to seem to be following them. I have been calm and extremely congenial on those rare occasions when I've been pulled over by the police.

And on late-evening constitutionals along streets less traveled by, I employ what has proved to be an excellent tension-reducing measure: I whistle melodies from Beethoven and Vivaldi and the more popular classical composers. Even steely New Yorkers hunching toward nighttime destinations seem to relax, and occasionally they even join in the tune. Virtually everybody seems to sense that a mugger wouldn't be warbling bright, sunny selections from Vivaldi's Four Seasons. It is my equivalent of the cowbell that hikers wear when they know they are in bear country.

Chapter Three

The Op-Ed Essay Assignment

Assignment Overview

Opposite Editorial[1]

An Opposite Editorial (or "Op-Ed") is an opinion piece often published in newspapers and, more recently, in online publications. The term describes the common placement of an Op-Ed piece on the page *opposite the editorial*. Op-Eds can focus on major national or international news stories or on local issues. In general, Op-Eds are written to educate members of the public about an issue beyond what the media may already be covering and to persuade readers to consider the author's point of view or to take action on an issue. Op-Eds also help to build the ethos or credibility of a writer by adding an alternative voice to a conversation, a perspective that authorities may previously have overlooked. Like academic research papers, the Op-Ed requires you to find your own voice and perspective in an already-existing community of voices and perspectives.

---

1   This assignment is adapted in part from *Directory Journal*, <http://www.dirjournal.com/articles/ what-is-an-Op-Ed/>. Do not duplicate outside an educational setting without the permission of the authors, including the editors of *Directory Journal*.

Unlike the Researched Argument, however, the Op-Ed calls for a civic argument rather than an academic one.

Content and Audience

As we continue to develop strategies of invention, arrangement, and revision, and the relationships among these, you'll practice these now on a significant news issue. Focus your Op-Ed by considering how your insights add something new to a current conversation on an issue of cultural, political, or humanitarian significance. Discuss how that issue affects you and others on our campus, in your hometown, in our nation, or in the larger world.

To find a focus, reflect on the readings we do throughout the unit, taking notes on perspectives that you feel are missing from these readings, or on viewpoints that you feel are incompletely expressed. Some questions for you to consider are as follows:

- What voices are missing from the conversation?

- How do your own experiences influence an alternative perspective on the issue?

- Does the writer misinterpret or unfairly represent certain points of view?

- Does the writer "get it right," but still leave important perspectives out of the conversation?

As you write and revise your Op-Ed, you will integrate relevant research that will allow you to both support your views and distinguish them from the views of others who have written on the issue. Be aware that typically, strong Op-Eds do not simply take an "either/or" argument, but rather concentrate on nuances about the issue that may have been missed or underdeveloped. In other words, powerful Op-Eds say something new rather than rehashing the same tired arguments. Finally, remember that your Op-Ed should develop a strong, well-supported argument, and that it should address the Binghamton University first-year community; that is, fellow students and faculty, some of whom may have little knowledge of the conversation you are entering.

Organization and Format

There are many ways to organize your Op-Ed piece and, as a class, we will analyze sample Op-Eds in order to articulate a general understanding of the conventions of the genre. Considering these conventions, you will have to decide the best way to arrange your Op-Ed to make your argument clear and persuasive.

In order to practice the skills necessary for our final assignment of the semester—the Researched Argument—you are required to use summary, paraphrase, and direct quotation in your Op-Ed, to incorporate appropriate in-text parenthetical citations, and to develop an end-of-text Works Cited page. Use no fewer than four recent sources. As with other essays written in this class, please follow MLA guidelines for citation and format. Your Op-Ed must be no fewer than four full pages, but no more than five.

You will be required to turn in a topic proposal and a preliminary Works Cited.

● INVENTION: **Op-Eds, Editorials, and Front Page News**

- Are the Op-Eds written by regular Op-Ed columnists? Do you recognize any of the names?

- If not, what's the connection of the writer to the subject? (ethos)

- Are the editorials truly by the editors, or are they "guest editorials?"

- Are the Op-Eds responding to news stories covered by the paper or are they syndicated columns?

- What is the focus and tone of a couple of Letters to the Editor that the editors choose to run?

- How is the intended audience addressed?

- How do writers of editorials and Op-Eds intend to affect the reader? What action or attitude do they want the reader to take, after reading their column? Discuss any accompanying graphics, section headlines, etc.

- Describe what rhetorical techniques you find engaging in the Op-Eds that you have read and list possible techniques you might choose to incorporate into your own essay.

INVENTION: **Preserving Your Academic Integrity**

Part 1

Read the original passage carefully. Select the acceptable paraphrase. Give a one-to-two sentence explanation of why each of the other paraphrases is unacceptable:

The original:

> "If each former smoker in the U.S. were given a yearly CT scan, lung-cancer mortality could be cut by 20%. But detection on that scale would require easier, cheaper tests. Researchers are developing a simpler blood test for a serum protein marker that could detect lung cancer earlier." (Saporito 34)

Paraphrase A

Lung cancer mortality, which often affects former smokers, could be reduced by as much as 20% if patients received a yearly CT scan. However, to achieve that rate of detection, it is necessary to develop less difficult and less expensive tests. Scientists are working on a less complicated blood test for a serum protein marker that would detect lung cancer in former smokers even earlier—and much less expensively—than an annual CT scan would (Saporito 34).

Paraphrase B

A major barrier to detecting cancer is cost. Death by lung cancer could decline by as much as one-fifth if former smokers underwent expensive CT scans annually. A blood test currently under development would detect lung cancer both earlier and much more cheaply (Saporito 34).

Paraphrase C

If everyone who had ever smoked underwent yearly CT scans, death by lung cancer could wane by one-fifth. However, the cost of performing such screening would be prohibitive. Therefore, researchers are working on a blood test to detect a substance in the blood that people with lung cancer have. The test would detect cancer even earlier than a CT scan would (Saporito 34).

Paraphrase D

20% of all people who smoke will develop lung cancer. CT scans can detect cancer early, but they are expensive and most insurance companies will not pay for a yearly CT scan. Researchers are working on a blood test that would detect lung cancer earlier than even a CT scan would and would be cheaper to administer (Saporito 34).

Paraphrase E

If every prior cigarette smoker in the United States received a Computed Tomography examination on an annual basis, lung-cancer death might be reduced by 20 percent. But detection of that magnitude would necessitate less difficult, more economical examinations. Investigators are creating a less complicated blood test for a serum protein indicator that can identify lung cancer more promptly (Saporito 34).

Part 2

Which of the following kinds of information do you need to cite?

a. quotations

b. facts in your geology textbook

c. contested theories in your geology textbook

d. loose paraphrase of the author's words or ideas

e. passages of your essay that you bought from the Internet

f. summary of an author's ideas that is not in the author's words

g. proverbs and folk-sayings

h. your own original ideas

i. essays published in academic journals

j. anything that TurnItIn recognizes as coming from another source

k. ideas you've had that you encounter in another writer's work

l. a chart, graph, or other visual text created by another person

m. a chart, graph, or other visual text that you create to illustrate others' data

n. knowledge or opinions you gained by speaking with others

o. photos, videos, compositions, or any other kind of artwork you have created

p. statistics

Part 3

Which of the following will *not* endanger your academic integrity?

a. recycling an essay you wrote or are writing for another class

b. asking mom or dad to revise your essay

c. talking with a friend, roommate, or classmate about your ideas

d. taking your paper to the Writing Center

e. praying

f. visiting paper sites on the internet just to get some ideas

g. consulting your research handbook to confirm you're not plagiarizing

h. talking to your instructor in class or in office hours

i. lending a draft to a friend in another section, class, or school—just for ideas

j. borrowing another's draft—just for ideas

k. exchanging essays during peer review that your instructor arranges

l. buying part or all of your paper

m. accepting part or all of your paper from a friend who hates seeing you struggle

n. changing your topic after your instructor approves it and before submitting your final portfolio

o. putting a subtle spin on the author's words to support your argument

Part 4

Which of the following will help you to avoid *unintentional* plagiarism?

a. performing the tasks in the order in which they're assigned

b. asking your instructor about anything you're uncertain about

c. meeting all deadlines for assigned work (including proposals/abstracts; annotated bibliography; peer-review, polished, and conference drafts)

d. reminding yourself that you've always worked best under pressure

e. considering that learning college-level research and writing will help you in all your classes

f. praying

g. substituting synonyms for every fifth word of the original

h. carefully noting the source and page number for each summary, paraphrase, and quotation

i. compiling your Works Cited page at the same time you write your essay

j. introducing borrowed words and ideas with a signal phrase that includes the author's name

k. summarizing or paraphrasing while not looking at the original, then checking that your summary or paraphrase is both accurate and in your own words

l. practicing good time management skills

m. writing about a topic that you care about and figuring out what you want to say about it

n. recognizing that college writing is more complex than high school writing

o. understanding that your reader is interested in your contribution to the discussion you've entered into

INVENTION: **Group Response Questions**

On the top of the paper to be submitted on behalf of your group, write the title of the reading or readings your group was asked to discuss. Respond to the following prompts in relation to the essay, essays, or visual argument your group has been assigned.

1. In a few sentences, summarize (don't quote) the writer's thesis or intended meaning.

2. Describe the uses of ethos, pathos, and logos in the essay. Where, how, and why are these appeals used? Are they effective? Why or why not? If any of these strategies is not present, how might the writer incorporate it into the essay?

3. Describe the overall tone of this essay. Highlight at least two passages from the essay to illustrate your point.

4. Describe the structure of this essay.

5. Describe alternative perspectives on the issue discussed in the essay.

6. Develop at least two thesis statements that you could develop if you chose this topic to focus your Op-Ed essay. How could you approach the issue in different or perhaps more nuanced ways?

● REVISION: **Reader-Response Comment Sheet**

Please place the following identifying information at the top of a piece of loose-leaf paper and clearly label your responses "Step 1," Step 2," etc. If you find you're repeating yourself, you may want to reference a previous response.

For the Writer: Before distributing your paper to peers, write out the specific kind of feedback you are looking for on your draft. Use the space in the heading of your paper to do so.

For the Reader: As you read your colleague's draft, challenge yourself to offer constructive feedback and to engage in the process with integrity. Label your responses "Step #1, #2," etc.

STEP #1: Read the essay completely through (without commenting on it) once. Give feedback on the issues the writer has identified.

STEP #2: Read the essay again, asking facilitative questions. In other words, ask questions that push the writer to think further or to consider something in a new light. (Why or how might some people pose counterarguments? What does the writer still need to consider?)

STEP #3: Focus on the introductory paragraph. Does it catch your attention? If so, tell the writer specifically why it is working. If not, make a concrete suggestion that might make the introduction stronger.

STEP #4: Read for a thesis statement. If you find one, note a) what paragraph you found it in; and b) whether or not it is clear. Then, restate the thesis in your own language. If you do not find a thesis statement or it is unclear, brainstorm one that might be appropriate for the paper.

STEP #5: As you read further, list the points that the writer makes in support of the argument. Comment on whether these points are clear, logical, etc. Is the writer's voice in control of the essay, or are sources dominating it? While source integration is important, let the writer know if you do not hear his or her voice in the paper, or don't hear it enough. Also, let the writer know if sources are integrated properly: are sources clearly introduced with author credentials, title, source context/summary, in-text citations and Works Cited entries?

STEP #6: Look for places where the writer needs to consider alternate points of view or interpretations. Can you think of ways in which some readers might disagree with the writer that he or she doesn't address? How would you engage such readers? Do you think that the writer fairly represents a range of views or interpretations? List your advice here.

STEP #7: Comment on the structure and organization of the essay. Are paragraphs or sections introduced with clear topic sentences that relate back to the thesis? Are transitions effective and clear? Make specific suggestions if you have any advice on how to develop more effective organizational strategies.

STEP #8: Do you see repeated punctuation or grammar errors? List here what those are and the paragraphs where the writer might find them.

STEP #9: Reflect on the "Characteristics of ABCD Writing." What is the most important piece of advice you would give the writer considering these evaluation criteria? What do you think is strongest about the paper in its present stage in regard to these evaluation criteria? Be specific when answering both questions.

STEP #10: List here any additional evaluation criteria your instructor may ask you to consider.

● REFLECTION: Op-Ed Essay Cover Letter

Statement Guidelines: Approximately 200 Words

Please consider the following categories in the format of an informal statement addressed to your instructor. You are not obligated to discuss all of these questions; instead, answer the three or four that will give your instructor the best insight into the present status of your draft. Instructors use these statements to guide their feedback, so do your best to reflect on both the strengths and weaknesses of your essay.

Before You Write Your Cover Letter

Prior to putting pen to paper, consider your most recent draft of the Op-Ed carefully.

Question 1: Getting Started

How did you start your Op-Ed? Did you take notes on the strategies writers used in the essays you found intriguing? Did you use in-class writing to identify a focus? Did you reread Op-Ed essays you found stimulating? Did you just jump in and draft from top to bottom? Or did you start in some other way? How did this process work or not work? Do you wish you had started differently? How did starting the Op-Ed differ from the way you started the Personal Essay?

Question 2: Focusing

What is your purpose with this piece? How was this different from the purpose of the Personal Essay? What thesis did you hope to communicate? Is this your original focus or has it changed? What opportunities can you imagine for refocusing in the future?

Question 3: Revising

During peer review, what advice did you seek from your classmates? What specific concerns and praise did they offer? What revision decisions did you decide to make and implement?

Question 4: What's Working Well? What's Not?

What are you happiest with in this piece? Did you try a particular technique that seemed to work for you? Did your workshop or peer group confirm that? What are you still dissatisfied with? Were there any approaches or techniques that you were trying out that didn't seem to work in your piece?

Question 5: Goals for Future Revision

When you revise this piece for your final portfolio, what priorities will you set for revision? What are your specific goals for improvement?

Question 6: Characteristics of ABCD Writing

Take a few minutes to reflect on the major criteria in the "Characteristics of ABCD Writing." Which of the three criteria (Content, Organization, Style and Mechanics) do you feel most confident about? Which one are you the least confident about? Why? Use the language within the criteria to help you determine your draft's strengths and weaknesses.

Preface to Related Reading

During this unit, you will take a library tutorial with your instructor and classmates, learn the conventions of research writing—most importantly, how to signal to your reader that you understand the contribution of other writers to your own work—and immerse yourself in a genre that's probably new to you: the civic argument, of which the Op-Ed is one example. While there are not many readings included in this textbook, you'll read lots of samples and examples of this genre, in *Binghamton Writes* and in current news publications, as you produce an Op-Ed yourself.

The Op-Ed is a timely response to a current situation, so it's important to keep up to date with whichever situation you're writing about. If you've never been a news follower, that will be a new role that you'll need to take on. Here are some resources to help you succeed in that new role and in this new genre.

- Check Blackboard. Your instructor will likely have readings and other resources there for you to read and discuss in class.

- Check the site www.dailyoped.com for samples of current and older editorials and Op-Eds from major newspapers.

- Many students find www.theopedproject.org to be of help in understanding why it's important to exercise their civic voice in this genre.

- Your instructor will help you to understand the library resources available to you, but in the meantime, check them out yourself. As a member of the Binghamton University community, you have free access to all the major newspapers and almost any smaller paper you can think of. There's no need to pay for news to succeed in research, and using the databases available will yield better results than using Google Scholar. Go to the Binghamton University Library homepage, then choose "Subject Guides" → "Writing 111."

  - That link will take you to "Resources for Writing 111." Explore the many links of that helpful page; it's there to help the hundreds of students who take Writing 111 each year to succeed in writing research papers, including the Op-Ed.

- Choose "Finding Articles" → "Current Events and News." You'll see nearly twenty databases listed. Take a few minutes to read the brief descriptions of each database and you'll see that some of them will be very helpful to you in this project. For example:

  · "Lexis-Nexis Academic" (a tutorial for using that database is on the Resources for WRIT 111 page) is a good place to start researching current issues.

  · "Access World News" will give you just that, plus *Pipe Dream* and likely even your hometown news.

  · "Gannet Newsstand" shows local and regional news across the country, including *Binghamton Press* and *Sun Bulletin.*

  · "ProQuest Congressional" enables you to research current and proposed legislation; that's what a lot of news, editorials, and Op-Eds are about.

  · "World News Connection" will show you sources that may not be in "National News Index" and can give an international perspective on major news.

  · A word of caution on "Opposing Viewpoints in Context": this can be a very helpful resource, but be sure to pay attention to the "in context" part. You want to show your understanding of multiple perspectives on important topics rather than taking a reductive "pro/con" approach.

Learn the skills, approaches, and techniques needed for this unit and you'll have a very good basis for the longest and most complex unit: the Researched Argument.

Related Reading

Rogerian Rhetoric: An Alternative to Traditional Rhetoric

by Douglas Brent, University of Calgary

As the Introduction to this volume points out, all of the approaches to argumentation collected here offer some form of alternative to the "argument as war" metaphor. In each approach, "argument" is redefined as one or another form of negotiated inquiry into common grounds for belief.

Rogerian rhetoric also moves away from a combative stance, but is distinct from other models of argumentation in three ways. First, it goes even farther than most other models in avoiding an adversarial approach. Second, it offers specific strategies based on nondirective therapy for building the co-operative bridges necessary for noncombative inquiry. Third, and in my opinion most important, it has the potential to offer students an opportunity for long-term cognitive and ethical growth.

Ever since Young, Becker and Pike introduced the discipline of composition to Rogerian rhetoric in 1970, our profession has remained deeply divided over whether such a rhetoric is conceptually sound, useful in practice, or even possible. Some have argued that it is nothing but warmed-over Aristotelian rhetoric (Lunsford 1979); others, that it is untrue to Carl Rogers' principles (Mader 1980), or that it is a cumbersome welding-together of persuasion and non-directive therapy, two fundamentally incompatible processes (Ede 1984). All of these criticisms point to real problems with the model, problems which often reflect the way it has been conceptualized by its proponents. Nonetheless, the literature of composition studies reflects a continuing fascination with Rogerian principles. Textbooks continue to suggest these principles as alternative methods of persuasion (Coe 1990; Flower 1993), and a recent collection edited by Nathaniel Teich (1992a) presents a wide variety of both philosophical and pedagogical investigations into Rogerian perspectives.

Brent, Douglas. Republished with permission of Sage Publications, from "Rogerian Rhetoric: Ethical Growth Through Alternative Forms of Argumentation" from *Argument Revisited, Argument Redefined: Negotiating Meaning in the Composition Classroom*. ed. Barbara Emmel, Paula Resch, and Deborah Tenney; permission conveyed through Copyright Clearance Center, Inc. © 1996.

In this chapter I will try to account for this continuing fascination with Rogerian rhetoric and explain what it can offer that no other approach to argumentation can quite match. To do so I will briefly survey the history of Rogerian rhetoric and outline its basic principles. Then I will discuss some of the ways in which Rogerian principles can be used in practice to teach both a technique of inquiry and an ethic of inquiry.

Background: Rogerian Therapy and Rogerian Rhetoric

Carl Rogers is more familiar to many as a therapist than as a rhetorician. However, the goal of therapy, like the goal of rhetoric, can be broadly described as "attitude change." Whereas the rhetorician may want his audience to adopt certain specific beliefs, the therapist may not—in fact, should not—have a clear model of specific behaviors which he wants the client to adopt in place of the dysfunctional ones that brought her into therapy in the first place. Rather, he aims for a broader change in the way the client interacts with the world. Nonetheless, the essence of both arts is to induce change through verbal means—Plato's "art of influencing the soul through words" (1956, 48).

Rogerian therapy informs rhetoric by offering a new way of thinking about the means of inducing change. Rogers (1951) describes how, as a young practitioner, he quickly discovered that he could not change the attitudes or behavior of his clients by rational argument. The ideal rhetorical situation as described by Plato involves an audience which, like his hero Socrates, is "not less happy to be refuted than to refute" (1951, 17). Alas, this attitude is rare among real, vulnerable human beings who are not characters in a Platonic dialogue. Clients in therapy, at the peak of their vulnerability, are particularly unhappy to be refuted. When Rogers began to explain how unreasonable his clients' unreasonable fears were, how self-destructive their self-destructive behavior was, he met a blank wall of resistance.

The problem, he decided, was that rational argument of this type always implies a form of evaluation. Argument may convince a person to buy this kind of car or to vote for that politician, but the closer the subject of argument comes to the beliefs that constitute the core of a person's sense of self, of identity, the more any attempt to change beliefs is perceived as a threat and met with walls of defence.

The way around these walls, Rogers discovered, was to change the role of the therapist. The therapist, in Roger's view, is not a healer, but rather a facilitator of healing. She does not explain her point of view to the client, but instead listens actively to the client as he gets in touch with his own thoughts and emotions and does his own healing.

For the art of rhetoric, the most immediately useful aspect of Rogerian therapy is the specific technique that Rogers developed to facilitate this self-healing process. This technique is called "restatement" or "saying back." Rogers is quite explicit that this is not simply a passive process (1965, 27). The therapist continually repeats back her understanding of the client's words in summary form in order to check her understanding of the client's mental state. Thus the therapist might say, "It sounds as though what you are really saying is that you hate your father." The client might respond, "No, that's not quite it," and the therapist would continue with more probes such as, "Well, perhaps you were just angry with him at that moment." Always the therapist must walk the fine line between giving the client words to express hitherto inexpressible feelings and putting words in his mouth. As a therapeutic tool, Rogerian reflection is both difficult—it can quickly degenerate into an irritating echo-chamber of voices—and breathtakingly successful when done well.

In this "pure" form, Rogerian therapy is not "argument." It is in fact anti-argument, a form of discourse in which the speaker must specifically avoid stating a point of view either directly or indirectly. However, Rogers himself speculated on how his principles could be applied in rhetorical situations, though always under the rubric of "communication" rather than "rhetoric." In his 1951 paper, "Communication: Its Blocking and its Facilitation," he proposes that the empathy and feedback model could be used to facilitate communication in emotion-laden situations outside the therapeutic relationship, such as political or labor negotiations. His formula is simple: "Each person can speak up for himself only after he has first restated the ideas and feelings of the previous speaker, and to that speaker's satisfaction" (332). In later articles he details Rogerian-style negotiation sessions that have produced astonishing results, including the Camp David negotiations conducted by Jimmy Carter, a conference involving health care providers and impoverished and embittered health care consumers, and even opposing sides in Northern Ireland (Rogers and Ryback 1984).

It is this power to create an atmosphere of co-operation that led Young, Becker and Pike to propose an alternative form of rhetoric based on Rogerian principles (1970). Rogerian rhetoric as recreated by Young, Becker and Pike is aimed at those situations in which more confrontational techniques are most apt to fail: that is, in highly emotional situations in which opposing sides fail to establish even provisional grounds for discussion. Young, Becker and Pike recommend that, rather than trying immediately to present arguments for her point of view and to refute her opponent's, the writer should first undertake a task similar to that of the Rogerian psychotherapist. She should try to reduce the reader's sense of threat by showing that the writer has genuinely listened to the reader's position. This reduction of threat will in turn induce an "assumption of similarity": the reader will see the writer as a human being more or less like herself and therefore be more likely to listen to what the writer has to say.

Although they argue that it should not be reduced to a mechanical formula, Young, Becker and Pike outline four basic stages through which a Rogerian argument should pass:

1. An introduction to the problem and a demonstration that the opponent's position is understood.

2. A statement of the contexts in which the opponent's position may be valid.

3. A statement of the writer's position, including the contexts in which it is valid.

4. A statement of how the opponent's position would benefit if he were to adopt elements of the writer's position. If the writer can show that the positions complement each other, that each supplies what the other lacks, so much the better. (283)

Not every version of Rogerian rhetoric emphasises exactly these stages, but the common denominator among all versions is that the writer must state the opposing viewpoint first, before stating her own, and do so honestly, with understanding, and without either overt or covert evaluation.

Rogerian Rhetoric in the Writing Classroom

Beginning with Maxine Hairston's seminal article (1976), a number of writers have recommended Rogerian rhetoric as an alternative form of argument to be used, as Young, Becker and Pike originally recommended, when emotions and a sense of threat preclude direct debate in the classical mode (Bator 1980, 1992; Coe, 1992).

Lunsford and Ede (1984), Gage (this volume) and others have argued that those who view classical rhetoric as inherently combative have been misled both by later misreadings of Aristotle and his contemporaries and by an incomplete understanding of the role of the enthymeme. They argue that the enthymeme, the heart of Aristotle's structure of argumentation, differs from the logical syllogism precisely in that it involves the rhetor in the building an argument from the opinions of the audience. Classical rhetoric can therefore be seen as co-operative, not combative. This in fact is the basis for Lunsford's argument that a Rogerian "alternative" to traditional rhetoric is unnecessary (1979).

Regardless of the merits of these arguments, the traditional conception of rhetoric still poses limitations. Traditional rhetoric as envisioned by Aristotle and by most modern textbooks on argument is typically triadic; that is, it is aimed at a third party who will judge the case on the basis of the arguments presented by competing advocates, politicians, researchers, advertisers, or other partisan arguers. In this case it matters little if one arguer threatens the beliefs and self-esteem of the other, for it is not the opponent he is trying to convince, but the audience as third party. The process of inquiry claimed for the enthymeme creates co-operation between rhetor and audience, not between rhetor and opponent.

But what about the instances—far more common in everyday life—in which two parties are directly trying to convince each other? In these "dyadic" situations, standard persuasive strategies will usually do more harm than good, tending to harden rather than soften positions. In such cases of dyadic argument, a technique is required that will create the grounds for reasonable discussion that classical rhetoric presupposes. Rogerian rhetoric offers such a technique (Coe 1992).

The challenge for the composition teacher, of course, is how to teach students to put Rogerian principles into practice. Rogerian rhetoric is often tried and dismissed as impractical, too difficult for students to use, too difficult to teach, or too easy for students to misinterpret as a particularly sly form of manipulation.

I believe that some of these problems stem from a failure to recognize just what Rogerian rhetoric really is. The basic model of Rogerian argument, particularly when abstracted from the rich context of heuristic techniques in which Young, Becker and Pike originally embedded it, looks like a form of arrangement: a recipe for what to say first. But arrangement is only part of the business of any rhetorical system. Logically prior to arrangement—and as I will argue, embedded in the process of arrangement, not separate from it—is the process of invention. In Rogerian terms, this means exploring an opposing point of view in sufficiently rich complexity that it is possible to reflect it back convincingly to an audience.

The problem of invention is accentuated by the written medium. A writer is in a much worse position than the therapist, for writing does not allow the back-and-forth movement of face to face conversation that makes possible the continual readjustment of the discourse. But if we are content to relax our standards somewhat, it is still possible for students to learn how to apply a form of Rogerian principles in writing. To do so, they must learn how to imagine with empathy and how to read with empathy.

By "imagining with empathy," I mean more than teaching students to imagine another's views. This would be little different from classical audience analysis. I mean teaching students to think carefully about how another person could hold views that are different from one's own. This is what Young, Becker and Pike mean by finding the "contexts in which the opposing viewpoint is valid." Rather than simply imagining an isolated set of arguments for an opposing viewpoint, the writer must imagine the entire worldview that allows those arguments to exist, that makes them valid for the other.

By "reading with empathy," I mean teaching students to use the printed words of another as a guide to this imagining process. In a sense, this is no more than what is usually known as "research." When preparing any written argument it is useful to do one's homework. But whereas students often associate "research" with the mere looking-up of "facts," research in a Rogerian context emphasises the looking-up of facts in the context of the arguments that support them, and looking at those arguments in the context of other worldviews, other ways of seeing.

This kind of imaginative reconstruction does not come easily. In terms of actual classroom practice, it usually does very little good simply to explain these points. Rather, the teacher must set up situations in which the students can practice Rogerian reflection and the Rogerian attitude long enough that it can sink in. For instance, the teacher can set up a dialectical situation in which they can practice on real, present people in a context more like the original therapeutic situations for which Rogerian principles were originally designed. The oral, face to face conversation serves as a bridge to the more difficult imaginative task of the distanced written conversation.

Though these tasks are in one sense designed to serve as preparation for another, they are in no sense mere warm-up drill or "prewriting" activities separate from the business of argument itself. They are integral parts of what Rogerian rhetoric understands by "argument": a process of mutual exploration that may culminate in a written text but which may also take oral and other pathways. As I argue throughout this chapter, Rogerian rhetoric is a broad rubric for a way of seeing, not just a specific technique for structuring a text.

Rogerian Rhetoric in Action: Some Closeups

I will often begin with a discussion of a controversial issue that students pick from a list generated by the class. For this exercise I usually depend on the knowledge that students already possess on the subject, though in more advanced classes I ask students to research the topic beforehand. I get students to identify themselves with one side or the other. Then I will call on a volunteer from each side to engage in a public Rogerian discussion (since my disastrous first experience with this technique I am careful not to use the word "debate").

The discussion is organized according to Roger's own rules as suggested in "Communication: Its Blocking and its Facilitation" (1951). Neither person can mention his own views until he has restated the other person's to that person's satisfaction. Thus the first "round" would consist of student A stating an argument, student B restating that argument in summary form, and student A either agreeing that the summary is accurate or attempting to correct it. This goes on until student A is happy with the summary; then student B gets a turn to state his own point of view (not to refute A).

The exercise often breaks down into a traditional debate in which one person either tries to refute the other's views or restates them in a way that will make them easier to attack. Emotional hot buttons get pushed, and more straw men begin flying about than in the monkey attack from The Wizard of Oz.

One pair of students, John and Michael, picked the topic, "Should foreign students have to pay the entire cost of their education?" Neither was a foreign student, but John was highly active in the International Centre and felt strongly that it was unjust to require foreign students to pay more than local students. He stated his reasons, including basic principles of equity and the important contribution that foreign students make to the university. Michael opened his "restatement" along the lines of, "So, you think it's okay to make our taxpayers pay for the education of a student from Singapore who won't even stay in this country?"

Obviously, this is hardly Rogerian reflection. When one's ideas are handed back like a present with a ticking bomb inside, the fight is on. But this is exactly the point. I want students to see the difference between this sort of rebuttal and true Rogerian discussion. Sometimes I involve the entire class in discussing whether a particular response is genuinely "Rogerian" or is really just a sneak attack on the other's values. After some discussion and more prompting from John, Michael eventually worked himself around to identifying the values behind John's statement:

> So, if I understand you correctly, you don't think that the cost of education should be tied directly to the amount of money one's family has paid into a given educational system, or the obvious financial returns that a country can get from educating people. Rather, you think that a more general principle of equity applies and that we need to look at a more global good.

He still didn't agree, but at least he understood John's point of view. Only John's assent that Michael had in fact got it right gave Michael permission to go on to state the reasons for that disagreement.

The process is exhausting and usually the class is over before the first exchange of views is complete. But by the end of the process, students (and the teacher!) have a greater appreciation of the difference between their own default mode of argument and the process of struggling toward a genuine understanding of another's point of view.

The point of this oral exchange is not so much to invent material for a particular piece of writing as to get the general feel of Rogerian discussion in its most "native" mode, face-to-face communication. Once I think students have got the hang of this, I move them on to the more difficult task faced by writers: recovering underlying values from other people's written texts. Again I pair them off and they begin by writing straight-ahead, univocal arguments for their own point of view on a controversial issue. Students exchange papers and try to write summaries that satisfy the original author, who in turn may write counter-summaries that extend and correct the reflected image of their ideas.

Kathy, for instance, felt quite passionate about the Young Offenders Act, a controversial Canadian law that severely limits the sentencing of criminals under sixteen years of age even if they have committed violent crimes. Her statement began like this:

I feel that we must dispose of the Young Offenders Act. It is a useless piece of legislation practically promoting crime. Hasn't our society enough evidence that the YOA doesn't work? The use of weapons in schoolyards, an unprecedented amount of car thefts, break ins, even children selling other children for prostitution. A slap on the hand prevents nothing. If greater punishment, including real time in jail were a threat, I guarantee that our youth would be a little more reluctant.

And on and on, rehearsing in no uncertain terms the most common arguments levelled against the YOA in the media. Her partner, Tracey, began her restatement like this:

You have expressed concern over the YOA. You are concerned that it actually encourages crime because of the lack of deterrence. You feel that a person under sixteen knows right from wrong and should be held responsible for his or her actions, regardless of the personal situation or background which might be used as an excuse for committing crimes. You believe that we should place the betterment of society above the protection of criminals, regardless of their age.

The important feature of this restatement is that it is not just a summary of the other's point of view, but, somewhat like Michael's, an attempt to get at underlying beliefs. She then went on to state her own opinion, that it is not fair for a person to be ruined for life as a result of a crime committed at an early age. But her response was moderate, and had to deal with the delicate balance between protection of society and protection of individual youths that she had detected in Kathy's position. The effect of the restating process was not simply to soften up Kathy by putting her in the right frame of mind to receive Tracey's argument. Rather, it put Tracey in touch with the complexities of the matter, enabling her to see the matter from another's point of view rather than just her own.

Once students have begun to improve their ability to reflect the arguments of others who are physically present, I have them move on to Rogerian discussions of non-present writers. One fruitful assignment is to have students reply to articles embodying worldviews that they do not share. Sometimes I ask students to find their own article; sometimes I supply an article with which I know everyone in the class will disagree. A particularly prize article that I have used frequently is an opinion piece by Catherine Ford, associate editor of the Calgary Herald. Ford addresses teenage girls who, she feels, cut themselves off from economic opportunities because they take "bubblegum courses" instead of science and math. She cites chilling statistics about how much time most women spend in the work force and how little most of them are paid, and equates science and math—which, she says, most girls have been "conned" into thinking are too difficult—with "one of the fastest ways to economic independence for women."

However, she begins by telling her audience that "the world is passing you by, while you're all out there spray-painting your hair purple and reading People magazine," and tries to get their attention by telling them that "you guys seem to have melted your brains with your stereo headphones." It's not hard to see that Ford is not exactly a master of Rogerian rhetoric, and the class usually has an entertaining few minutes raking her over the coals for her unsupported generalizations and unflattering portrayal of the very people she is supposedly trying to convert. Students taking a Humanities course are particularly irritated by being accused, by implication, of having chosen a "bubblegum" course. Then I set my students a dyadic task: to write a letter directly to Ford herself that uses Rogerian techniques to convince her to moderate her position.

To do so, we discuss not only the areas of validity in Ford's argument, but also try to understand both the rhetorical situation—why she might decide to adopt such an aggressive tone to get her point across—and also who she is as a person. Nobody in the class ever knows much about her personally, but with a little exploratory discussion, we begin to think about the implications of being a woman in her forties—to judge by her picture—who has fought her way up to associate editor of the city's major newspaper. From this and years of experience with Ford's writing, we build up a picture of a woman who prides herself on pulling no punches, who is easily angered by behavior that she perceives as foolish, and whose feminism frequently takes the form of being disgusted by girls who cut themselves off from the opportunities that she herself fought so hard to make for herself. Her insistence on "economic independence" suggests someone with a fierce personal pride and a hard-nosed attitude to life, but not—judging by other columns in which she discusses government fiscal policy—someone who values money for its own sake. In short, the students are applying consciously the reader-response process of constructing both a text and the person behind the text. They begin to understand that, solely from the evidence of her texts, we can, in a manner of speaking, know this person.

None of these personal details need to find their way into the final written product, of course. There is not much to be served by presenting Ford with a detailed picture of herself that is not directly relevant to the issue and could very well be inaccurate. The object of this part of the exercise is simply to sensitize the students to the idea that arguments come from somewhere, and if you can understand where they are coming from, you can negotiate meaning more effectively.

Here is an example of the sort of texts students produce when they sit down to produce their actual written responses:

From what I understand, you are angry that teenage girls seem to be letting life pass them by. They are playing into the roles society seems to have laid out for them, even though the deficiency of women in math and science is an enormous myth. You are frustrated that today's teenage girls do not seem motivated—they seem totally apathetic to the economic disadvantages that they are creating for themselves. I see young girls in shopping malls who seem to be wasting their lives away, concerned more with buying the right kind of makeup than with insuring that they will have the resources to lead independent lives.

However, I have to ask you this—what about all the successful women in fields other than math and science? I think there are many opportunities in math and science—opportunities that many teenage girls overlook because they think that these fields are too difficult. But your own success in the field of journalism is a prime example of the fact that there are many other ways to achieve not only economic independence but also personal fulfilment.

I don't think we should make girls feel inferior because they have genuinely chosen to enter a non-science field. But I guess the point is that girls should not feel locked out of any profession, and they should not take advantage of every strength they have and every opportunity life offers them. Otherwise they are going to end up being dependent on some guy because they don't have the skills they need to look after themselves.

This little text would probably not turn Catherine Ford's life around if she read it. But it would be more likely to engage her in honest debate than would a text that began "How dare you tell me that I'm lazy and ignorant because I'm majoring in the humanities!" More important, it reflects a new understanding on the student's part. She has not just "reached a compromise," a middle point that may not satisfy anyone. Rather, she has thought through what she and Catherine Ford might genuinely share on a subject that she has surely discussed before, but perhaps not explored in this way.

The skills learned in this sort of reconstructive reading will, I hope, carry over from civil to academic discourse. As Booth long ago argued (1974), and as rhetorics of science and rhetorics of academic disciplines increasingly make us aware, there is no field of knowledge in which "facts" emerge unencumbered by values. A history paper or even the literature review section of a laboratory report can be enhanced by a Rogerian belief that points of view come from somewhere, that the lenses other people choose to hold up to reality are worthy of honest, empathic understanding.

One may ask, if Rogerian principles go so much beyond mere form, why is all of this Rogerian apparatus needed at all? My answer is that, even if Rogerian rhetoric is best seen as fundamentally a matter of invention, this invention is driven by the Rogerian form. As Richard M. Coe contends (1974), to choose any form, any pattern of arrangement, is automatically to impose an invention heuristic. If students are attempting to "fill in the form" of Rogerian rhetoric, they know that they must produce a statement of another's beliefs that the other person can recognize as his own and can take seriously. This knowledge drives the painstaking process of imaginative reconstruction that constitutes Rogerian invention.

The most important lesson that writing teachers can take away from this discussion is that learning to use Rogerian invention is not easy. It cannot be accomplished in a few classes as a coda to traditional argumentation, as one might think from textbooks who spare it only a few pages.

I don't mean to suggest that an entire composition course ought to built around explicit instruction in Rogerian rhetoric from beginning to end. Dialogic communication is only one kind of communication, and Rogerian rhetoric is only one kind of dialogic communication. As a form of arrangement, Rogerian rhetoric may not always be appropriate: if communicative bridges are already in place, it may not be necessary to build them, and in some forms of triadic communication it may be desirable to underline only one's own point of view. Students therefore need to be taught a variety of rhetorical forms.

However, the general spirit of Rogerian invention should be woven into the fabric of the course through a variety of exercises that help students learn to understand others' points of view. Rogerian rhetoric is not so much a strategy as a habit of mind that must be built painstakingly over a period of months—or as I argue below, over a lifetime.

Criticisms of Rogerian Rhetoric

Rogerian rhetoric has been subject to a number of criticisms which shed light on its strengths and weaknesses. In particular, these criticisms illustrate the importance of treating Rogerian rhetoric as part of a larger system of knowing and valuing, not as an isolated "technique."

One criticism of Rogerian rhetoric is that it can be manipulative. In formal structure, it looks suspiciously like the often-described "indirect structure" in which a writer buffers unwelcome news or an unpalatable request by flattering the reader. (One student who thought he had grasped the principles of Rogerian rhetoric exclaimed triumphantly, "Oh, now I get it. First you get the reader on your side, then you hit 'em with your own ideas at the end.")

Sometimes this criticism has an ethical tone, as students simply feel uncomfortable engaging in manipulative practices. (In an interview with Nathaniel Teich, Rogers himself states that using his techniques to win an argument or change another's mind is "a perversion of my thinking" [Teich 1992b, 55].) Sometimes it has a more practical tone. Students frequently protest that Rogerian rhetoric is too idealistic to be used in day-to-day life. People are too hostile, they say, have too often been burned by smooth talkers, to be moved into a more co-operative mindset by Rogerian techniques.

Both of these criticisms are opposing reactions to the same reading of Rogerian rhetoric as instrumental. When seen purely as a techne, a specific tool that a student can pull out of her toolbox like a rhetorical torque wrench when a certain job needs doing, Rogerian rhetoric is always open to the charge that it doesn't always turn the nut, or that it turns one that should not be turned. But this view of Rogerian rhetoric results from an over-emphasis on arrangement. When Rogerian arrangement becomes divorced from the therapeutic roots of Roger's philosophy, it becomes little more than an updated version of the benivolentiae captatio (securing of good will) recommended in medieval and modern letter-writing practice. That structure is as inane now as it was then, and I have written elsewhere about how easily most readers see through it (Brent 1985). Aside from the ethical issues, foregrounded flattery just doesn't work very well in an age in which readers have been inoculated by a lifetime of exposure to sales techniques that would have made Gorgias envious.

However, when Rogerian techniques are taught more as a matter of invention than of arrangement, the emphasis falls more on the underlying attitude rather than the form, the mutual exploration rather than the attempt to convince an "opponent." The goal of Rogerian rhetoric is to identify genuine grounds of shared understanding, not just as a precursor to an "effective" argument, but as a means of engaging in effective knowledge-making. It is a way of activating the Kantian imperative to pay as much attention to others' ideas as you would have them pay to yours. If the result sometimes looks manipulative to a cynical audience, this is simply the price we pay for living in an imperfect world in which we can never be sure of each other's intentions.

A deeper criticism comes from feminist approaches to language. On the surface, Rogerian rhetoric might appear to be an ideal instantiation of feminist discourse. Studies of women's language suggest that women in conversation tend to engage in more transactional and co-operative rather than linear and competitive behavior. "Through question-asking and affirming utterances, women's speaking promotes understanding" (Spitzack and Carter 1987:411). Rogerian rhetoric, because it privileges co-operative construction of meaning over goal-directed persuasion, the building of relationships over the winning of an argument, seems to fit neatly into the feminist perspective.

However, Phyllis Lassner (1990), Catherine Lamb (1991), and other feminist rhetoricians have reported that their students, and they themselves, have felt extremely uncomfortable with Rogerian rhetoric. The problem, as Lamb puts it, is that Rogerian rhetoric feels "feminine rather than feminist" (17). Although studies of women in conversation frequently show them working harder than men at promoting understanding and maintaining relationships, the typical method of doing so, especially in gender-mixed groups, is through self-effacement (Lakoff 1975). Their tendency to interrupt less than men, to ask more questions and to avoid direct confrontation, can be seen not just as a "maternal" desire to focus on relationships, but also as a willingness to give in, to let the conversation be directed by men. "It has always been women's work to understand others," claims Lamb. "Often that has been at the expense of understanding self" (17).

For men, who have been brought up to value the individualist, goal-directed construction of self, the challenge is to connect with others. For women, brought up to see themselves as socially constructed through their relationships with others, the challenge is to find ways of having a well-defined self without sacrificing that connectedness. Elizabeth Flynn's comparison of compositions by male and female students ("Composing as a Woman" 1988) dramatically illustrates these differences in orientation to self and other. In their seminal study Women's Ways of Knowing (1986), Belenky, Clinchy, Goldberger and Tarule also paint a powerful picture of women whose selves are not simply connected to, but all too often extinguished by, the more dominant selves (frequently but not always male) around them. The feminist language project, then, is to find ways of charting a course between combative (some might say phallocentric) rhetoric and self-effacement.

Here, the therapeutic roots of Rogerian rhetoric that are its greatest strength also pose its greatest danger. The role of the Rogerian therapist is precisely to efface the self in order to enable the client to use language as a tool of self-exploration. Even for the therapist, this is risky. Because the client in a therapeutic relationship is by definition dysfunctional in some way, the possibility of the therapist's personality being significantly changed by the client's is not necessarily an attractive prospect. "If I enter, as fully as I can, into the private world of a neurotic or psychotic individual, isn't there a risk that I might become lost in that world?" (Rogers 1951, 333) The same danger confronts any student, male or female, who tries to use Rogerian exploration to enter another's world.

Moreover, as Lassner points out (1990), the detached, unemotional tone recommended by standard Rogerian rhetoric goes against the grain of most women's preferred ways of knowing. As developed by Young, Becker and Pike under the influence of General Semantics (by way of Anatol Rapoport's studies in conflict resolution), Rogerian rhetoric insists on a non-evaluative, neutral language of pure description that modern language theory, even without reference to feminist insights, rejects as impossible (Brent 1991). This privileging of rationalist objectivity, with its concomitant assumption that emotional involvement destroys the purity of reason, can be seen as yet another variant on the old theme that women make poor scientists, poor speakers and poor leaders of society because they are inclined to be emotional.

Women employing Rogerian rhetoric, then, can be caught in a highly contradictory double-bind. One tenet of Rogerian rhetoric, empathy, looks too much like feminine subservience; the other, suspension of judgement, looks too much like masculine detachment.

To deal with the first problem, it is important to keep in mind the differences as well as the similarities between Rogerian rhetoric and

Rogerian therapy. Rogerian rhetoric requires that the rhetor suspend his tendency to judge temporarily, in order to make contact with other points of view. But the process does not end there; the Rogerian rhetor, unlike the Rogerian therapist, has his own point of view as well, and puts it forward in concert with the picture he has constructed of the other's view. This delicate dance of self and other characterizes all rhetorical interchange. If Rogerian rhetoric is to take its place as a means of participating in this dance, it must be a whole rhetoric, a rhetoric in which the rhetor's views and those of others collaborate in a dialectical process of meaning-making.

When students use Rogerian reflection to understand other points of view, then, it is important that they use the glimpses of other selves not just to understand those other selves but also to gain a fuller understanding of their own beliefs and what has caused them to think differently from the others they take in. In classroom practice, this means that the teacher needs to direct discussion toward differences as well as similarities, and toward understanding the roots of those differences. The students coming to grips with their first defensive reaction to Ford's article, for instance, explored not only what might have made Ford such an outspoken advocate of math and science, but also their own experience of gender differences, the reasons for their varied choices of specialization, and their relationship with different forms of knowledge in their high school years. As part of this process they use not only Rogerian reflection but group conversation, storytelling and freewriting—all methods of exploration that can be and have been used without a Rogerian context, but which take on new depth in a Rogerian frame.

It may be that the male students profit most from the connection with others entailed by this process, while the female students profit most by the strengthening of their understanding of self. I do not, however, wish to buy into the politics of separation by setting up Rogerian exercises differently for male and female students. Rather, I try to allow space for all differences in meaning-making by emphasising the connections between the two parts of the process—the exploration of self and the exploration of other.

To deal with the second problem, "neutral" language must be valued, not as a pure good in itself, but in a dialectical relationship with emotional language and the connection with self that emotion entails. As noted above, students get a chance to try out their first reactions to an opposing point of view, responding for instance to Ford's caricature of teenage girls with the derision that an overstated viewpoint deserves. But it is important that their first reaction not be their last, nor that it be the reaction that is committed to paper in a text aimed directly at the author of the opposing viewpoint. And even when they are passing through the most overt stage of Rogerian reflection, in which hostile language is to be avoided at all costs, I do not make them feel that avoiding overt hostility means adopting a tone of total detachment. We can strive for empathy, understanding, and the completest possible construction of the other, without supposing that language can ever be a fully neutral descriptor.

In short, most of the more problematic aspects of Rogerian rhetoric result from insufficiently complex uses of the technique and a failure to bring it into line with views of language, gender and politics appropriate to the nineties. Neither Rogers nor Young, Becker and Pike ever pretended that their ideas were anything but a stage in the development of new paradigms of communication. To teach Rogerian rhetoric as if Young, Becker and Pike's twenty-year-old formulation were the last word is to ignore the promptings of teacherly common sense as well as the work of Bator, Teich, Coe, and many others in constantly updating the spirit of non-adversarial rhetoric.

Rogers and the Ethics of Rhetoric

Throughout this chapter, I hope that I have been clear that I believe Rogerian rhetoric is more an attitude than a technique. The specific form of Rogerian discourse, in which one must be able to reflect another's point of view before stating one's own, is not just a technique to get someone else to listen to you. It's a technique that helps students learn to connect with other points of view, explore them fully, and place them in a dialectical relationship with their own as part of a process of mutual discovery.

I believe, in consequence, that the benefits of Rogerian rhetoric go far beyond teaching students an alternative model of argument. An important goal of a liberal education is to create citizens who are fully equipped to take their place in society. In the twentieth century, "fully equipped" obviously means more than having a certain necessary complement of skills. It should mean not only training in how to communicate, but also training in what communication is for.

Once a person has fully internalized the process of inquiry into another's beliefs—not just the surface of those beliefs but the underlying experiences and values from which they spring—it will be proportionally more difficult for him to treat others as mere instruments for the fulfilment of his own desires. He will be in a better position to find, as Booth puts it, "grounds for confidence in a multiplicity of ways of knowing" (1974; see also Bator, 1992).

This growth in understanding of others is frequently placed under the heading of "cognitive" growth by developmental researchers such as William Perry. This name is certainly not inappropriate, for the ability to think through one's own position relative to those of others, and to find grounds for at least provisional confidence in an intellectual position, is certainly a cognitive act. But it is also an ethical act.

Cognition is concerned with understanding and ethics is concerned with valuing, but the one presupposes the other. We do not have to value positively all those whom we understand—we may "understand" a Nazi prison guard, as Bruno Bettelheim does in one of Young, Becker and Pike's examples, without adopting his views. But we certainly cannot make informed ethical choices without being able to explore other points of view.

Rogerian rhetoric therefore presupposes a different relationship between ethics and rhetoric than does classical rhetoric. Quintilian for instance insists on virtue as a precondition to good rhetoric: rhetoric is "a good man speaking well." If "virtue" includes being able to achieve understanding of other people, not only those with whom we must argue directly but also those countless others, alive and long dead, who contribute to the rhetorical building of our selves, then Rogerian rhetoric reverses the equation. Rogerian training in speaking well helps to create a "good" person by contributing to ethical as well as cognitive growth. Good rhetoric is a precondition to virtue.

This is a heavy burden, and of course Rogerian rhetoric cannot be expected to carry it alone. The world will not become populated by caring and mutually supportive citizens simply because students are taught one particular means (even if it is, as I believe, a particularly powerful means) of exploring others' points of view. But we could certainly do worse than to take up Rogers' challenge to "take this small scale answer, investigate it further, refine it, develop it and apply it to the tragic and well-nigh fatal failures of communication that threaten the very existence of our modern world" (1951: 337).

Coda: Beyond Rogerian Rhetoric

Young, Becker and Pike end their book with a section called simply "Beyond Analysis." With almost no comment they reproduce A. M. Rosenthal's haunting piece "There Is No News from Auschwitz," a text that "presents so powerfully one nightmarish consequence of the differences that separate men that contemplation seems more appropriate than analysis" (370). It is an eloquent testimony to the need to develop and teach any textual practices, however imperfect and in need of continued development, that we can find which might help our students bridge such tragic differences.

I would like to end, with equally little comment, with an incident that suggests a more optimistic counterpart to Rosenthal's dark vision: a renewed faith in the healing power of language.

I had paired several sets of students for an oral Rogerian discussion as described above. One pair decided to discuss drunk driving. They are not exactly on "opposing sides"—who would be for drunk driving?—but they had very different views of the problem and its consequences. Was that all right? I told them that it was; in reality, differences of opinion seldom divide along neat bipolar lines of cleavage that allow pat "yes/no" sides.

Lisa went first. Her initial "statement of position" was much fuller than usual. In somewhat abbreviated form, it went like this:

> The year I was born, my grandmother was killed by a drunk driver.
>
> She was the stabilizing force in my grandpa's life, so when she died he became a bitter and miserable man. The only time I've ever spent with my grandpa is when he lived with our family after he was seriously injured in another drinking and driving incident. This time he was the drunk. This accident left him crippled and even more miserable.
>
> I see my grandpa once a year. He is usually in his wheelchair complaining. All I think is, "You did this to yourself." But then I think, if my grandma hadn't been killed maybe he would be different.
>
> The driver that killed her robbed me. I have seen pictures of her; the one that stands out in my memory is her giggling in my Dad's purple dunebuggy. She was wearing a short skirt, had a beehive and was 50 years old. I never got to meet her.
>
> My family does not dwell on what happened so many years ago. We never talk about what happened to the other driver. But we never drink and drive.

Gayleen went through the motions of reflecting back Lisa's statement, appreciating the pain and the anger contained within it. But there really wasn't much to uncover. Lisa's eloquent narrative hid little that needed to be dug out by Rogerian techniques, and they reached agreement very quickly that Gayleen had "got it."

Gayleen's opening statement was equally full:

I also learned a very hard lesson, but from a different perspective than you, Lisa. I too was the victim of a drunk driver, and I too lost something that day that I will never be able to regain. The difference is that a member of my family was not killed by a drunk driver—a member of my family was the drunk driver.

When I was nineteen years old, my fiance went to a stag one night. They all drank and then drove home. On the way home, he went through a stop sign and broadsided a car, killing a woman in the back seat.

From that day on, my life was never the same. While the court case dragged on, I was trying to plan a future. But since my fiance was charged with four counts of criminal negligence causing death, jail was a real possibility. Several people who didn't feel comfortable confronting my fiance said terrible, hurtful things to me, as if I condoned this act he had chosen. "Friends" dropped us as if we had a contagious disease, including the same guys my fiance had grown up with and partied with that night, and who also drank and drove themselves home. I also grieved for the family of the woman who was killed, a woman about my mother's age—I kept thinking that it could have been her.

My fiance was never able to talk about his feelings about that night. Though we got married and were together for twenty years, it set a pattern for him of avoiding difficult situations and emotions. He continued to drink and drive—perhaps ten times in twenty years, but it was ten times too many, and it was the one thing we argued about until our marriage fell apart.

I always wanted to tell the woman's family how truly sorry I was for their loss. I thought of her every day for many years, so that now the incident is a part of the fabric of my being. I don't drink and drive, yet I feel the same shame as if I had been behind the wheel that day.

What more could be said? What could be "reflected back"? Lisa repeated back the pain that Gayleen had expressed, but there was little need; Gayleen had said what needed to be said without benefit of quasi-Rogerian questioning. And as for working through propositions to isolate areas of mutual validity—well, as you might imagine, we never got that far.

At the end of their "Rogerian discussion," they shared the background of their topic. Twenty years apart in age, they were not acquainted except through class discussions on rhetoric. Gayleen had recognized Lisa's name at the beginning of term, but they had not discussed the incident until they were paired by random number draw. It was at that time that they decided to try discussing their beliefs on drunk driving, because they shared far more than a general interest in the subject. The accidents they had discussed were actually the same accident. Gayleen's fiance had killed Lisa's grandmother.

The class was left speechless by the courage they displayed in talking about this incident in front of people who until two months ago had been total strangers. They also had the courage to revisit the longstanding grief and anger with each other and with their families. Lisa, who had never really talked with her parents about the incident and what it had meant to her family, talked now, and gave a copy of Gayleen's speaking notes to her father. A renewed process of healing through language was begun.

Rogerian rhetoric is lauded for its power to build bridges. But in this instance, the elaborate scaffolding of Rogerian rhetoric was unnecessary because Gayleen and Lisa, through the most impossible of chances, had already found the opportunity to work through their long-separated feelings in both private and public rhetoric. The bridges were already in place when they stood to speak.

There is no news from Auschwitz, but there is news from Communications Studies 461. One news item is that Rogerian rhetoric is not always necessary if the conversants have the will to communicate. But the more important news is that the power of rhetoric, Rogerian or not, to heal is as powerful as its ability to persuade. It has a power that is beyond analysis.

Notes

1. It is instructive to watch Rogers in action in films such as *Three Approaches to Psychotherapy II—Dr. Rogers*. I do not necessarily suggest showing these films to a composition class, as they set up such a powerful image of Rogers' methods as therapy that it may be difficult for students to make the transition to written rhetoric. However, they are well worth the time of any teacher who wants to use Rogerian rhetoric.

2. For a more thorough critical analysis of the strengths and weaknesses of Young, Becker and Pike's entire project, as well as a more complete discussion of the criticisms that have been levelled at Rogerian Rhetoric over the years, see my article "Young, Becker and Pike's 'Rogerian' Rhetoric: A Twenty-Year Reassessment," College English, 53: 452–66.

3. Nathaniel Teich recommends exactly the opposite. Because controversial arguments tend to produce intractable position, Teich suggests avoiding them and concentrating on less emotionally taxing ones ("Rogerian Problem-Solving" 57–58). I take his point, but because emotional situations are precisely the ones in which Rogerian rhetoric is most necessary, I tend to damn the torpedoes and let students argue about gun control, nuclear disarmament and such. Perhaps the main criterion for choosing between these paths is how long the course is—that is, how much time the instructor is able to spend on damage control.

4. In Reading as Rhetorical Invention (Urbana: NCTE 1992), I extend this argument to claim that all research, even into the most apparently "factual" information, is strongest when it consists of this sort of imaginative reconstruction of the person behind the text. That we can never do so perfectly—that all reading is fundamentally indeterminate—ought not to dissuade us from teaching our students to come as close as they can.

References

Bator, P. 1980. Aristotelian and Rogerian rhetoric. *College Composition and Communication.* 31:427–32.

Bator, P. 1992. Rogers and the teaching of rhetoric and composition. In *Rogerian Perspectives: Collaborative Rhetoric for Oral and Written Communication*, ed. Nathaniel Teich, 83–100. Northwood, N.J.: Ablex

Brent, D. 1985. Indirect structure and reader response. *Journal of the American Business Communication Association.* 22: 5–8.

Brent, D. 1991. Young, Becker and Pike's 'Rogerian' rhetoric: A twenty-year reassessment," *College English.* 53:452–66.

Coe, R. M. 1974. An apology for form, or, who took the form out of the process? *College English.* 49:13–28.

Coe, R. M. 1990. *Process, Form, and Substance: A Rhetoric for Advanced Writers.* Englewood Cliffs: Prentice Hall.

Coe, R. M. 1992. Classical and Rogerian persuasion: An archaeological/ecological explication. In *Rogerian Perspectives: Collaborative Rhetoric for Oral and Written Communication*, ed. Nathaniel Teich, 83–100. Northwood, N.J.: Ablex.

Ede, L. 1984. Is Rogerian rhetoric really Rogerian? *Rhetoric Review* 3 (1984):40–48.

Flower, L. 1993. *Problem-Solving Strategies for Writers.* 4th ed. Fort Worth: Harcourt Brace Jovanovich.

Flynn, E. 1988. Composing as a woman. *College Composition and Communication* 39:423–35.

Hairston, M. 1976. Carl Rogers' alternative to traditional rhetoric. *College Composition and Communication.* 27:373–77.

Lakoff, R. 1975. *Language and Women's Place.* New York: Harper and Row.

Lamb, C. E. 1991. Beyond argument in feminist composition. *College Composition and Communication.* 42:11–24.

Lunsford, A. A. 1979. Aristotelian vs. Rogerian argument: A reassessment. *College Composition and Communication.* 30:146–51.

Lunsford, A. A., and L. S. Ede. 1984. On distinctions between classical and modern rhetoric. In *Essays of Classical and Modern Discourse*, ed. Robert J. Connors, Lisa S. Ede and Andrea A. Lunsford, 37–49. Carbondale and Edwardsville: Southern Illinois University Press.

Mader, D. C. 1980. What are they doing to Carl Rogers? Et Cetera. 37:314–20 kPlato. 1951. Gorgias, trans. W. C. Helmbold. Indianapolis: Bobbs-Merrill.

Plato. 1956. Phaedrus, trans. W. C. Helmhold and W. G. Rabinowitz. Indianapolis: Bobbs-Merrill.

Rogers, C. R. 1961. This is me. Chapter 1 of *On Becoming a Person*. Boston: Houghton Mifflin.

Rogers, C. R. 1951. Communication: Its Blocking and its Facilitation. Rpt. in *On Becoming a Person*, C. R. Rogers, 1961, 329–337, Boston: Houghton Mifflin.

Rogers, C. R. 1965. *Client-Centered Therapy*. Boston: Houghton Mifflin.

Rogers, C. R., and D. Ryback. 1984. One alternative to planetary suicide. *The Consulting Psychologist*. 12(2):3–12. Rpt. in *Rogerian Perspectives: Collaborative Rhetoric for Oral and Written Communication*, ed. Nathaniel Teich, 35–54. Northwood, NJ: Ablex, 1992.

Spitzack, C. and K. Carter. 1987. Women in communication studies: A typology for revision. *Quarterly Journal of Speech*. 73:401–23.

Teich, N., editor. 1992a. *Rogerian Perspectives: Collaborative Rhetoric for Oral and Written Communication*. Northwood, N.J.: Ablex.

Teich, N. 1992b. "Conversation with Carl Rogers. In *Rogerian Perspectives: Collaborative Rhetoric for Oral and Written Communication*, ed. N. Teich, 55–64. Northwood, N.J.: Ablex.

Young, R. E., A. L. Becker and K. L. Pike. 1970. *Rhetoric: Discovery and Change*. New York: Harcourt.

Chapter Four

The Researched Argument Assignment

Assignment Overview

Researched Argument

Making an argument—expressing a point of view on a subject and supporting it with evidence—is often the aim of academic writing, even if the
word "argument" is never used. Your college instructors may assume that
you know this and thus may not explain the importance of arguments to
you in class. Someone, somewhere, has debated most material you learn in
college at some time. Even when the material you read or hear is presented
as simple "fact," it may actually be one person's interpretation of a set of
information. In your writing, instructors may call on you to question that
interpretation and defend it, refute it, or offer some new view of your
own. In short, in writing assignments, you will almost always need to do
more than just present information that you have gathered or regurgitate
facts that were discussed in class. You will need to select a point of view
and provide evidence to develop your own considered argument.

Content and Audience

In a Researched Argument, you should examine scholarly articles that discuss a range of perspectives on contemporary issues being debated in various cultures, including academic disciplines. You should put scholarly articles into conversation with each other, analyzing the ways writers offer diverse perspectives in different ways. As a new member of the academic community, you should find where your voice, perspective, and argument fit into the existing conversation. So, unlike a research report (a popular high school genre that summarizes or explains ideas), a Researched Argument asks writers to interpret a wide spectrum of perspectives and offer creative insights.

This assignment asks you to build on the source citation and argumentation skills you developed in your Op-Ed, engage in the critical examination of texts you practiced in the Rhetorical Analysis, perform the careful observation and development of voice you rehearsed in the Personal Essay, and work within the broad and diverse conventions of scholarly research. You may choose to use in-class readings as a touchstone for your writing and/or expand on an issue you've already written about in Writing 111. Whatever you decide, you should investigate an issue that you are genuinely interested in learning more about.

When you find an issue to focus on, ask yourself the following questions:

- What are the core controversies at the heart of the issue?

- What do I need to define or explain to readers so they can make sense of the issue?

- What sources will I use and what gaps are there in these sources?

- What information am I seeking from additional sources to fill these gaps?

- Do sources agree on an issue? Disagree? Are they somewhere in between? How do I respond to these sources? Given my own life experiences or analysis, what do I think?

As with other assignments in this course, you will write for a specific audience: the Binghamton University first-year community, but particularly scholars within this community. As such, you should explain important concepts to your readers (who are intellectually curious, but who have different knowledge bases and areas of expertise); you should also seek to persuade readers that your perspectives are worth considering.

Organization and Format

As you begin your research and brainstorming, look to the readings that we have examined in class and other academic arguments to help imagine an appropriate structure. Consider the following questions:

- What kinds of research questions are writers trying to answer?
- How do they begin and end their pieces?
- How do they use evidence, including summary, paraphrase, quotation, and analysis?
- How do they signal that they are moving on to another portion of their argument?
- How do they show their willingness to listen to and engage with alternative viewpoints?

You will develop a general understanding of the conventions of researched argumentation, as you work to arrange your ideas in ways your readers will recognize: develop a clear thesis; demonstrate a range of perspectives on the issue; analyze and complicate those perspectives; and offer new insights to the academic conversation. If you are just documenting and summarizing sources, you may be merely writing a report. If you are summarizing or drawing on sources revolving around a common focus and engaging with each of them related to an argument you support in your thesis statement, you are probably writing a Researched Argument.

Your essay must be no fewer than eight full pages and no more than ten, and must use MLA style formatting conventions. You must integrate a variety of sources in your paper, **three of which must be scholarly sources** (published in a scholarly peer-reviewed journal or collected in an anthology of scholarly articles published by a university press), and two of which must be sources not read in our class.

Supporting Materials

These are required of all students and are considered a vital part of the Researched Argument process and therefore an integral part of your participation grade. Satisfactory completion of supporting documents counts toward your participation grade. These materials will help to ensure your success.

In order to ensure that your paper starts off on the right track, you will submit a 250-word abstract that outlines your argument and gives a short overview of the sources you will incorporate.

You will also submit a four-page Annotated Bibliography in which you summarize and explain your intended use of each of the four sources, three of them academic/scholarly sources. Each entry should begin with the source listed in the proper MLA style for a Works Cited page and be followed with a lengthy paragraph related to that entry. For more info on Annotated Bibliographies, see the OWL at Purdue's handout: http://owl.english.purdue.edu/owl/resource/614/01/ and samples at http://owl.english.purdue.edu/owl/resource/614/03/.

Oral Presentation

Make sure that you practice and time your oral presentation carefully. It should be four to five minutes long: students who exceed five minutes will be stopped. Tell the class what your argument is and how you came to it. What is your research question? What is the range of perspectives on your issue? How do you respond to them? What unique contribution are you making? As time allows, your teacher may ask your peers to pose questions and/or give you feedback on the basic premises of your Researched Argument.

● INVENTION: **The Researched Argument**

1. List five topic/themes that you are interested in outside of school. For example, video games, anime, Victorian parlor music, home automation, broom hockey.

2. List five topic/themes that relate to your school/professional interests. For example, someone interested in accounting might be fascinated with the idea of a tax code revision. Someone who majors in literature might be interested in the impact of e-books on the future of print books. Someone interested in music might be itching to engage in a discussion on the effect of classical music on infants.

3. List five topic/themes related to something new that you find interesting. For example, you may have just learned about Google Glasses or the popularity of the new Tesla electric car. Or perhaps you saw a news article about a new work from Mark Twain that was recently published.

4. List five topic/themes related to something old that you think others may have overlooked. Think about history and how it relates to themes or topics that are interesting to you. Think about how history informs present developments. For example, past rural educational models included one-room schoolhouses. As urban schools get bigger and bigger, a researcher might suspect that older models may be better models. Another student might look at the history and politics surrounding the U.S. decision to drop the bomb in WWII and make a new argument regarding the reasoning around that decision and how our current understandings relate to our ethical or moral judgments in times of war.

5. List five topic/themes that you think are cool or interesting or wacky but totally not possible for a researched argument. For example, terraforming Mars, the benefit of conspiracy theories for democracy, 10th century Gregorian chants, internet memes, historical pirates as a lens for viewing Internet media "piracy."

Be sure to collect some info on the following two items so you can explain them to your class. For example, what form do they want the material in? How many words? Is an abstract required? Etc.

Journal or Conference Possibility 1:

Journal or Conference Possibility 2:

● INVENTION: Cubing Your Topic

Subject: A broad category. For example, global warming might be a subject you'd like to begin with in order to find a topic.

Topic: A subset of the subject. Using the subject of global warming, you might settle on the topic of wind farms.

You'll notice that the movement from subject to topic is contextual. Wind farms may still be a broad topic and might be narrowed down further.

For example, you may have driven through West Virginia and seen billboards supporting coal mining through scare tactics related to employment (i.e., "If you want to keep your job in the mine next year, don't vote for candidate X"). You might be wondering if a solution to the reduction of coal mining could be the development of new renewable energy sources in that particular region. Effectively argued, this could respond to the issue related to employment raised on the billboards. The argument that wind farms should replace coal mining in Appalachia might be something more specific, but still broad enough. The goal here is to establish an argument in an ongoing conversation that is expansive enough, but specific enough. You will be continuing to revise your thesis/ideas as you conduct research and write about it.

Run through "Cubing" together as a class with the above scenario (Wind farming in Appalachia in order to replace the economic benefit of coal mining) or one generated together.

In order to help us consider different angles, cubing is a pre-writing activity that asks us to think of a subject or topic in different dimensions and from different perspectives.

- Generate a list of possible subjects/topics for your paper.

- Consider your list and narrow items down, if you can.

- Conduct the "Cubing."

- Afterwards, share your work with one other classmate. What might they add to the list?

● INVENTION: **Cubing Activity**

As you write the responses to this activity out on a separate sheet of paper, please clearly mark each section of this exercise with the headings and numbers below.

Subject:

Topic/Question/Argument:

1. Describe it.

2. Compare it. (What is it like?)

3. Associate it. (What does it make you think of? What other things are connected to it?)

4. Analyze it. (How can you break it down? How do the parts of it contribute to the whole?)

5. Apply it. (How can you use it to understand or see something else?)

6. Argue for or against it. (What kind of support will back up your assertion?)

INVENTION: **Abstract and Annotated Bibliography**

While Writing 111 is designed to focus on three genres (the Personal Essay, the Op-Ed, and the Researched Argument) in general, many other genres of supporting documents surround the kind of writing we do in academic contexts. Two important genres of supporting documents are the abstract and the annotated bibliography.

Supporting documents usually attend to at least two goals. First, they prepare you for your major assignment by requiring you to think about important sources and/or the purpose of your essay and to represent that critical thinking in writing. Thus, supporting documents support major assignments not as supplemental texts, but as texts that build writing and a body of knowledge that is directly transferrable to the end document. Second, these supporting documents will give readers a condensed look at your understanding and interpretation of important sources and information and of your evolving essay.

Content and Audience

Sometimes, an abstract is completed after an essay is produced. Other times, abstracts are required as part of a proposal process. We believe that going through the cognitive process of developing your proposal as an abstract will help you narrow your objectives as you are writing. The abstract will also offer your instructor more information on your vision of your project, which will help them respond to you with feedback during conferences. For more information on the process of creating your abstract, please refer to the "How to Write an Abstract" activity that follows this one.

While the abstract chronicles what you argued or plan to argue in your work, often giving nods to those who came before you in the scholarly conversation, whose ideas you are now adding to, disputing, or complicating, an annotated bibliography is basically a list of sources with information and critical thinking provided by you following each source.

The annotated bibliography is a more formal kind of system for taking notes and recording thoughts regarding a list of sources a writer is working with. Although it can serve the writer well as they complete an essay, it is also a genre of writing of its own. Your annotated bibliography should include **four** sources you are planning on using for your Researched Argument essay, **three** of which must be your scholarly sources. In each of your annotations, you should use summary, direct quotation, and paraphrase as you cover that particular source. For more information on how to use summary, direct quotation, and paraphrase, please see the "Summary, Paraphrase, and Quotation" handout. For more info on Annotated Bibliographies see the OWL at Purdue's handout at: http://owl.english.purdue.edu/owl/resource/614/01/ and samples at http://owl.english.purdue.edu/owl/resource/614/03/.

As with other assignments in this course, you will write for a specific audience: the Binghamton University first-year community, but particularly scholars within this community. As such, you should explain important concepts to your readers (who are intellectually curious, but who have different knowledge bases and areas of expertise).

Organization and Format

Your abstract and annotated bibliography document should begin with the 250 word abstract on the first page. The annotated bibliography should follow. Start by listing your source in MLA Works Cited format and then following the entry with your writing that includes summary, paraphrase and quotation from the source. Be sure to use MLA in-text citation to appropriately document your use of the source. Each of the four sources should be on a new page and should include approximately a full page of writing. The final document should be at least five full pages.

INVENTION: **How to Write an Abstract**

An effective abstract does the following:

- Begins with a research question that identifies a debatable issue.

- States a clear thesis that establishes what the writer will argue in relationship to the issue.

- Lists the major claims that the writer will use to support the thesis, identifying important sources the writer will use to make particular claims.

- Communicates at least one major counterargument that the writer will explore.

- Identifies the primary research strategies the author will employ and the purpose for integrating these strategies in relation to the argument. This will appropriately lead into the sources you cover in your Annotated Bibliography.

Your abstract should be about 1 page (approximately 250 words). This means you will have to be clear and succinct.

Sample Abstract

While most citizens in the United States agree that a college education is key to economic success, educators disagree over what kind of education young adults should receive. In essence, many educators seek to answer the question: What kind of education will best prepare young people to lead productive, civically engaged adult lives? In this paper I will argue that while curricula that focus on "Great Books" and "education for the professions" are both valuable parts of the college experience, "multicultural education" is a necessary component of education that prepares student for the demands of American life. When initiated well, multicultural education not only gives students exposure to important books and professional preparation, it prepares them to work productively in a diverse, democratic society. In order to explore this issue and help readers understand the range of opinions that erupt in this debate, I will briefly define each of the three educational philosophies listed above. I will support my thesis using two central claims: 1) _____ and 2) _____ .

To support claim #1, I turn to both Jane Smith's essay "_____ _____" and Frieda Doe's chapter "_____." To support claim #2, I will explore ideas presented by Martha Naussbaum in her essay "The Idea of World Citizenship in Greek and Roman Antiquity." While I will ultimately refute his argument, I will also explore a common argument against multicultural education, namely one that states _____: John Q. Academic makes this argument in his essay "_____." I also examine another counterargument, which is represented in the work of _____.

You may want to answer to the following prompts to help you write your abstract:

- First, what is your research question?

- Now articulate your thesis.

- List the major claims you will use to support your thesis, identifying important sources you will use to make these particular claims.

- Tell us about at least one major counterargument you will explore.

- Identify the primary research strategies you will employ and the purpose for integrating these strategies in relation to your argument.

- Now use the Word Count feature to see how many words you have used. Even if you have less than 300 words, you may want to read back through your abstract to see if there are places where you can cut unnecessary words.

- Read (or have a friend read) your abstract aloud. Does it flow smoothly from one sentence to the next?

- Now, read your abstract one more time, completing any minor editing that may be needed.

● REVISION: **The Researched Argument**

1. What is interesting about the introduction? How does it catch and/ or hold your attention?

2. What is the thesis? How is it engaging for a general Binghamton audience?

3. Are there transitions between new ideas? How is the essay organized?

4. What is the function of the conclusion in the paper? Does it sum everything up? Does it point towards future action? Does it address the reader? What could add to the conclusion?

5. Does the paper reach the minimum complete page requirements of the assignment (not counting the MLA Works Cited, if one is included)? How can it be extended? If it's too long, what could be cut?

6. Are there any sources mentioned? Is the title of the source correctly formatted? (Underline or use italics for bigger works and put quotation marks around smaller works.)

7. Is the source included in a Works Cited page in MLA style?

8. Is the quote properly integrated within the text? Does the author introduce the source? Are the page numbers included in parentheses? Is the punctuation properly placed after the parentheses for both short-form and block-form quotations?

9. If appropriate, is there an adequate mix of summary, paraphrase, and quotation in terms of work with sources?

10. Prepositions are words like "about, on, in, around, through, of, etc." Does the author use the proper prepositions? For example, you wouldn't say I stood *on* line for a ticket, but instead, I stood *in* line for a ticket. Check all the prepositions.

11. Are possessives used in the paper? Does the author properly use apostrophes for possessive? Are it's/its and there/they're/their used correctly?

12. Given your analysis, what is one concrete improvement in the area of content that the author could work towards in a final revision?

● REVISION: **Reader-Response Comment Sheet**

Please place the following identifying information at the top of a piece of loose-leaf paper and clearly label your responses "Step 1," Step 2," etc. If you find you're repeating yourself, you may want to reference a previous response.

For the Writer: Before distributing your paper to peers, write out the specific kind of feedback you are looking for on your draft. Use the space in the heading of your paper to do so.

For the Reader: As you read your colleague's draft, challenge yourself to offer constructive feedback and to engage in the process with integrity. Label your responses "Step #1, #2," etc.

STEP #1: Read the essay completely through (without commenting on it) once. Give feedback on the issues the writer has identified.

STEP #2: Read the essay again, asking facilitative questions. In other words, ask questions that push the writer to think further or to consider something in a new light. (Why or how might some people pose counterarguments? What does the writer still need to consider?)

STEP #3: Focus on the introductory paragraph. Does it catch your attention? If so, tell the writer specifically why it is working. If not, make a concrete suggestion that might make the introduction stronger.

STEP #4: Read for a thesis statement. If you find one, note: a) what paragraph you found it in; and b) whether or not it is clear. Then, restate the thesis in your own language. If you do not find a thesis statement or it is unclear, brainstorm one that might be appropriate for the paper.

STEP #5: As you read further, list the points that the writer makes in support of the argument. Comment on whether these points are clear, logical, etc. Is the writer's voice in control of the essay, or are sources dominating it? While source integration is important, let the writer know if you do not hear his or her voice in the paper, or don't hear it enough. Also, let the writer know if sources are integrated properly: are sources clearly introduced with author credentials, title, source context/summary, in-text citations and Works Cited entries?

STEP #6: Look for places where the writer needs to consider alternate points of view or interpretations. Can you think of ways in which some readers might disagree with the writer that he or she doesn't address? How would you engage such readers? Do you think that the writer fairly represents a range of views or interpretations? List your advice here.

STEP #7: Comment on the structure and organization of the essay. Are paragraphs or sections introduced with clear topic sentences that relate back to the thesis? Are transitions effective and clear? Make specific suggestions if you have any advice on how to develop more effective organizational strategies.

STEP #8: Do you see repeated punctuation or grammar errors? List here what those are and the paragraphs where the writer might find them.

STEP #9: Reflect on the "Characteristics of ABCD Writing." What is the most important piece of advice you would give the writer considering these evaluation criteria? What do you think is strongest about the paper in its present stage in regard to these evaluation criteria? Be specific when answering both questions.

STEP #10: List here any additional evaluation criteria your instructor may ask you to consider.

● REFLECTION: **Researched Argument Activity**

Now that you have a completed draft of your Researched Argument, take a little time to freewrite about the genre and your writing process. Respond to the following questions. Digressions are okay. Be prepared to share your responses.

- What are the major skills you've practiced in order to complete your Researched Argument?

- How do the characteristics of the genre relate to or diverge from the other genres in Writing 111? Be specific.

- Which skills for the Researched Argument will be most likely to transfer to the kind of writing you will do in your other classes? What skills from the other genres will transfer? Why?

- Describe your writing process for this paper. Was it similar to or different from the processes you employed for the other genres? Why?

- If you were speaking to a student in Writing 111 who was just beginning the Researched Argument unit, what advice would you give to that student?

- Create a quick checklist of the things you need to do in order to prepare for the final portfolio.

REFLECTION: Researched Argument Essay Cover Letter

Guidelines: Approximately 200 Words

Please consider the following questions in the format of an informal letter to your instructor. You are not obligated to discuss all of these questions; instead, answer the three or four that will give your instructor the best insight into your work and your experience with this assignment. Instructors will use this statement to guide their feedback, so do your best to reflect on both the strengths and weaknesses of your project.

Before You Write Your Cover Letter

Prior to putting pen to paper, consider your most recent draft of the Researched Argument carefully.

Question 1: Getting Started

Explain how you went about starting the assignment. How did classroom activities shape your thinking, and which seemed the most fruitful for you as a writer? Did you jump in and plan your essay from top to bottom? Or did you start in some other way?

Question 2: Focusing

What is your purpose with the essay? If you have a traditional thesis, paraphrase it again here. If you have a less traditional focus statement, how did you develop it, and where is it in your essay?

Question 3: Revising

During peer review, what advice did you seek from your classmates? What specific concerns and praise did they offer? What revision decisions did you decide to make and implement?

Question 4: What's Working Well? What's Not?

What are you happiest with in this essay? Did you try a particular rhetorical technique that seemed to work for you? Did your classmates confirm that technique's success? What's not working at this point? Were there any techniques that you tried that didn't seem to work?

Question 5: Goals for Future Revision

When planning for your final portfolio, what priorities will you set for revision? What are your specific goals for improvement?

Question 6: Characteristics of ABCD Writing

Take a few minutes to reflect on the Characteristics of ABCD Writing. Which of the criteria do you feel most confident about? Which one are you the least confident about? Why?

In Search of New Frontiers:
How Scholars Generate Ideas

by Robert L. Hampel

In my second year of graduate school, the historian Michael Kammen brought a file folder to the first session of his Colonial America seminar. In it were several dozen term-paper topics that Kammen believed could yield publishable articles or dissertations. Our own ideas were not barred, but we all chose one of the subjects suggested by the man who had just won a Pulitzer Prize for People of Paradox.

What we did not know was how he had decided that those particular topics deserved study. On what basis had he selected them as GTFR (good topics for future research), as I labeled the folder that I kept while writing my dissertation?

After several years of teaching a seminar for first-year Ph.D. students, I started to doubt the topic-selection advice I offered: Fill a gap in the literature, identify a problem that has not been studied adequately, and add a brick to the wall of knowledge. That might be how I and others justified our research, but was it how we came upon the topic in the first place?

In the 35 years since my seminar with Kammen, I never asked my colleagues if they had similar folders to store their seed corn for the time when their current projects came to an end. After reconsidering my topic-selection advice, I did. I wanted to know how other professors kept track of and, more importantly, generated ideas for future research. So last year I asked a dozen full or chaired professors in my school how they discovered research topics.

When I talked to my colleagues, I found that they rarely decided to pursue a project because they had seen a gap in the literature that needed filling. Several acknowledged that while reading was a crucial source of ideas for them, they relied on other sources of inspiration more often. Here are the four key lessons I gleaned from my conversations with those colleagues to pass on to new doctoral students:

- ***Future research arises from current research.*** We mislead our doctoral students when we say that a study is finished. Often we cannot

Hampel, Robert L. "In Search of New Frontiers: How Scholars Generate Ideas" as appeared in *The Chronicle of Higher Education*, 55.17, 2008. Reprinted by permission of the author.

fully explain our findings. Something happened that we did not expect. There is usually an unpredictable interplay of careful planning and sheer serendipity, especially for researchers who are alert to puzzles and surprises. When things don't work out as initially envisioned, it is not necessarily a failure. The tidiness of the results in journal articles can be misleading. They are presented so neatly, telling the clearest story possible, but that is like telling a life story as if it were scripted from infancy.

- ***Future research can be autobiographical.*** Research is often "me-search," a friend of mine likes to say. Ideas for research topics can stem from brief personal experiences from childhood or threads that run throughout their professional lives. For example, gender equity in science education has riveted a colleague since she majored in chemistry in college. Another colleague's passion is the give-and-take of arguments, "so I think that's why I'm studying fifth graders' persuasive writing." What "voice" means for minority scholars fascinates an African-American academic who feels that the traditional norms of scholarly discourse stifle her own creativity. For those colleagues, their lives are inspiration, but not evidence—in other words, they are not autoethnographers.

Sometimes a good project arises from family life. A child psychologist extended her work on infant communication when her 14-month-old son was pointing incessantly to the refrigerator. "I'd take one thing out after another, and he finally seemed to find what he wanted," she said. "So I got excited and found three families, studying how kids make their ideas known and how they correct your misconceptions when you're wrong about what they want."

- ***Future research often arises from conversations.*** A new assistant professor who thinks she's too busy to have lunch with her colleagues should remember that such talk is a fertile source of GTFR. The Vygotskian notion of co-constructing ideas rings true for many of us: We get insights together that none of us would have developed alone.

In the case of my colleagues, none sat down with friends for the purpose of generating GTFR; ideas were generated through chance and serendipity instead. For a friend in special education, a few words in the elevator with a statistician led to a three-year collaboration. For a math educator, an hour in a friend's office spawned two studies, spanning eight years, that analyzed mathematics instruction in eight countries. Lucky accidents, perhaps, but all the people involved were already keen on collaboration before those episodes occurred. They were in the habit of spending time with colleagues; for instance, when a former dean at my institution served on advisory boards, he tried to arrive the afternoon before so he could have dinner with the other panelists.

Conversations at conferences can also spark GTFR. Hearing, giving, or commenting on papers was less valuable for my peers than the impromptu talk in the hallways. So when a department chair saw a former colleague at an annual meeting, their reunion sparked his interest in aggregation error as a new twist on his continuing research.

- *Future research can derive from what others want and might pay for.* Here someone else supplies the creative spark and imaginative leap: An editor solicits a contribution to a handbook or Festschrift, the federal government seeks grant proposals for particular projects, a local district needs a program evaluation. In my school of education, faculty members tend to use such invitations as one way to decide which of several possible topics for future research they will take off the back burner. The invitation is an incentive and a catalyst to choose one of those worthwhile topics.

There are caveats to those four approaches, however. The me-researcher who relies solely on personal history could narrow her scope and miss other rewarding topics to explore. The eager lunch partner might discount his own flashes of inspiration. Everyone who depends on grants runs the risk of selling their souls if they take on projects beyond their expertise in order to fatten their paychecks. Each source of creative work can become counterproductive if it stifles the flexibility and curiosity necessary to envision unexplored subjects or imagine new ways to tackle familiar topics.

Surprisingly, no one I spoke with had been taught how to generate topics for future research during their years in graduate school. Several said that since research had pervaded the ethos of their university, they had merely absorbed the spirit of curiosity. Initially, many had been handed topics to study or had imagined topics much too broad to tackle within a semester or year. For those with postdoctoral fellowships, that was the time when their ideas took shape.

That lack of formal coaching may explain not only the variety of approaches that my colleagues take to identify ideas for future research but also the different mechanical ways that they keep track of them. One used a single folder; another had a separate folder for each idea. Two kept journals—one was strictly about research, the other resembled a personal diary. Three used computer files ranging from the very simple to the elaborate, cross-referenced array with shorthand and symbols throughout. Another had index cards. The only common pattern held for the four people who used no system, preferring to carry the ideas in their heads, confident that they would never run short of topics.

I was also surprised that no one had made plans for what to do with their topics for future research if they suddenly died. The two professors in their 70s, each of whom has faced serious health issues, have rich accumulations of material that warrant special instructions to their heirs and executors. None of my colleagues share the urgency felt by the psychologist Abraham Maslow, who began keeping journals primarily to let posterity have "everything unfinished, all that is ¼ or ½ done—it will save all of my forgotten insights, beautiful ones that are lost because I have too many of them to work them all out or even to classify & save efficiently." At age 57, he fretted that "much of my work will die with me."

Fortunately, it did not. And the notes for future research accumulated by scholars in all fields deserve a better fate than oblivion.

If graduate students cannot see how senior scholars generate and manage their ideas, then their induction is incomplete. Our students dutifully take research-methods courses, but every graduate seminar should discuss the wide range of sources of creative work. Otherwise our students will think in terms of the assignments we give them, when they should really be thinking about the assignments they can give themselves: interesting topics for future study.

Robert L. Hampel is a professor and former director of the school of education at the University of Delaware.

From Topics to Questions

by Wayne C. Booth, Gregory G. Colomb, and Joseph M. Williams

In this chapter we discuss how to explore your interests to find a topic, narrow it to a manageable scope, question it to find the makings of a problem, then turn it into a problem that guides your research.

If you are free to research any topic that interests you, that freedom can be frustrating—so many choices, so little time. At some point, you have to settle on a topic, but beyond a topic, you also have to find a reason beyond your assignment to devote weeks or months pursuing it and writing up what you find, then to ask readers to spend their time reading your report.

As we've said, your readers expect you to do more than just mound up and report data; they expect you to report it in a way that continues the ongoing conversation between writers and readers that creates a *community* of researchers. To do that, you must select from all the data you find just those data that support an answer to a question that solves a problem your readers think needs solving. In all research communities, some problems are already "in the air," widely debated and deeply researched, such as whether personality traits like shyness or an attraction to risk are genetically inherited or learned. But other questions may intrigue only the researcher: *Why do cats rub their faces against us? Why do the big nuts end up at the top of the can?* That's how a lot of research begins—not with a "big" question known to everyone in a field, but with a mental itch that only one researcher feels the need to scratch.

If you have such an itch, good. But as we've said (and will say again), at some point, you have to decide whether the answer to your private question is also significant to others: to a teacher, colleagues, other researchers, or even to a public whose lives your research could change. At that point, you aim not just to answer a question, but to pose and solve a *problem* that others also think is worth solving.

Now that word *problem* is itself a problem: commonly, a problem means trouble, but among researchers it has a meaning so special that we devote all of the next chapter to it. It raises issues that few beginning researchers are able to resolve entirely and that can vex even advanced ones. But before you can address a research problem, you have to find a topic that might lead to one. We'll start there, with finding a topic.

From an Interest to a Topic

Most of us have more than enough interests to pursue, but beginners often find it hard to locate among theirs a topic focused enough to support a research project. A research topic is an interest defined narrowly enough for you to imagine becoming a local expert on it. That doesn't mean that you already know a lot about it or that you will have to learn more about it than your professor has. You just want to know more than you do now.

If your assignment leaves you free to explore any topic within reason, we can offer only a cliché: Start with what interests you most deeply. Nothing contributes to the quality of your work more than your commitment to it. Start by listing two or three interests that you'd like to explore. If you are undertaking a research project in a course in a specific field, skim a recent textbook, talk to other students, or consult your teacher. You might try to identify an interest based on work you are doing or will do in a different course.

If you are still stuck, you can find help either on the Internet or in your library. The Internet may seem the easier way, but it is more likely to lead you astray, especially if you are new to research. Start with the standard guides:

- For a project in a general writing course, start in the library. Look at the headings in a general bibliography such as the *Reader's Guide to Periodical Literature*. If you already have a general focus, use more specialized guides such as the *American Humanities Index* or the *Chicano Index*.

Scan headings for topics that catch your interest. They will provide not only possible topics, but up-to-date references on them. If you already have an idea for a topic, you can check out the Internet, but if you have no idea what you are looking for, what you find there may overwhelm you. Some indexes are available online, but most don't let you skim only subject headings.

- For a first research project in a particular field, skim headings in specialized indexes, such as the *Philosopher's Index,* the *Psychological Abstracts,* or *Women's Studies Abstracts.*

Once you identify a general area of interest, use the Internet to find out more about it and to help you narrow your topic. (If you are really stuck, see the Quick Tip at the end of this chapter.)

- If you are doing an advanced research project, you might look first for what resources are easily available *before* you settle on a topic.

If you pick a topic and then discover that sources are hard to find, you may have to start over. If you *first* identify resources available in your library or on the Internet, you can plan your research more efficiently, because you will know where to start.

At first, you may not know enough about a general interest like *the use of masks in religious and social contexts* to turn it into a focused topic. If so, you have to do some reading to know what to think about it. Don't read randomly: start with entries in a general encyclopedia, then look at entries in a specialized encyclopedia or dictionary, then browse through journals and websites until you have a grip on the general shape of your topic. Only then will you be able to move on to these next steps.

From a Broad Topic to a Focused One

At this point, you risk settling on a topic so broad that it could be a sub-heading in an encyclopedia: *Spaceflight, history of; Shakespeare, problem plays; Natural kinds, doctrine of.* A topic is usually too broad if you can state it in four or five words:

Free will in *War and Peace*	The history of commercial aviation

With a topic so broad, you may be intimidated by the idea of finding, much less reading, even a fraction of the sources available. So you have to narrow it, like this:

Free will in *War and Peace*	→	The conflict of free will and historical inevitability in Tolstoy's description of three battles in *War and Peace*
The history of commercial aviation	→	The crucial contribution of the military in the development of the DC-3 in the early years of commercial aviation

We narrowed those topics by adding words and phrases, but of a special kind: *conflict, description, contribution,* and *development.* Those nouns are derived from verbs expressing actions or relationships: *to conflict, to describe, to contribute,* and *to develop.* Without such words, your topic is a static thing—*free will in War and Peace, the history of commercial aviation.* But when you use nouns derived from verbs, you move your topic a step closer to a *claim* that your readers might find significant.

Note what happens when these topics become statements. Topics (1a) and (2a) change almost not at all:

TOPIC		CLAIM
1a. Free will and historical inevitability in Tolstoy's *War and Peace*	→	There is free will and historical inevitability in Tolstoy's *War and Peace.*
2a. The history of commercial aviation	→	Commercial aviation has a history.

Topics (1b) and (2b), on the other hand, are closer to claims that a reader might find interesting:

1b. The *conflict* of free will and historical inevitability in Tolstoy's *description* of three battles in *War and Peace*	→	In *War and Peace,* Tolstoy *describes* three battles in a way that makes free will *conflict* with historical inevitability.
2b. The *crucial contribution* of the military in the *development* of the DC-3 in the early years of commercial aviation	→	In the early years of commercial aviation, the military *crucially contributed* to the way the DC-3 *developed.*

Such claims will at first seem weak, but you will develop them into more specific ones as you develop your project.

A more specific topic also helps you see gaps, puzzles, and inconsistencies that you can ask about when you turn your *topic* into a research *question* (more about that in a moment). A specific topic can also serve as your working title, a short answer when someone asks you what you are working on.

Caution: Don't narrow your topic so much that you can't find enough data on it:

TOO MANY DATA AVAILABLE	TOO FEW DATA AVAILABLE
The history of commercial aviation	The decision to lengthen the wingtips on the DC-3 prototype because the military wanted to use the DC-3 as a cargo carrier

From a Focused Topic to Questions

In taking this next step, researchers often make a beginner's mistake: they rush from a topic to a data dump. Once they hit on a topic that feels promising, something like *the political origins and uses of legends about the Battle of the Alamo,* they go straight to searching out sources—different versions of the story in books and films, Mexican and American, nineteenth century and twentieth. They accumulate a mound of summaries of the stories, descriptions of their differences and similarities, ways in which they conflict with what modern historians think happened. They write all that up and conclude, "Thus we see many interesting differences and similarities between…"

Most high school teachers would give such a report a passing grade, because it shows that the student can focus on a topic, find data on it, and assemble those data into a report—no small achievement for a first project. But in any advanced course, including a first-year writing course in college, such a report falls short because it offers only random bits of information. If the writer asks no *question* worth pondering, he can offer no focused answer worth reading. Readers of research reports don't want just information; they want the answer to a question worth asking. To be sure, those fascinated by a topic often feel that *any* information about it is worth reading for its own sake: collectors of Japanese coins or Elvis Presley movie posters will read anything about them. Serious researchers, however, do not report data for their own sake, but to support the answer to a question that they (and they hope their readers) think is worth asking.

233

The best way to find out what you do not know about a topic is to barrage it with questions. First ask the predictable ones of your field. For example, a historian's first questions about the Alamo stories would concern their sources, development, and accuracy. Also ask the standard journalistic questions *who, what, when,* and *where,* but focus on *how* and *why.* Finally, you can systematically ask four kinds of analytical questions, about the composition, history, categorization, and values of your topic. Record the questions, but don't stop for answers. (And don't worry about fitting the questions into the right categories; use the categories only to stimulate you to ask them and to organize their answers.)

Identify the Parts and How They Interrelate

- What are the parts of your topic, and how do they relate to one another?

  In stories about the Alamo, what are the themes, the plot structure, the main characters? How do the characters relate to the plot, the plot to the actual battle, the battle to the characters, the characters to one another?

- How is your topic part of a larger system?

  How have politicians used the story? What role does it have in Mexican history? What role does it have in U.S. history? Who told the stories? Who listened? How does their nationality affect the story?

Trace Its Own History and Its Role in a Larger History

- How and why has your topic changed through time, as something with its own history?

  How have the stories developed? How have different stories developed differently? How have audiences changed? How have the storytellers changed? How have their motives to tell the stories changed?

- How and why is your topic an episode in a larger history?

  How do the stories fit into a historical sequence of events? What caused them to change? How did they affect national identity in the United States? In Mexico? Why have they endured so long?

Identify Its Characteristics and the Categories that Include It

- What kind of thing is your topic? What is its range of variation? How are instances of it similar to and different from one another?

  What is the most typical story? How do others differ? Which is most different? How do the written and oral stories differ from the movie versions? How are Mexican stories different from those told in the States?

- To what larger categories can your topic be assigned? How does that help us understand it?

  What other stories in U.S. history are like the story of the Battle of the Alamo? In Mexican history? How do the stories compare to other mythic battle stories? What other societies produce similar stories?

Determine Its Value

- What values does your topic reflect? What values does it support? Contradict?

  What moral lesson does the story teach, if any? Whose purposes does each story serve? Who is praised? Who blamed? Why?

- How good or bad is your topic? Is it useful?

  Are some stories better than others? More sophisticated than others? What version is the best one? The worst one? Which parts are most accurate? Which least?

Evaluate Your Questions

When you run out of questions (or think, *Enough!*), it's time to evaluate them. First, set aside questions whose answers you could look up in a reference work. Questions that ask *who, what, when,* or *where* are important, but they may ask only about matters of settled fact (though not always). Questions that ask *how* and *why* are more likely to invite deeper research and lead to more interesting answers.

Next, try to combine smaller questions into larger, more significant ones. For example, several Alamo questions revolve around the issue of the interests of the storytellers and their effects on the stories:

How have politicians used the story? What role does it have in U.S. history? How have the storytellers changed? How have their motives to tell the stories changed? How did the stories affect national identity in the United States? How do the stories compare to other mythic battle stories? Is its moral lesson worth teaching? Whose purposes does each story serve?

Many of these can be combined into a larger, more significant question:

How and why have tellers of the Alamo story given a mythic quality to the event?

Once you settle on a question or two, you have a guide to doing your research more systematically. A question narrows your search to only those data you need for its answer. And once you have an answer you think you can support, you know it's time to stop hunting. But when you have only a topic, the data you can find on it are, literally, endless; worse, you will never know when you have enough.

Through all this, though, the most important goal is to find questions that challenge you or, better, arouse your intense curiosity. Of course, you can't be sure where any particular question will lead, but this kind of questioning can send you in directions you never imagined, opening you up to new interests, new worlds of research. Finding good questions is an essential step in any project that goes beyond fact-grubbing. With one or two in mind, you are ready for the next steps.

From a Merely Interesting Question to Its Wider Significance

Even if you are an experienced researcher, you might not be able to take this next step until you are well into your project. If you are a beginner, you may feel that this step is still deeply frustrating even when you've finished it. Nevertheless, once you have a question that grabs your interest, you must pose a tougher question: *Why should this question also grab my readers? What makes it worth asking?*

Start by asking, *So what?* At first, ask it for yourself:

So what if I don't know or understand how snow geese know where to go in the winter, or how fifteenth-century violin players tuned their instruments, or why the Alamo story has become myth? So what if I can't answer those questions?

Eventually, you will have to answer this question not just for yourself but for your readers. Finding its answer vexes all researchers, beginners and experienced alike, because it's so hard to predict what will really interest readers. Instead of trying to answer instantly, though, you can work toward an answer in three steps.

Step 1: Name Your Topic

If you are just beginning a project, with only a topic and maybe the glimmerings of a few good questions, describe your topic in a sentence as specific as you can make it (glance back at pp. 231–233):

I am trying to learn about (working on, studying) _____

Fill in the blank with your topic. Be sure to use some of those nouns based on verbs or adjectives:

I am studying *diagnostic processes* in the *repair* of cooling systems.

I am working on Lincoln's *beliefs* about *predestination* in his early speeches.

Step 2: Add a Question

As soon as you can, add to that sentence an indirect question that specifies something that you do not know or understand about your topic but want to:

1. *I am studying X*
   2. *because I want to find out* who/what/when/where/whether/why/how _____

1. *I am studying* diagnostic processes in the repair of cooling systems
   2. *because I am trying to find out how* expert repairers diagnose failures.

1. *I am working on* Lincoln's beliefs about predestination in his early speeches
   2. *because I want to find out how* his belief in destiny influenced his understanding of the causes of the Civil War.

When you add that *because-I-want-to-find-out-how/why* clause, you state why you are pursuing your topic: to answer a question important to you.

If you are doing one of your first research projects and you get this far, congratulate yourself, because you have framed your project in a way that moves it beyond the kind of aimless collection and reporting of data that afflicts too much research. But now go one step more, if you can.

Step 3: Motivate Your Question

This step is a hard one, but it lets you know whether your question is not just interesting to you but possibly significant to others. To do that, add another indirect question, a bigger and more general one that explains why you are asking your first question.

Introduce this second implied question with *in order to help my reader understand how, why,* or *whether:*

1. *I am studying* diagnostic processes in the repair of cooling systems
   2. *because I am trying to find out how* expert repairers analyze failures,
      3. *in order to help my reader understand how* to design a computerized system that can diagnose and prevent failures.

1. *I am working on* Lincoln's beliefs about predestination in his early speeches
   2. *because I want to find out how* his belief in destiny and God's will influenced his understanding of the causes of the Civil War,
      3. *in order to help my reader understand how* his religious beliefs may have influenced his military decisions.

It's your answer to the third step that will give you a claim on your readers' interest. If that larger question touches on issues important to your field, even indirectly, then you have reason to think that your readers should care about its answer, and so care about your answer to the smaller, prior question you raise in step 2.

A few researchers can flesh out this whole pattern even before they start gathering data, because they are working on a well-known question, some widely investigated problem that others in their field are already interested in. In fact, advanced researchers often begin their research with questions that others have asked before but not answered thoroughly or maybe even correctly. But many researchers, including at times the three of us, find that they can't flesh out these steps until they're nearly finished. And too many write up their research results without having thought through these steps at all.

At the beginning of your project, you may not be able to get past the first step of naming your topic. But regularly test your progress by asking a roommate, relative, or friend to *force* you to question your topic and to flesh out those three steps. Even if you can't take them all confidently, you'll know where you are and where you still have to go.

To summarize: Your aim is to explain

1. what you are writing about—your topic: *I am studying...*

2. what you don't know about it—your question: *because I want to find out...*

3. why you want your reader to know about it—your rationale: *in order to help my reader understand better...*

If you are just beginning serious research, don't be discouraged if you never get past that second step. As long as your question is interesting to *you,* plow ahead. Your teacher should be satisfied, because you have changed the terms of your project from simply gathering data to asking and answering a question.

If you are a graduate student doing advanced research, however, you *must* take that last step, because answering that last question will help you create the relationship you are working to establish with the rest of your research community. It's your ticket into the conversation.

In the following chapters, we will return to those three steps and their implied questions, because as you'll see, they are crucial not just for finding good specific questions that you want to answer, but for finding and then expressing the problem that you want your readers to recognize and value.

QUICK TIP: Finding Topics

If you have experience in your field but are stuck for a topic, you can find one with some quick research. Read recent articles and review essays and, if they are available, recent dissertations. Look closely at the conclusions: they often suggest further lines of research. You can also browse the archives of an Internet discussion list in your field: look for points of current controversy.

But if you are a beginner and your teacher has not suggested specific topics, try these steps.

FOR GENERAL TOPICS

1. What special interest do you have—sailing, chess, finches, old comic books? The less common, the better. Investigate something about it you don't know: its origins, its technology, how it is practiced in another culture, and so on.

2. Where would you like to go? Surf the Internet, finding out all you can about it. What particular aspect surprises you or makes you want to know more?

3. Wander through a museum with exhibitions that appeal to you—artworks, dinosaurs, automobiles. If you can't get there in person, browse a "virtual museum" on the Internet. Stop when something catches your interest. What more do you want to know about it?

4. Wander through a shopping mall or store, asking yourself, *How do they make that?* or, *I wonder who thought up that product?*

5. Leaf through a Sunday newspaper, especially its features sections, until something catches your eye. Skim reviews of books or movies, in newspapers or on the Internet.

6. Browse a large magazine rack. Look for trade magazines or those that cater to specialized interests. Investigate whatever catches your interest.

7. If you can use an Internet newsreader, look through the list of "alt" newsgroups until you find one that sounds interesting. Read the posts, looking for something that surprises you or that you disagree with.

8. Tune into talk radio or interview programs on TV until you hear a claim you disagree with. Or find something to disagree with on the websites connected with well-known talk shows. See whether you can make a real case to refute it, instead of just shouting back.

9. Use an Internet search engine to find websites about something people collect. (Narrow the search to exclude dot-com sites.) You'll get hundreds of hits, but look only at the ones that surprise you.

10. Is there a common belief that you suspect is much too simplistic, or just plain wrong? Or a common practice that you detest? Don't just pronounce the belief or practice wrong, but instead probe for something you can show about it that might lead others to reconsider.

FOR TOPICS FOCUSED ON A PARTICULAR FIELD

1. Browse through a textbook of a course that is one level beyond yours or a course that you know you will have to take some time in the future. Look especially hard at the study questions.

2. Attend a lecture for an advanced class in your field, and listen for something you disagree with, don't understand, or want to know more about.

3. Ask your instructor about the most contested issue in your field.

4. Find an Internet discussion list in your field. Browse its archives, looking for matters of controversy or uncertainty.

5. Surf the websites of departments at major universities, including class websites. Also check sites of museums, national associations, and government agencies, if they seem relevant.

First-Year Composition as an Introduction to Academic Discourse

by M. J. Braun and Sarah Prineas

This essay is a revision of material that originally appeared in A Student's Guide to First-Year Composition, *20th ed., edited by Sarah Prineas, Lori Church, and Adrian Wurr (Edina, MN: Burgess, 1999).*

A Background for Instructors

From the inception of the composition course in the late nineteenth century, composition instructors and the professoriate at large have assumed that a student would emerge from first-year composition prepared to write for all academic purposes, with little regard for whether the course's content included instruction in academic conventions. Only in the last thirty years of composition studies, however, have scholars attempted to identify what these conventions are. This work spawned debates over the wisdom of teaching what came to be called academic discourse. Although the debate has been far reaching, its terms have coalesced around three issues: the advisability of teaching students academic discourse (scholars have argued that first-year students do not need this type of instruction); the ethics of teaching academic discourse (scholars have argued that academic discourse reproduces hegemonic power relations that suppress the voices of oppressed groups); and the very existence of such a genre (scholars have argued that academic conventions are more dependent on disciplinary than academic concerns). As a result of these challenges, few composition scholars now write unproblematically about academic discourse; in fact, most discussions about the need to prepare students to write for the university have been relegated to scholarly work on writing across the disciplines. But through all of this, the expectations of many composition programs and the professoriate at large have never strayed far from the now century-old assumption that once students leave their first-year composition course, they will be better able to write in any future course they take.

Braun, M. J. and Sarah Prineas, "First Year Composition as an Introduction to Academic Discourse" revised, originally from *A Student's Guide to First-Year Composition*, 20th edition, edited by Sarah Prineas, Lori Church, and Adrian Wurr. Reprinted by permission of M. J. Braun.

As graduate associate teachers in the Department of English at the University of Arizona, we participated in a two-year pilot study to redesign the first-year composition course, English 101, so that it would better prepare students to read and write for academic purposes. But we did not want the new design to jettison a widely recognized strength of the course: introducing students to rhetorical analysis. Rhetorical analysis, as defined in the University of Arizona's *A Student's Guide to First-Year Composition,* is a method of judging the effectiveness of a writer's choices by analyzing the purpose, audience, and context of a text, its arguments, claims, and assumptions, and its appeals using the Aristotelian categories of ethos, pathos and logos. We emerged from the two-year study conceiving of the course as one in which students are asked to investigate the rhetoric of scholarship by offering them a chance to engage in what David Bartholomae has called "an academic project." Like Bartholomae's, our purpose for teaching academic discourse is not gatekeeping—that is, guarding the hallowed halls of academe from the barbarous hordes. Rather, our purpose is to arm young scholars with the frameworks they will need to be able to assess scholarship critically, even from their nonexpert positions within the university.

In the following slightly edited excerpt from *A Student's Guide to First-Year Composition,* we invite students to enter the world of scholarly research in the way scholars do. We use Bartholomae's distinction between the novice and the expert scholar to help students segue from high school to university standards of research. We define these two sets of standards by identifying the following distinctions: purpose of research, generating a topic, method of inquiry, and evaluation of sources. We begin by introducing the students to the master trope for the process of engaging in an academic project—the Burkian parlor.

Suggested Reading

Bartholomae, David. *Facts, Artifacts and Counteracts: Theory and Method for a Reading and Writing Course.* Upper Montclair, NJ: Boynton/Cook, 1986.

———. "Interchanges: Response." *College Composition and Communication* 46 (1995): 84–87.

———. "Writing with Teachers: A Conversation with Peter Elbow." *College Composition and Communication* 46 (1995): 62–71.

Bizzell, Patricia. *Academic Discourse and Critical Consciousness.* Pittsburgh: U of Pittsburgh P, 1992.

Bridwell-Bowles, Lillian. "Discourse and Diversity: Experimental Writing within the Academy." *College Composition and Communication* 43 (1992): 349–68.

———. "Freedom, Form, Function: Varieties of Academic Discourse" *College Composition and Communication* 46 (1995): 46–61.

Elbow, Peter. "Being a Writer vs. Being an Academic: A Conflict in Goals." *College Composition and Communication* 46 (1995): 72–83.

———. "Interchanges: Response." *College Composition and Communication* 46 (1995): 87–92.

———. *Writing without Teachers.* New York: Oxford UP, 1973.

Geisler, Cheryl. "Exploring Academic Literacy: An Experiment in Composing." *College Composition and Communication* 43 (1992): 39–54.

The Process of Research: Joining the Conversation

Why Do University Scholars Research?

University scholars not only make knowledge accessible to each new generation entering higher education, but they also work at developing new lines of inquiry and producing new knowledge in their various fields of study. This activity is known as scholarly research, and the ways of thinking, speaking, and writing that emerge from the act of research are often referred to as academic discourse. In *The Philosophy of Literary Form,* Kenneth J. Burke uses the metaphor of conversation to describe academic discourse:

> Imagine that you enter a parlor. You come late. When you arrive, others have long preceded you, and they are engaged in a heated discussion, too heated for them to pause and tell you exactly what it is about. In fact, the discussion had already begun long before any of them got there, so that no one present is qualified to retrace for you all the steps that had gone before. You listen for a while, until you decide that you have caught the tenor of the argument; then you put in your oar. Someone answers; you answer him; another comes to your defense; another aligns himself against you, to either the embarrassment or gratification of your opponent, depending upon the quality

of your ally's assistance. However, the discussion is interminable. The hour grows late, you must depart. And you do depart, with the discussion still vigorously in progress. (110–11)

Because these academic conversations have been going on, as Burke says, "interminably," a scholar cannot expect to join them until she has done some research. Once the scholar has situated herself in the ongoing conversation through research and reading, she will be ready to become an active "speaker" in that conversation. In order to produce new knowledge, she considers what has been left out of the academic conversation. She asks, "What questions need to be raised? What arguments need to be made? What issues have been left unexamined?" Once she has found such a site for further argument, the scholar continues her research. Most scholars pursue a particular line of inquiry throughout their lives. Over the years, they develop theories about the phenomena they have researched, resulting in the production of new knowledge. This knowledge is often developed in opposition to previously held theories.

Because the scholar conducts research in this way, her work follows certain conventions. For example, she will cite authoritative sources to give her own work academic *ethos,* or credibility, in the eyes of scholarly readers. Second, she conducts research in order to sustain the conversation within her own work so that the other voices who have spoken on her issue can be heard speaking within her own work. Because sustaining this conversation is so important to scholars, they also value proper citation format for quotations and paraphrasing and always include an accurate record of sources—a bibliography or works cited. By including citations and a bibliography, the scholar makes it possible for the next person who picks up the conversation to become well informed on the issue by going back and studying the works cited.

How Do Scholars Decide upon a Topic?

Before starting research, it is important to be aware that in the university scholars choose topics that have relevance to the academic community. Topics for research do not begin and end with unexamined personal biases, because scholars expect to have their assumptions challenged by the academic conversations in their disciplines. For students at the university, topics arise from class discussions and from class readings—from any class, not just English composition. Beginning scholars and researchers need to become aware of the conflicts in their classrooms: What issues are under debate? What are scholars arguing about? What terms do different groups define in different ways? For example, English majors become aware that there is extensive debate about the "canon," or the list of texts considered by some scholars to be "authentic" literature. Some scholars insist that the traditionally assigned texts by revered authors—Chaucer, Shakespeare, Milton, Johnson, Dickens, or T. S. Eliot—must remain required materials. Other scholars working from different theories and assumptions call attention to the fact that the authors just mentioned represent a limited literary tradition that privileges the work of middle- and upper-class European males and insist that the canon must be expanded to include works previously not considered to be literature because of the gender, sexual orientation, religion, or ethnic or racial background of its authors. A novice scholar, for example, might explore the canon debate, analyze the arguments put forth by each player in the debate, and conclude by making an informed argument. Here's another example: In the medical field, nursing students and professors may be concerned about the issue of euthanasia and the role they should play as professionals within that debate. Other disciplines have other hot issues about which scholars argue. These are the sites where established assumptions have been called into question, and these questions are up for debate.

What Research Methods Do Scholars Use?

Less experienced researchers who are just entering the scholarly conversation should be careful not to jump to hasty conclusions, because they need to follow their research where it leads. That way they can leave their options open, allowing possibilities for new arguments to arise from the research. Often, novice researchers have been taught to find bits and pieces of texts that will fit smoothly into the argument they already want to make, glancing quickly through articles, circling only those quotations which support their previously determined position, and dismissing views which contradict their own. They may not consider the possibility that they might want to revise their original argument because the issue has broader implications than they had realized.

Experienced researchers approach research as a necessary step *before* participating in the scholarly conversations occurring in their disciplines. They realize the need to read first, to keep an open mind as they read, and to revise their original assumptions in the face of new knowledge. They recognize the complexity of issues and thus do not claim to have simple answers to complicated problems. Scholars generally respect opposing views because they know that issues can be approached in varied ways and that one can learn a great deal from other approaches, even those that challenge one's own assumptions. Experienced researchers keep careful track of their sources and evidence because they know they may have to give a careful accounting of their evidence if their conclusions or reasoning is challenged. Finally, scholars are aware that research takes time; they do not expect to complete their research in one trip to the library.

For example, as English 101 student Guy Natale began working on his academic project, he decided that as an aerospace and mechanical engineering major he wanted to research the military's use of unmanned aerial vehicles. Unlike most novice researchers, though, Natale did not begin his research with a set thesis in mind. As his instructor relates,

> While conducting his research Guy stumbled upon a topic that needed to be pursued further. Most of Guy's research in the beginning of the assignment centered on finding out how unmanned aerial vehicles (UAVs) are made and what they are used for, but as he slowly became an expert on UAVs, he realized that he did not approve of their potential use as weapons-bearing vehicles in warfare. Guy did not come upon this argument in a professional journal or read it in the newspaper; instead he developed his ideas about the ethical use of UAVs in conjunction with his research. At the time he wrote this essay, these little, computer-controlled crafts were not being used to deliver missiles, but Guy could sense that this would be the next step. He proceeded to research and write a position paper that had a complex purpose: the goal was to take a stand against using unmanned aerial vehicles as weapon delivery systems and also to reaffirm the horrific nature of war by pointing out some of humanity's past mistakes.

Defining a Topic

Once students have begun to identify an area of inquiry—say, for example, the canon debate in English literature, or the euthanasia controversy among health professionals—it is time for them to learn more about the history of the issue, the players involved in the debate, and the kinds of arguments that are being deployed in the debate. The best way to go about this is to begin by visiting the library's computerized catalog of holdings. The first search through this database will be most effective if students approach the task with the attitude that they are engaging in play—they are exploring, searching for useful terms, following promising leads, getting ready to enter the stacks where the books and journals are waiting for them. After they've written down some call numbers, they will be ready to explore the library to track down the sources themselves. When they get to the stacks and find the book they were searching for, they should sit down right there and leaf through the book. They check the table of contents, the index, and the bibliography. They evaluate the chapter or essay titles, skim the introduction and conclusion, and figure out what type of source they have in front of them. They decide right there whether the book might be useful. If it is, they take a look at the shelf where they found that book and examine some of the nearby texts. By browsing the stacks and exploring texts in this way, they begin to get a feel for the debate they are researching. Possibly, certain names will appear several times—these are the players in the debate, the people engaged in the continuing argument. After checking the publication dates of each text, they begin to get a sense of the history of the debate. After reading a few introductions, the positions (rather than rhetorical choices) of those involved in the debate will become more evident.

Evaluating Sources

As scholars assemble research material, they are aware that there is a hierarchy of credibility among sources. This section analyzes the difference between scholarly and nonscholarly texts.

What Is a Scholarly Text?

A scholarly text is distinguished by the fact that the author makes evident in the text that he or she is making an argument as part of a continuing conversation. The author does so through literature reviews, bibliographies or works cited, footnotes or endnotes, and indexes. In other words, scholarly texts make the other voices—the voices of scholars who have previously written or spoken about the issue—"heard" and therefore present in the text. In nonscholarly texts, usually only the voice of the author can be heard.

Some examples of scholarly texts can include the following:

Singly and collaboratively authored books: These scholarly texts contribute something that has not been argued before in a scholarly conversation. These new arguments always build on knowledge that came before: sometimes they take an oppositional stance to that previous knowledge; sometimes they examine previously unconsidered aspects of the argument. Scholarly books are most often published by university, not commercial, presses. Books are published only after they have undergone a rigorous review process. A panel reviews the book to ensure that the author has a thorough understanding of the scope of the scholarly conversation; however, the panel does not evaluate the veracity of the argument. Scholarly works that have undergone this review process are considered credible sources among academics. Be aware that some books may seem to follow these scholarly conventions, yet their credibility is nonexistent in the academic community. For example, in *The Bell Curve: Intelligence and Class Structure in American Life* by Richard J. Herrnstein and Charles A. Murray, the authors argue that intelligence levels, not environmental circumstances, poverty, or lack of education, explain many of our social problems.

In making their argument, the authors assert that intelligence is biologically, not environmentally, determined, and based on their data, they find that blacks are less intelligent than whites or Asians. The book *seems* to follow academic conventions, is written by two Harvard professors, is well documented, and acknowledges the theories on which the authors rely. Yet despite its semblance of credibility, as soon as the book came out scholars across the country, including scholars from Harvard, began to make academic arguments against it, questioning its use of evidence, the authors' manipulation of data, and the authors' suspect conclusions. Geneticists, biologists, and social scientists have challenged the book's premises, pointing out that the authors never clearly define "race," and, referring to the body of knowledge in their various disciplines, arguing the premise that race is in fact socially constructed. According to academic standards, *The Bell Curve* may seem to be a credible text; however, experts in many fields have rigorously questioned its "truth."

One thing to remember when reading scholarly texts is that the introductory chapter usually presents a concise overview of the author's central argument. The introduction often contains a literature review (a review of the major voices in the conversation whose purpose is to review and then problematize what has been said before).

Journal articles: An academic journal, by definition, contains articles relevant to a specific discipline. Journal articles, authored singly or collaboratively, do the same work as a book, in the sense that they are scholarly texts that present an argument and participate in the scholarly conversation. Before an article can be published in an academic journal, it must be refereed, which means that it has been reviewed by a panel of scholars expert in that field. The panel reviews the article to ensure that the author has a thorough understanding of the scope of the conversation; however, the panel does not evaluate the veracity of the argument. Note that while journals are usually found in hard-copy format, they are increasingly appearing in online format. An example of a journal article is R. G. Newby and D. E. Newby's "'The Bell Curve'— Another Chapter in the Continuing Political Economy of Racism," which appeared in *American Behavioral Scientist* in 1995. The authors critique Herrnstein and Murray's *The Bell Curve: Intelligence and Class Structure in American Life* as part of their argument about the role that intellectuals have played in different historical periods in producing knowledge about intelligence and race. They argue that such pseudoscientific arguments about race arise under certain political and economic conditions. Therefore, for Newby and Newby, Herrnstein and Murray's "data" are less important than the political and economic conditions in which their book was produced.

Anthologies: Anthologies are collections of scholarly writings about a common subject. The materials published in anthologies are edited by scholars in a field. The articles republished in anthologies usually appeared first in academic journals or at academic conferences. Anthologies have a theme; all of the articles address some specific topic within the field. *Current Problems in Sociobiology* is an example of an anthology of academic papers presented at a conference at Cambridge University in 1980. The theme of this particular anthology, obviously, revolves around problems facing scholars engaged in sociobiological research.

What Is a Textbook?

While scholarly work seeks to produce new knowledge, textbooks construct a canon of knowledge, in the sense that they present previously theorized knowledge as information that is "true" without interrogating that "truth." In other words, textbooks do not employ the conventions of scholarly writing, because scholars always interrogate "truths." Because a textbook usually presents knowledge as, essentially, dead information, the conversation ends. At the same time, textbooks often come out in new editions in order to update the knowledge contained within, as the conversations have continued.

What Is a Nonacademic Text?

Nonscholarly texts are intended for a general, or popular, audience. While scholarly texts make evident their participation in a conversation, nonacademic texts derive their authority from a huge range of sources—from scholarly work, to received knowledge, to ideology. In this sense, nonacademic texts are problematic because the theoretical assumptions in the texts are less evident and require a more actively analytical and knowledgeable reader. One problem with nonacademic sources is that novice readers lack the analytical skills to recognize whether the theoretical assumptions underlying the text are credible, sometimes to the extent that anything that appears in print may seem credible. In nonscholarly texts, only the voice of the author is heard, while other voices—the voices of scholars who have previously written or spoken about the issue—are usually not present in the text. In academic texts, the voices of other participants in the conversation can be heard.

Singly and collaboratively authored books. These nonacademic texts don't make a scholarly argument; their theoretical assumptions are either unexamined or buried. For example, in *You Just Don't Understand: Women and Men in Conversation,* author Deborah Tannen, writing for a popular audience, argues that men's and women's conversational styles differ. In this book, she presents numerous examples from men's and women's speech to illustrate her point; however, Tannen does not explicitly refer to the large body of linguistic theory which informs her analysis. In her scholarly work on the same subject, *Gender and Discourse,* Tannen supports her method of analysis by citing the linguistic theory that informs it. Nonacademic texts pose a problem more for the uninformed than the informed reader because those readers who are, in this case, unfamiliar with linguistics are unaware of the author's knowledge of linguistics itself and her standing as a scholar in that field. A reader unfamiliar with conventions of academic texts has no way of knowing if a book by Deborah Tannen on gender and conversation is more credible than a book by Oprah Winfrey on the same subject.

Oprah Winfrey might have interesting things to say about the differences in men's and women's conversational styles, but her observations would not be based on accepted linguistic theory or current research, but rather on passively received ideas. For example, according to linguistic theory, gender differences in conversational styles are explained as socially, not biologically, contingent. On the other hand, a nonlinguist may recognize that there are gender differences in conversation styles but attribute these differences to testosterone rather than the social roles men and women play.

Anthologies. Nonacademic anthologies are collections of popular rather than scholarly writings about a common subject. The materials published in popular anthologies are not necessarily edited by scholars and usually appeared first in popular sources such as books, newspapers, or magazines. An example of a nonacademic anthology is *The Bell Curve Wars: Race, Intelligence, and the Future of America,* edited by Steven Fraser, containing articles written by scholars for a popular audience. The anthology contains many articles arguing against the claims made by sociologists Herrnstein and Murray in *The Bell Curve: Intelligence and Class Structure in American Life,* including articles by biologist Stephen Jay Gould and literary theorist Henry Louis Gates Jr. These articles are not scholarly in that Gould, for example, does not write for an audience of biologists, but for a more general audience interested in the debate.

Magazines may seem to provide current information, but they are generally not considered by scholars to be reliable sources. Often, they do not acknowledge their sources, as scholars do, and they are usually not aimed at an academic audience. Magazine articles may even be authored by someone not trained to speak on the subject. For example, a magazine reporter has been trained in journalism, not the subject about which he or she is writing.

Newspapers. Newspaper articles have the same limitations for scholarly use as magazine articles. Reporters, rather than scholars, usually but not always write the articles. Because sources for newspaper articles are unacknowledged, there is no way of knowing what sources are informing a reporter's version of events.

Web pages. In the hierarchy of credibility, Web pages are less credible than print or hard-copy texts for a variety of reasons: anyone (not necessarily an "expert" or scholar) can publish a Web page; Web pages are ephemeral (that is, they can be revised without warning, unlike print sources); sometimes the organizations that publish Web pages can construct the site in such a way that it seems "official" and credible, when in fact it is not. In addition, the Web itself was originally developed by the military and adopted for commercial purposes. Therefore, the format and content of the Web may serve hidden purposes outside of scholarly inquiry. Recently, some scholarly journals have begun to publish on the Web and follow all of the conventions of hard-copy journals.

Works Cited

Burke, Kenneth. *The Philosophy of Literary Form*. Baton Rouge: Louisiana State UP, 1941.

Current Problems in Sociobiology. Ed. King's College Sociobiology Group. New York: Cambridge UP, 1982.

Fraser, Steven, ed. *The Bell Curve Wars: Race, Intelligence, and the Future of America*. New York: Basic, 1995.

Herrnstein, Richard J., and Charles A. Murray. *The Bell Curve: Intelligence and Class Structure in American Life*. New York: Free, 1994.

Newby, Robert, and Diane Newby. "'The Bell Curve'—Another Chapter in the Continuing Political Economy of Racism." *American Behavioral Scientist* 39 (1995): 12–24.

Tannen, Deborah. *You Just Don't Understand: Women and Men in Conversation*. New York: Morrow, 1990.

Introductions and Conclusions

by Wayne C. Booth, Gregory G. Colomb, and Joseph M. Williams

> *In this chapter, we show you how to introduce your research report with a problem that motivates readers to read it and conclude it in a way that emphasizes its significance. Nothing is more useful than a strong introduction and conclusion that help readers see the significance of your work.*

Once you have a revised first (or second or third) draft, you're ready to revise your working introduction so that readers know where you will take them and why they should go there. Some writers think that means following the old advice: *Grab their attention with something snappy or cute.* That advice is not useless, but those who read research reports look for more than cute. What grabs readers is a problem they think is in need of a solution, and what holds them is the hope that you've found it.

In this chapter we show you how to write an introduction that frames your report so that readers can read it faster and understand it better, because they know both what to expect and why they should care. We then show you how to conclude your report so that readers come away not only with a clear understanding of your claims but also with renewed appreciation of their significance. The time you spend on your introduction and conclusion may be the most important revising you do. As we've said, you can always work with readers inclined to say, *I don't agree.* What you can't survive are readers who shrug and say, *I don't care.*

The Three Elements of an Introduction

As we've steadily emphasized, different research communities do things in different ways, but nowhere do those differences seem more striking than in their introductions. These three, for example, are from the fields of cultural criticism, computer design, and legal history. They look different on the surface, but in fact, they are much alike in their structure:

> (1) Why can't a machine be more like a man? In almost every episode of *Star Trek: The Next Generation,* the android Data wonders what makes a person a person. In the original *Star Trek,* similar questions

were raised by the half-Vulcan Mr. Spock, whose status as a person was called into question by his machinelike logic and lack of emotion. In fact, Data and Spock are only the most recent "quasi-persons" who have explored the nature of humanity. The same question has been raised by and about creatures ranging from Frankenstein to Terminator II. But the real question is why characters who struggle to be persons are always white and male. As cultural interpreters, do they tacitly reinforce destructive stereotypes of what it is about a person that we must think of as "normal"? The model person, to which we all must aspire, seems in fact to be defined by Western criteria that exclude most of the people in the world.

(2) As part of its program of Continuous Quality Improvement ("CQI"), Motodyne Computers plans to redesign the user interface for its Unidyne™ online help system. The specifications for the interface call for self-explanatory icons that will allow users to identify their function without an identifying label. Motodyne has three years' experience with its current icon set, but it has no data showing which icons are self-explanatory. Lacking such data, we cannot determine which icons to retain and which to redesign. This report provides data for eleven icons, showing that five of them are not self-explanatory.

(3) In today's society, would Major John André, a British spy captured behind American lines in civilian clothes in 1780, be hanged? Though considered a noble patriot, he suffered the punishment mandated by military law. Over time, our traditions have changed, but the punishment for spying has not. It is the only offense for which death is mandated. Recently, though, the Supreme Court has rejected mandatory death sentences in civilian cases, creating an ambiguity in their application to military cases. If Court decisions apply to the military, then Congress may have to revise the Universal Code of Military Justice. This article concludes that to be the case.

The topics and problems posed in those three introductions differ as much as their intended readers, but behind them is a shared rhetorical pattern that readers look for in all introductions, regardless of field. That common structure consists of three elements:

- contextualizing background,
- a statement of the problem,
- a response to the problem.

Not every introduction has all three of those elements, but most do, and the vast majority state at least part of a problem.

We can see that structure of *Context + Problem + Response* in all three of those introductions:

(1) OPENING CONTEXT: Why can't a machine be more like a man?... The same question has been raised by and about creatures ranging from Frankenstein to Terminator II.

PROBLEM: But the real question is ... do they tacitly reinforce destructive stereotypes of what it is about a person that we must think of as "normal"?

RESPONSE: The model person, to which we all must aspire, seems in fact to be defined by Western criteria that exclude most of the people in the world.

(2) OPENING CONTEXT: As part of its program of Continuous Quality Improvement ("CQI"), Motodyne Computers plans to redesign the user interface.... Motodyne has three years' experience with its current icon set,

PROBLEM: but it has no data showing which icons are self-explanatory. Lacking such data, we cannot determine which icons to retain and which to redesign.

RESPONSE: This report provides data for eleven icons, showing that five of them are not self-explanatory.

(3) OPENING CONTEXT: In today's society, would Major John Andre... be hanged [for spying]?... It is the only offense for which death is mandated.

PROBLEM: Recently, though, the Supreme Court has rejected mandatory death sentences in civilian cases, creating an ambiguity in their application to military cases.... Congress may have to revise the Universal Code of Military Justice.

RESPONSE: This article concludes that to be the case.

Each of those elements of an introduction plays it own role not only in helping readers understand, but in motivating them to read. We will discuss them in their order.

Establishing Common Ground

We call contextualizing information *common ground,* because it establishes a shared understanding between reader and writer about the general issue the writer will address. But it does something even more crucial, illustrated best with the opening of a fairy tale:

> One sunny morning, Little Red Riding Hood was skipping happily through the forest on her way to Grandmother's house, when suddenly Hungry Wolf jumped out from behind a tree, frightening her very much.

Like the opening to most fairy tales, this one establishes a stable, unproblematical, even happy context:

> STABLE CONTEXT: One sunny morning, Little Red Riding Hood was skipping happily through the forest on her way to Grandmother's house *stable context* [imagine butterflies dancing around her head to flutes and violins].

That stable context is then disrupted with a problem:

> DISRUPTING PROBLEM: ... When suddenly Hungry Wolf jumped out from behind a tree *condition* [imagine trombones, tubas, and bass fiddles], frightening her [and, if they lose themselves in the story, little children as well].*cost*

The rest of the story develops that problem and then resolves it.

Unlikely though it may seem, introductions to most research reports follow the same strategy. They open with the stable context of a common ground—some apparently unproblematic account of research, a statement of the community's consensus on a familiar topic. The writer then disrupts it with a problem: *Reader, you think you know something,* **but** *your knowledge is flawed or incomplete.*

> (3) OPENING CONTEXT: In today's society, would Major John André, a British spy ... be hanged? ... [Spying] is the only offense for which death is mandated.

> PROBLEM: Recently, **though**, the Supreme Court has rejected mandatory death sentences. ...

Not every research report opens with common ground. Here is an introduction that opens directly with a problem:

> Recently the chemical processes that have been thinning the ozone layer have been found to be less well understood than once thought. We may have labeled hydrofluorocarbons as the chief cause incorrectly.

Some readers might find that problem already disturbing enough to motivate their reading, but you can heighten its rhetorical punch by introducing it with an unproblematical context of prior research, not just to orient readers toward the topic, but specifically to create an apparently stable context just so that you can disrupt it:

> As we have investigated environmental threats, our understanding of many chemical processes such as acid rain and the buildup of carbon dioxide has improved, allowing us to understand better their eventual effects on the biosphere. *common ground (Sounds good.)* **But recently the chemical processes that have been thinning the ozone layer have been found to be less well understood than once thought.** *destabilizing condition* We may have labeled hydrofluorocarbons as the chief cause incorrectly. *cost*

Readers now have not one but two reasons to see their self-interest in the problem: the problem itself, and also their ignorance of it.

Common ground can describe a general misunderstanding:

> **The Crusades in the eleventh century are widely believed to have been motivated by religious zeal to restore the Holy Land to Christendom.** *common ground* In fact, the motives were at least partly, if not largely, political.

Or survey current but perhaps flawed research:

> **Few sociological concepts have fallen out of favor as fast as Catholicism's alleged protective influence against suicide. Once one of sociology's basic beliefs, it has been called into question by a series of studies in both Europe and North America.** ... *common ground* However, certain studies still find an effect of religion ...

Or it can point to a misunderstanding about the problem itself:

> Education in the U.S. has focused on teaching children to think **critically, to ask questions and test answers.** *common ground* But the field of critical thinking has regularly been taken over by special programs based on fads and special interests. Until we recognize that there is no silver bullet way to teach critical thinking, it will not achieve what we wish it would. *problem*

Some inexperienced researchers skimp on common ground, thinking they can open their report as if they were picking up a class conversation where it left off. Their introductions are so sketchy that only others in the course would understand them:

> In view of the controversy over Hofstadter's failure to respect the differences among math, music, and art, it was not surprising that the response to *The Embodied Mind* was stormy. What is less clear is what caused the controversy in the first place. I will argue that any account of the human mind must be interdisciplinary.

When you draft your introduction, imagine you are writing to another person who has read the same books and thought about some of the same issues, but does not know what happened in your particular class.

Stating Your Problem

Once you establish common ground, you can disrupt it with a problem. Typically, the statement of a research problem has two parts:

- some *condition* of incomplete knowledge or understanding, and
- the *consequences* of not fully knowing or understanding.

You can state the condition directly:

> Motodyne has no data showing which icons are self-explanatory.

Or you can imply it in an indirect question:

> The real question is why these characters are always white and male.

This condition of ignorance or misunderstanding is part of a *full* research problem only when you then spell out a *consequence* as an answer to *So what?* You answer that question by stating a cost:

So what if you don't have that data?

> Lacking such data, we cannot determine which icons to redesign. *cost*

Or you can transform the cost into a benefit:

> With such data, we can determine which icons to keep and which to redesign. *benefit*

This is not entirely a stylistic choice. Some research suggests that readers are more motivated by a certain cost than by a possible benefit.

That's the straightforward version of a problem; there are variations.

When Should You State Conditions Explicitly?

Occasionally, you tackle a problem so familiar that you can imply it just by naming its condition. Such familiar conditions are found in fields like mathematics and the natural sciences, in which many research problems are widely known. Here again, for example, is that abbreviated introduction to perhaps the most significant article in the history of molecular biology, the one in which Crick and Watson report their discovery of the double-helix structure of DNA (this is substantially condensed):

> We wish to suggest a structure for the salt of deoxyribose nucleic acid (D.N.A.). This structure has novel features which are of considerable biological interest. A structure for nucleic acid has already been proposed by Pauling and Corey. They kindly made their manuscript available to us in advance of publication. Their model consists of three intertwined chains, with the phosphates near the fibre axis, and the bases on the outside. In our opinion, this structure is unsatisfactory ...

By saying that they will suggest a structure for DNA, Crick and Watson implied that their readers did not know it. They did not have to say that, because they knew readers were already keen on the problem. (Note, though, that they do raise a problem to solve by mentioning Pauling and Corey's *incorrect* model.)

In the natural sciences and most social sciences, researchers typically address questions familiar to readers. Even so, readers won't know what *particular* flaw in their knowledge your research will address unless you tell them. In the humanities and some social sciences, researchers typically address questions that they alone have found or even invented, questions that readers find new and often surprising. In that case, you must explicitly describe the particular gap in knowledge or flawed understanding that you believe your readers can't resolve but should.

When Should You Spell Out Costs and Benefits?

To convince readers that your problem should matter to them, you must convince them to care about it because they will pay a cost if it is not resolved and gain benefits once it is. Sometimes you can describe tangible costs that your research helps your readers avoid:

> Last year the River City Supervisors agreed that River City would benefit if it added the Bayside development project to its tax base. That argument, however, was based on little economic analysis. If the Board votes to annex Bayside without understanding what it will cost the city, **the Board risks worsening River City's already poor fiscal situation.** When the added burden of expanding city schools and bringing sewer and water service up to city code are included in the analysis, the annexation is less advantageous than the Board assumes.

This is the kind of problem found in applied research. The area of ignorance (no economic analysis) has tangible consequences in the world (unanticipated costs or benefits).

In pure research, you formulate the same kind of problem when you explain the cost not in dollars and cents, but as even greater flawed knowledge or misunderstanding, or alternatively, as the benefit of better understanding:

> Since 1972 American cities have annexed upscale neighborhoods to prop up tax bases, often bringing disappointing economic benefits. But that result could have been predicted had they done basic economic analysis. The annexation movement is a case study of how political decisions at the local level fail to use expert information. What is puzzling is why cities do not seek out those with expertise. **If we can discover why cities fail to rely on basic economic analyses, we might better understand why their decision-making fails so often in other areas as well.** This paper analyzes the decision-making process of three cities that annexed surrounding areas but ignored economic consequences.

Testing Conditions and Costs

Previously, we suggested a way to test how clearly you have articulated the costs of not solving a problem: after the sentences that best state your condition of ignorance or misunderstanding, ask, *So what?* You have articulated your problem persuasively when what comes before the *So what?* plausibly elicits that question and when what follows plausibly answers it.

> Motodyne has no data showing which icons are self-explanatory. *(So what?)* With such data, it could determine which icons to retain and which to redesign.

> Stories about the Alamo in Mexican and U.S. versions differ in obvious ways, but U.S. versions from different eras also differ. *(So what?)* Well, hmmmmmm . . .

Answering that question is not just difficult; it can be exasperating, even dismaying. If you fall in love with stories about the Battle of the Alamo, you can pursue them to your heart's content, without having to justify your pursuit to anyone but yourself: *I just like knowing about it.* But for others to appreciate your research, you have to "sell" them on its significance. Otherwise, why should they spend time on it?

If you write a paper for a class, your teacher is obliged to read it, but when you address your research community, you have to convince them that your problem is *their* problem, that if they go on without knowing, say, how those stories about the Alamo have evolved, how Hollywood turned the story into myth, they will be neglecting something about their identity as North Americans.

Now, to be sure, some readers will ask again, *So what? I don't care about myth and history or our identity.* To which you can only shrug and think, *Wrong audience.* Successful researchers know how to find and solve interesting problems and how to convince readers that they have. But a skill no less important is knowing where to find readers who appreciate the kind of problem that you have solved.

If you are sure your readers know the consequences of your problem, you might decide not to spell them out. Crick and Watson did not specify either costs or benefits, because they knew that their readers knew that they would not understand genetics until they understood the structure of DNA. Had Crick and Watson stated those costs, they might have seemed both redundant and condescending.

If you are tackling your first research project, no reasonable teacher will expect you to articulate your problem in detail, because you probably do not yet know what other researchers think is significant. But you take a big step in that direction if you can state explicitly just *your own* incomplete knowledge or flawed understanding in a way that shows that *you* are committed to improving it. You take an even bigger step when you can explain why it is important to resolve that flawed understanding, when you can show that by understanding one thing better, you understand better something else much more important, *even if it is for you alone.*

Stating Your Response

Once you disrupt your readers' stable context with a problem, they will expect you to resolve it, either by explicitly stating the gist of your solution or by implicitly promising them that you will do so later on. They look for that response in the last few sentences of your introduction. You can state it in one of two ways.

State the Gist of Your Solution

You can state your solution explicitly. When you announce your main point in the introduction, you create a "point-first" paper (even though that point appears as the *last* sentence of the introduction).

> As we have investigated environmental threats, our understanding of many chemical processes such as acid rain and the buildup of carbon dioxide has improved, allowing us to understand better their eventual effects on the biosphere. *common ground (Sounds good.)* But recently the chemical processes that have been thinning the ozone layer have been found to be less well understood than once thought. *condition (So what?)* We may have labeled hydrofluorocarbons as the chief cause incorrectly. *cost* **We have found that the bonding of carbon** ... *gist of solution/main point*

Promise a Solution

Alternatively, you can put off stating your main point by stating only where your paper is headed, thereby implying that you will present your solution in your conclusion. This approach provides a "launching point" and creates a "point-last" paper:

> As we have investigated environmental threats, our understanding...
> has improved.... But recently the chemical processes... [have proved
> to be] less well understood.... *(So what?)* We may have labeled hy-
> drofluorocarbons as the chief cause incorrectly. *(Well, what* have *you
> found?)* **In this report, we describe a hitherto unexpected chemical
> bonding between**...

This introduction launches us into the body of the paper not with a point
or summary of its solution, but with a sentence that promises a solution
to come.

The weakest form of a launching point is one that merely announces
a topic:

> This study investigates the chemistry of ozone depletion.

If you have good reason to save your point for the end of your paper, be
sure that your launching point does more than just announce a topic. It
should suggest the conceptual outlines of your solution or announce a
plan (or both).

> There are many designs for hydroelectric turbine intakes and diversion
> screens, but on-site evaluation is not cost-effective. A more viable al-
> ternative is computer modeling. **To evaluate the hydraulic efficiency
> of hydroelectric diversion screens, this study will evaluate three
> computer models, Quattro, AVOC, and Turboplex, to determine
> which is most cost-effective in reliability, speed, and ease of use.**

This kind of plan is common in social sciences, but less frequent in the
humanities, where many readers consider it ham-handed.

Fast or Slow?

A final decision is how quickly to raise your problem. That depends on
how much your readers know. In the following, the writer begins flat out,
announcing a consensus among well-informed engineers; then, in the second sentence, he briskly disrupts that consensus:

> Fluid-film forces in squeeze-film dampers (SFDs) are usually obtained
> from the Reynolds equation of classical lubrication theory. However,
> the increasing size of rotation machinery requires the inclusion of
> fluid inertia effects in the design of SFDs.

We have no idea what that means, but we can see the pattern clearly.

This next writer also addresses technical concepts but begins with more familiar ones, implying readers who do not already possess vast technical knowledge:

> A method of protecting migrating fish at hydroelectric power developments is diversion by screening turbine intakes ... [*another 110 words explaining screens*]. Since the efficiency of screens is determined by the interaction of fish behavior and hydraulic flow, screen design can be evaluated by determining its hydraulic performance ... [*40 more words explaining hydraulics*]. This study resulted in a better understanding of the hydraulic features of this technique, which may guide future designs.

When you open quickly, you imply an audience of peers; when you open slowly, you imply readers who know less than you. If your readers are knowledgeable and you open too slowly, you may sound as if *you* know too little. But if you open too quickly, you may seem inconsiderate of their needs.

Organizing the Whole Introduction

All this may seem formulaic, but when you master a rhetorical pattern, you have more than a formula for writing. You also have a tool for thinking. By forcing yourself to work through a full statement of your problem, you have to explore what your audience knows, what they don't, and, in particular, what they should.

By now you may feel overwhelmed with too many choices, but they all follow what is in fact a simple "grammar." A full introduction consists of just three elements:

Common Ground + Problem + Response

You don't need all three elements all the time:

- If the problem is well known, omit the common ground; begin with the condition of the problem.

- If the consequences of the problem are very well known, you can also omit them.

- If you want to show how you worked through the problem and solved it, state your main point in the conclusion; at the end of your introduction, frame your response as launching point.

Like all structural summaries, this one feels mechanical. But when you flesh this pattern out in a real paper, readers lose sight of the form and notice only the substance. In fact, the expected form helps them find the substance they are looking for. That form also encourages you to think harder than you might have.

Conclusions

Not every research paper has a section formally called *Conclusion,* but they all have a paragraph or two that serves as one. You may be happy to know that you can use the same elements that you used in your introduction for your conclusion. You just use them in reverse order.

Start with Your Main Point

- If you end your introduction with your main point, state it again at the beginning of your conclusion, but state it more fully. It should not simply repeat your introduction.

- If you end your introduction not with your main point but with a launching point, state your point at the beginning of your conclusion, and be sure to use the key terms you used at the end of your introduction.

Add a New Significance or Application

Once you state your claim, say why it's significant: paraphrase the consequences of your problem or point to a new significance not mentioned in your introduction. This new significance should be another answer to the question *So what?* in the introduction.

For example, in this next conclusion, the writer introduces for the first time an additional cost of the Supreme Court's decision on military death sentences: the military may have to change the culture of its thinking.

> In light of recent Supreme Court decisions rejecting mandatory capital punishment, then, the mandatory death provision for treason is apparently unconstitutional and must therefore be revised by Congress.

> More significantly, **though, if the Universal Code of Military Justice is changed, it will challenge a fundamental value of military culture: ultimate betrayal mandates the ultimate penalty. Congress will then have to deal with the military's universal sense of what is just.**

The writer could have used that implication in his introduction, as a potential cost resulting from new Supreme Court decisions, but he may have felt that it was too volatile to raise early.

As you write your conclusion, take care not to broaden a possible significance so much that it seems to be your main point. You can be clear about its role by introducing it almost "by the way," as an additional, *possible* practical implication of your solution.

Add a Call for More Research

Just as you can survey research already done in your common ground, you can also call for more research still to do at the end of your conclusion:

> These differences between novice and expert diagnosticians clearly define the starting and ending points in their maturation and development. We know how novices and experts think differently. **What we do not understand is which elements in the social experience of novices contribute to that development and how. In particular, we need longitudinal studies on how mentoring and coaching affect outcomes, whether active explanation and critique help novices become skilled diagnosticians more quickly.**

When you conclude by pointing out what remains to be done, you show your readers that you haven't had the last word on your problem, that there is still more to say. That keeps the conversation alive. Those who pursue your suggestion will review your work, respond to it, and move beyond it. So before you write your last words, imagine someone fascinated by your work who wants to follow up on it: What would you suggest they do? What more would you like to know? After all, that may have been one of your strategies in finding a problem of your own.

QUICK TIP: Opening and Closing Words

Many writers find the very first sentence or two especially difficult to write, and so they fall into clichés:

- Don't start by citing a dictionary entry: Webster's *defines* ethics *as* ... If a word is important enough to define in a report, it is too complex for a dictionary definition.

- Don't start grandly: *The most profound philosophers have for centuries wrestled with the important question of* ... If your subject is grand, it will speak its own importance.

- Don't repeat the language of your assignment: If you are struggling to start, prime your pump with a paraphrase, but when you revise, drop it.

Here are three choices for your first sentence or two.

OPEN WITH A STRIKING QUOTATION

Do this only if its language is like the language in the rest of your introduction:

> "From the sheer sensuous beauty of a genuine Jan van Eyck there emanates a strange fascination not unlike that which we experience when permitting ourselves to be hypnotized by precious stones."
>
> Edwin Panofsky, who had a way with words, suggests here something magical in Jan van Eyck's works. His images hold a fascination ...

OPEN WITH A STRIKING FACT

> Those who think that tax cuts for the rich stimulate the economy should contemplate the fact that the top 1 percent of Americans own as much wealth as everyone in the bottom 40 percent.

OPEN WITH A RELEVANT ANECDOTE

Again, do this only if its language or content connects to your topic and if it vividly illustrates an aspect of your problem. The following paper addressed the economics of school segregation:

This year Tawnya Jones begins junior high in Doughton, Georgia. Though her classmates are mostly African American like herself, her school system is considered legally racially integrated. But except for a few poor whites and Hispanic students, Tawnya's school still resembles the segregated and economically depressed one that her mother entered in 1962....

When you open with any of these devices, be sure to use language that leads to your context, your problem, and a focused statement of its solution.

CLOSE WITH AN ECHO

You bring your conclusion to a graceful, even literary close by echoing your opening fact, anecdote, or quotation with another at the end. Here, for example, is an introduction that begins with a quotation, an epigraph that highlights the themes of spiritualism and modernity. The writer echoes those themes with a parallel quotation at the end of her conclusion (note, too, how the title pulls together key themes):

> Flannery O'Connor and the Spiritual Foundations of Racism:
> Suffering as Southern Redemption in the Modern World
> *"I write the way I do because ... I am a Catholic peculiarly*
> *possessed of the modern consciousness."*
>
> Although Flannery O'Connor's stories give us insights into southern culture, some have said her attitude toward race was the product of "an imperfectly developed sensibility" and that "large social issues as such were never the subject of her writing." But that criticism ignores ...

Here is the conclusion:

> Thus we see that those who claim that O'Connor ignored racism fail to see that she understood racism as a deeper crisis of faith, as a failure to recognize the healing knowledge of suffering, insights that put her among a few southern writers who saw the modern world as spiritually bankrupt. Seen in this light, a rereading of her private correspondence might reveal ... **As she said in one letter (May 4, 1955), "What I had in mind to suggest [was ... the redemptive quality of the Negro's suffering for us all. ... I meant [a character in the story to suggest] in an almost physical way ... the mystery of existence."** *conclusion*

This echoing device may seem a bit literary, but it is not at all uncommon.

Appendix

Homestretch Final Portfolio Planning

Your portfolio is meant to represent your very best work. Since it is the culmination of the class, its expectations are higher than they have previously been for earlier drafts.

Requirements for each draft in the portfolio:

Content

- Should be revised based on instructor and peer feedback, sometimes up to your discretion, sometimes not. If someone catches a simple formatting error or typo, you are required to fix it. If someone offers you a suggestion on a tactic you might or might not try, you will decide.

- Should include revision choices that fall outside the scope of instructor or peer feedback. You should be able to demonstrate that there are revisions to your piece that YOU decided to make. Your instructor is a coach, not the player in the game. You can do everything the coach says and still have problems in the game.

- Should be interesting to read and not repeating ideas others have written or your audience will already know.

- Should show that you understand the differences between genres and that you use conventions suitable to each genre.

Sentence Structure, Punctuation, and Formatting

- Should have all titles properly formatted in MLA style.

- Should have any commas or periods next to quotation marks moved to inside the quotation marks. Example: In the story, "I Stand Here Ironing," by Tillie Olsen, the narrator is a cruel mother.

- Should have possessive apostrophes for any possessives. Example: Paul's rules are draconian.

- Should have correct prepositions. Not "I waited on the line" but "I waited in line."

- Have subjects and verbs in agreement. Example: The three boys agrees with me (problematic). The three boys agree with me (correct).

- Should use past tense to talk about the past.

- Should have any direct or indirect quotations or paraphrases cited in MLA style in-text.

- Should have longer quotes correctly formatted in MLA style for block quotes.

- Should have shorter quotes correctly formatted in MLA style.

- Should include an MLA formatted Works Cited page if there are any sources used at all.

Final Portfolio Directions and Checklist

1. Make sure each finished draft attends to the minimum requirements for that assignment. Remember, MLA style requires 1-inch margins all around, which is different than the default margins for Microsoft Word.

    -   Does your Personal Essay do more than just summarize chronological events from your life?

    -   Are your Op-Ed sources recent and credible?

    -   Do you have at least four sources for your Researched Argument? Are at least three scholarly sources (published in a peer-reviewed journal or part of a book published by an academic press)?

    -   Did you follow the page requirements? Remember, if it says four pages, that means four complete pages. If it says eight to ten pages, that means no more than ten full pages.

2. Edit each finished draft to ensure it conforms to academic conventions for spelling, punctuation, and sentence structure.

3. Edit each draft to ensure it conforms to MLA style conventions for page formatting, in-text quotations, and Works Cited.

4. The portfolio is due during the final class session. It is a good idea for you to print out your materials the night before they are due, even if you plan on fine-tuning. This will ensure you have a draft to submit in the portfolio if printers are tied up or something else happens. Your instructor will provide a file folder for your portfolio and distribute that in or before the final class session.

5. Portfolios are evaluated holistically without written feedback and are kept by the Writing Initiative for one full academic year.

General Revision Strategies for Portfolio Assignments

Personal Essay

Content

- Make sure that you make a claim about your personal experience in order to connect it to a broader range of general human experience via the context of "Coming of Age in the Twenty-first Century." Think of your personal experience as evidence to support your claim. Consult the Personal Essay Assignment Overview.

Organization

- Because part of the challenge of this essay is to illustrate your claim in the space of limited pages, successful essays in this genre typically develop one or a few detailed examples to illustrate the claim rather than relying on many. Don't cover your entire high school year if one important event—such as a valedictorian speech—is the essential focus.

- Use thick description and sensory details to develop your examples and—by extension—illustrate your claim and its connection to the larger world. In other words, you've got to do more than simply "tell" readers about your life; you must also "show" them through the use of thick description.

Style and Mechanics

- The essay will probably depend on the "I" pronoun and a more casual style than some of the other papers you wrote this semester. It should be engaging and persuasive, as well as descriptive and vivid.

Op-Ed Essay

Content

- While all good writing seeks to shed new light on an issue, this is particularly important in your Op-Ed essay. If you are simply re-hashing old arguments and not contributing something new to the conversation, you're not satisfying a key convention of the genre. Successful Op-Ed essays carefully and clearly introduce sources. In most circumstances, this means that in the paragraph where a source first appears, you must name the author, state her credentials, list the title of the source, and briefly summarize the key argument made in the source. Successful Op-Ed essays also use both paraphrase and direct quotation, although the genre typically uses paraphrase more often than direct quotation.

Organization

- Remember that one important convention of the Op-Ed genre is to "hook" readers with an interesting introduction that leaves readers wanting to finish the essay. If your introduction doesn't hook readers, you're not fulfilling a key requirement of the genre.

Style and Mechanics

- Although typically written in a more formal register than the personal essay genre, you should strive to write Op-Eds in the clear, straightforward style represented in the writing anthologized in journalistic writing: this essay should be written with the average American citizen in mind, someone who has a high school education or above, but who will need you to avoid jargon and define or explain technical- or discipline-specific language.

Researched Argument Essay

Content

- Develop an issue-based thesis statement that integrates counterarguments in order to build credibility and focus your argument. While there are many ways to design a successful thesis statement in an academic essay, by using the "While some argue X, I will argue Y" thesis model, you set up a solidly persuasive argument, one which readers are likely to find even-handed, sophisticated, and credible. Remember, the claim in a good thesis statement is typically an argument that a reasonable reader can disagree with. The rest of your paper serves as evidence to convince the reader that your perspectives are reasonable, interesting, and worth considering.

Organization

- In addition to making sure that you examine counterarguments in relationship to your own argument, it is vital that you focus your paragraphs in such a way that readers understand how they relate to your thesis. As such, you'd be wise to develop sophisticated topic sentences that let readers know the focus of a paragraph or series of paragraphs. Paragraph cues such as "One reason why people believe X is..." or "another example of why critics disagree with X is..."

Style and Mechanics

- The ways in which you introduce, contextualize, quote from, cite, and analyze your sources are key to building your argument and your credibility as an academic writer. Make sure that you follow the conventions for sources use as outlined in the various textbooks we use in this class. In general, when integrating sources for the first time in your paper, you should introduce the author and source—"Jane Smith, Professor of History at the University of California, writes in her book *The American History of Crime*, that..." After quoting or paraphrasing a passage or idea from a source, it is also essential that you analyze that passage or idea, showing your readers how it relates to the argument you are making. Don't expect readers to know what you are thinking: you need to "connect the dots" of your thinking in your writing.

- Following MLA format precisely is one of the biggest ways to signal to your readers that you are a legitimate researcher who cares about her writing and her reputation as serious student and scholar. This is especially the case in portfolio system, in which more than just your own instructor evaluates your work. Following MLA format isn't hard, but it is time-consuming. Do it well, or your grade is at risk. Both your in-text citations and your end-of-text Works Cited page need to be developed accurately and with care. MLA manuscript format directions and sample student essay models can be found in a variety of places in the course textbooks.

Binghamton Writes **Submission Information**

NOTE TO SELF: Get published in *Binghamton Writes!*

Current Writing 111 students—here's why you should publish your work:

- Getting published looks great on your resume: it's a distinctive accomplishment.

- Getting published feels great: you'll feel proud of your work.

- You'll learn a lot about the process of publication.

- You'll help future students and instructors see how differently students can successfully tackle the Writing 111 assignments.

- You'll earn fame, prestige, and a *complimentary copy*!

On the last day of classes (the day you turn in your portfolio), send your very best final drafts of Writing 111 essays to

BinghamtonWritesEditor@gmail.com

to be considered for publication in next year's edition of *Binghamton Writes*. Send one, two, or all three essays, but please send each in a separate email.

1. In the subject line, just give your last name and the genre of your essay (r.e., "Perez: Researched Argument;" "Jones: Personal Essay;" "Ahmad: Op-Ed"). No cover letter is necessary.

2. Remember to attach the essay as a Word .doc or .docx file (not odt, pages, PDF, or any other format).

3. Make sure your Works Cited is included as part of the file. Do not send it as a separate file.

To give yourself the best chance, don't send work before you've completed final revisions during the last two weeks of classes.

Authors who submit their work in the Spring semester will be contacted by mid-October if their work is chosen. Those submitting work in the Fall semester will hear by late February if their work is selected.

Good luck and happy writing!